"Linda Goudsmit warns that attacks on the nuclear family are attacks on the nation:

> *Political predators attacking the cohesion of our national American family is a macrocosm. The simultaneous radical leftist attack on the cohesion of America's nuclear family is the microcosm. The destruction of the nuclear family is foundational to the attack on America's national identity and America's cultural identity.*
>
> *It is important to understand the combatants in terms of competing ideologies. Leftism is rooted in Marxist collectivism and loyalty to the state. Americanism is rooted in individualism and loyalty to the family. Consider the Chinese Communist Revolution 1946–1949. Thousands of years of family veneration were extinguished and replaced with loyalty to the newly established People's Republic of China (PRC).*

How privileged we are to have a masterful new book by the internationally recognized conservative star Linda Goudsmit. Linda's rise to the top echelons of journalism has been mercurial because the hallmark of goudsmit. pundicity.com quickly drew avid followers of her high-level insightful grasp of the evils that have been weakening our Western culture for decades. No other writer manifests Linda's unique 'way with words.' In her new book, *The Collapsing American Family*, Linda's arguments are indisputable and her deep reach into historical trends showcases the depth of her comprehension of the dangerous global (and national) mechanisms that threaten us all. Buy Linda's book and spread the word among your friends. This is a serious MUST READ product of an acutely intelligent, highly educated political analyst. Linda Goudsmit's books and commentaries will live through the ages. *The Collapsing American Family* belongs in the Library of Congress."

—**Charlotte Baker**, conservative editor, aggregator-distributor, and commentator

"There can be no more dangerous yet subtle agenda used to take over humankind than psychological operations (psyops) grounded in socialism/communism—carefully hidden behind the use of deceptive equivocal language (same term, different meaning). Psychological warfare has been used successfully for millennia. I experienced this psyops/linguistic fraud myself while teaching medical ethics in Romania just one year after their Communist dictator had been killed. Interestingly, a group of Romanians understood such Communist linguistic maneuverings and took the genuine Romanian language underground until it was safe to bring it back out to the public again! Our State Department concluded that most of the Romanian adults were psychologically too far gone by that time and so profoundly schizophrenic because of such psyops/linguistic experiences that they said it was too late to help them; best to just focus on the Romanian children who had survived! Carefully and meticulously identifying the psychological grid of the disastrous psyops/linguistic agenda currently moving swiftly throughout the world under various deceptive "pretenses" is the reason why Linda Goudsmit's new book is so critically important and a must-read. Save yourself years of research and read her book *now*— before it's too late and schizophrenia sets in; then we'll be incapable of ever thinking again. We'll just *obey...*"

—**Dianne N. Irving, M.A., Ph.D.** A retired university professor at Georgetown and Catholic universities, Dr. Irving holds doctorates in biochemistry, bioethics, and history of philosophy, and has a career appointment at the National Institutes of Health as a bench research biochemist/biologist.

"Linda Goudsmit's newest book, *The Collapsing American Family: From Bonding to Bondage*, continues her tradition of educating and elucidating. She always punches hard—but accurately. The following three sentences from *The Collapsing American Family* are not only well stated but also exemplify that, once again, she knows what she's talking about economically as well as socially, politically, and psychologically.

> *The Tavistock-generated identity politics of leftist victimhood has duped two generations of Americans into believing that one-world government will provide "social justice" for their perceived victimhood. The reality is that one-world government has no middle class, no upward mobility, no national sovereignty, and no individual freedoms. One-world government is a binary socio-political system consisting of a small ruling class and an enslaved population that serves them.*

You do not get more accurate than that. If you really want to understand the events of the day, read Linda's wonderful new book. It explains not only what's going on, but why."

—**Marilyn MacGruder Barnewall**, author, International Banking Consultant (Ret.), "Guru" of North American Private Banking, started the first private bank in the United States.

"Linda Goudsmit's new book, *The Collapsing American Family: From Bonding to Bondage*, should be mandatory reading in colleges and universities in this age of identity politics, cancel culture, anti-Americanism, critical race theory, and globalism.

The book brings a unique perspective and deeper understanding of the dangers confronting America in a covert war that seeks to destroy our constitutional republic. It brilliantly explores the nature, the goals, and the vehicles by which our society is transforming, not with new and innovative ideas, but with the same failed totalitarian concepts of the past.

Mrs. Goudsmit writes:

> *In contemporary America, radical leftist Democrats are imitating the Maoist cancel-culture model. They target the three supporting pillars of Americanism: family, faith, and freedom. Cancel culture is asymmetric warfare used by the advancing leftist army to prepare America for socialist replacement ideology.*

Beginning with the disintegration of the American family, the book takes us on a terrifying journey through the deconstruction of society. There can be no religion, family unit, or individualism in the new normal, a new world of collectivism launched by the pandemic and orchestrated by the globalist elite.

The indoctrination is all around us, in our schools, on our televisions, and in the news. Mrs. Goudsmit dives into the insidious nature of the beast we see growing in our own children, who now reject our traditions and even us as parents.

> *Freedom of speech is no longer a part of many American families. Leftist censorship has infiltrated American family life.... Children are now demanding their conservative parents surrender to their demand for censorship.... When parents surrender to emotional extortion and conform to their children's ideological indoctrination and demands, the parents no longer pose a threat to the Marxist movement.*

Globalist ambition does not end with Marxist collectivism. Mrs. Goudsmit explains that socialism is just the required stepping-stone for imposition of the new normal in a totalitarian managerial state. This book is essential for understanding the war on America today. It is this understanding that will wake people up to the reality of the existential threat we face—from the Sophist perversion of our language to the demonization of individualism—and how it can be beaten down.

This book is a classic."

—**Maureen Dowling**, author, publisher of Independent Sentinel

"Linda Goudsmit has once again created a masterpiece, superbly elucidated, founded in principle, critical thought, objective reality, and irrefutable truth; and applied meticulously to our current battle for Judeo-Christian and Western Civilization. As Linda clarifies in her book, *"Family is the most fundamental, universal, and powerful social structure in human society. America was founded with the infrastructure of a nuclear family—a man and a woman and their children."* Abraham, known to be the *Father of Nations* (Old Covenant); Joseph, the foster father of Jesus Christ (New Covenant); and God Himself honored and obeyed the biblical family structure, the foundational target of the Godless/Marxist Left.

Linda, with surgical precision, identifies and bravely confronts institutions and methodologies developed by entities such as the Tavistock Institute to foster globalism by conditioning the American public to reject Americanism and embrace globalism through psychological manipulation. As she so succinctly states, *"Globalism is the existential enemy of a sovereign United States of America as a constitutional republic."* In totality, this book is literally a necessity."

—**Dr. Scott Keller, Ph.D.**, Strategic Security and Counter Terrorism (DSS), President and founder of Strategic Synergies Inc., fighter pilot, Joint/Multi-Service (USMC/USN/USAF/International) operations

THE

COLLAPSING

AMERICAN

FAMILY

FROM BONDING TO BONDAGE

—— THE ——
COLLAPSING
AMERICAN
FAMILY

FROM BONDING TO BONDAGE

LINDA GOUDSMIT

CONTRAPOINT PUBLISHING
ST. PETE BEACH, FL

Publication date 2022

Contrapoint Publishing
St. Pete Beach, FL
contrapointpublishing.com

The Collapsing American Family: From Bonding to Bondage

ISBN: 978-1-953255-18-1 Paperback
ISBN: 978-1-953255-20-4 Hardcover
ISBN: 978-1-953255-19-8 ePub

Library of Congress Control Number: 2021925786
Printed in the United States of America

FIRST EDITION

Designer: Baris Celik

To my beloved husband, Rob

here is the deepest secret nobody knows
(here is the root of the root and the bud of the bud
and the sky of the sky of a tree called life;which grows
higher than soul can hope or mind can hide)
and this is the wonder that's keeping the stars apart

i carry your heart(i carry it in my heart)

—e e cummings

CONTENTS

ACKNOWLEDGMENTS

To Rita Samols, my gifted editor and gentle friend, with heartfelt appreciation for her extraordinary skills.

With profound gratitude to all the brave writers and publishers who fight the good fight for liberty and justice with written words. I have benefited enormously from the courage of your convictions.

War is peace

Freedom is slavery

Ignorance is strength

—George Orwell

War is war

Peace is peace

Freedom is freedom

Slavery is slavery

Ignorance is ignorance

Strength is strength

—Linda Goudsmit

Freedom is an adult enterprise.

PREFACE

Dear America,

I am writing to express my profound sadness and deepest concerns for the future of my beloved country. I am outraged by the deliberate tearing asunder of the nation our forefathers fought to build, and the destruction of ideals that generations of patriots loved and protected with their lives. Our Founding Fathers longed for freedom, sacrificed for freedom, and died for freedom. Their hopes and dreams created the single greatest experiment in individual freedom the world has ever known.

Freedom in a constitutional republic requires adult independence from its citizens; socialism demands childish dependence. The preface to my previous book, *The Book of Humanitarian Hoaxes: Killing America with 'Kindness'*, introduces the theme of dependence vs. independence in America. *The Collapsing American Family: From Bonding to Bondage* expands on that theme by exposing the multifaceted attack on the American family as the primary political strategy and tactic for destroying our American constitutional republic, and replacing it with socialism.

Socialism is the necessary intermediate step required to shatter America's middle class, centralize government control, and prepare America for globalism's seismic reset. The Great Reset, globalism's relabeled New World Order, is a catastrophic regression to the binary, feudal socio-political structure of rulers and ruled on a planetary scale.

My trilogy of books, *Dear America: Who's Driving the Bus?* (2011), *The Book of Humanitarian Hoaxes: Killing America with 'Kindness'* (2020), and *The Collapsing American Family: From Bonding to Bondage* (2021), connects the theoretical, philosophical, psychological, and political dots necessary to understand the comprehensive operational plans for defeating America from within, and transferring loyalty from the family to the state.

American independence begins with fishing.

Ancient Chinese philosopher Lao Tzu, founder of Taoism, famously said, "Give a man a fish and you feed him for a day. Teach him how to fish and you feed him for a lifetime."

In two simple sentences Lao Tzu expresses the fundamentals of dependence and independence. His 2600-year-old maxim is key to understanding not only family life and politics, but also the asymmetric warfare attacking America's nuclear family in globalism's 21st-century battle for America's soul.

Families and entire countries can be encouraged to become independent, or taught to remain dependent. America's founding ethos, which prevailed for over two hundred years, was one of fierce independence. The trinity of American life—family, faith, and freedom—cooperated in common cause to produce proud, independent, rational, autonomous, patriotic adult citizens prepared for the responsibilities of sustaining freedom.

Americans were known worldwide for their swagger and the self-confidence that derives from competence and self-sufficiency. In the 1990s, however, I began to notice a disturbing trend in society toward dependence and away from independence.

I wrote down my observations, analyzed why chronological adults were behaving like narcissistic young children, and developed a theory of behavior to explain the dynamic. In 2011, I published the theory in my philosophy book, *Dear America: Who's Driving the Bus?*

My editor casually remarked that the book was very political. *Political?* I was stunned. I had written *Dear America* to help people understand why they behave the way they do, and to provide a useful paradigm that would help them lead more productive adult lives.

The paradigm is a universal prism that reveals how we are each individually the sum of our parts and are collectively a society that interacts with each of those parts. We begin life in a state of infantile narcissism: "I am everything and everything is me."

The universal task of childhood is to emerge from the state of boundaryless infantile narcissism. The universal task of parenting is to teach the child that others exist in the world whose lives are equal to our own. The child must accept the concept of *other* or that child will never mature into an emotional adult.

As we grow and develop, our life's experiences create historical inner entities in our minds. These entities, buried deep within us, are often totally unknown to us yet remain active passengers on our individual metaphorical buses. When we reach chronological adulthood, we function emotionally along a continuum from infantile narcissism to rational adulthood.

Thought precedes behavior. When life circumstances create a threat that shouts "Danger!" to an inner entity, it mobilizes that entity to take control of the bus and respond to the perceived threat. If our adult identity allows an inner child to take the wheel and dictate our response, the child is driving the bus and making our decisions. No rational adult would allow a real child to drive a bus, and so it must be with our inner children.

The question "Who's driving the bus?" seeks to identify which part of us is making our decisions at any given moment. The answer to that question determines the quality of life in our society. The paradigm shows us how we can change the bus driver to a more rational and developed part of ourselves, thereby improving life in our society.

In 2011, when I published *Dear America*, I did not understand that the pervasive pressure for regression on individuals and families in society was sinister, deliberate, and intensely political.

I began to question the situation. What was the motive for giving people fish instead of teaching them to fish? What could possibly explain deliberate societal pressures toward dependence and infantile narcissism in adults? I remembered a helpful tip on parenting: "If you want to know the motive, look at the result." I began to consider who would benefit from an infantilized America.

I thought about how our extraordinary individual freedoms and ordered liberty require a citizenry of emotional adults. That was when I realized that a nation of emotional children is easily controlled, and that the enemies of the United States of America were deliberately infantilizing Americans! It was a kaleidoscopic moment—the patterns and elements of my worldview were rearranged forever.

Of course *Dear America* is political! Freedom is an adult enterprise. Regression has the ravaging political purpose of infantilizing America in order to collapse it from within. A strong, independent, rational, adult citizenry would never accept the political tyranny of socialism's centralized government and totalitarian social control. The enemies of American freedom are colluding to infantilize the public and move society from freedom to socialism—from family bonding to government bondage.

It is difficult for the civilized mind to process such intentional destruction, but doing so is essential for understanding political deceit and how menacing it is to freedom.

The choice between globalism and national sovereignty is the essence of Lao Tzu's wisdom. Globalism promises to give us fish and keep us dependent upon a permanent ruling class. President Donald Trump tried to teach Americans to fish again, to be independent, sovereign, and free—a profound return to government of the people, by the people, and for the people.

The Collapsing American Family: From Bonding to Bondage demonstrates how our constitutional republic derives its strength and longevity from the generational bonds and support of the nuclear American family. The nuclear family is the microcosm that supports participation in the macrocosm, our national American family. The American nuclear family is an existential threat to and competing ideology of the globalist enemies of American freedom.

The war on America is an information war targeting the American family. Globalism's leftist institutions are indoctrinating Americans and recruiting our children and grandchildren to embrace socialist collectivism, reject American individualism, and repudiate the American family.

The United States of America must remain a constitutional republic and deny globalism's dystopian Great Reset.

It is time for Americans to be fishermen again.

Most sincerely,

Linda Goudsmit

USA 2021

INTRODUCTION

KAHLIL GIBRAN

Kahlil Gibran, the gifted Lebanese-American poet, philosopher, and artist, writes about family in his 1923 masterpiece, *The Prophet*. In the book, the prophet describes the role of parents:

> You are the bows from which your children as living arrows are sent forth.

> The archer sees the mark upon the path of the infinite, and He bends you with His might that His arrows may go swift and far.

> Let your bending in the archer's hand be for gladness:

> For even as He loves the arrow that flies, so He loves also the bow that is stable.

Gibran's poetry captures the American Judeo-Christian ideal of family love, growth, independence, and continuity. His exquisite image of the archer and bow is an iconic depiction of idealized parenthood—the preparation and exemplary launching of children into adulthood. The stillness of the archer's pose contrasts with the perpetual motion of the children being launched into the future, becoming parents who will prepare their own children for adulthood in the magnificent, ongoing cycle of life.

Family is the most fundamental, universal, and powerful social structure in human society. America was founded on the infrastructure of the nuclear family—a man and a woman and their children. Parents providing for, protecting, and preparing their children for a future in a free society. The nuclear family is the source of family love, family loyalty, and family appreciation for the unparalleled individual freedoms guaranteed by our U.S. Constitution.

The nuclear family is the foundation of American freedom, American ideals, and American morality rooted in the Judeo-Christian tenets of the Ten Commandments. Family is the supporting structure that provides stability and continuity for the American Constitution, American sovereignty, and the American dream.

My purpose for writing this book is to expose the multidimensional, coordinated attacks on the American family as strategic, operational, tactical, asymmetric warfare.

The enemies of America have targeted the American family, intentionally inverting the natural growth process and interrupting the cycle of life. The war on America is a war on children. Centuries of American parents preparing their children for independence and launch into responsible adulthood are being disparaged, discredited, and replaced by a socialist movement determined to keep the children eternally dependent. Socialism is unapologetic in its goal to destroy the American family as a competing ideology.

The war on America is an ideological war—a battle between Americanism and socialism, between individualism and collectivism, between freedom and slavery. The war on America is a multipronged information war that must destroy the American family in order to succeed.

The immediate political goal is to overthrow our constitutional republic and replace it with socialism, which is presented as the superior replacement ideology. This book exposes the humanitarian hoax of socialism, its fraudulent narrative of social justice and economic equality, and its purpose in the war on America. Socialism is the deceitful stepping-stone to a New World Order.

Socialism is the *beginning* of the war on America. This book connects the sequential dots that begin with socialism and end with transhumanism in a dehumanized planetary managerial state, where *you will own nothing and be happy*. Private property, the hallmark of freedom in a constitutional republic, is being threatened with extinction. Ownership and upward mobility will be replaced with totalitarian control of the population and all its resources by world government managers empowered to distribute all goods and services. The process of reordering the world economy and its resources is called the *Great Reset.*

Sequentially, the collapse of the American family is required to transform America into socialism. Socialism is required to centralize government power and surrender American sovereignty to globalist one-world government. One-world government is required to enslave the global population in the New World Order of a planetary managerial surveillance state.

Socialism establishes a collectivist nation of dependent citizens who, like children, are easily controlled—for our own good, of course. The socialist authoritarian state denies the archer, discredits the bow, and deliberately prevents the arrows from being sent forth. The socialist state replaces parental authority with state authority, and replaces family loyalty with state loyalty.

The collapse of the American family awards total centralized social control to the authoritarian state. The end of the American nuclear family is the end of the greatest experiment in individual freedom the world has ever known. A nation of children cannot sustain itself. To survive, it requires a central government that usurps the traditional roles of parents.

The ideological war between socialism and Americanism being fought today on U.S. soil is part of the greater globalist effort to regress the world back to feudalism and establish a New World Order of planetary governance. Today's Marxist-Leninist soldiers are the legions of radical leftist Democrats, socialists, communists, and anarchists who graduated college in the 1960s, cut their hair, put on suits, and entered the American workforce with the goal of destabilizing and collapsing our country from within.

This socialist army successfully infiltrated every sphere of American life, and it particularly targeted education. Educational indoctrination is asymmetric warfare. The children and grandchildren of America's 1960s activist generation are being indoctrinated to become citizens of the "equitable" globalized world deceitfully promised by United Nations Agenda 2030.

Students of history know that socialism's familiar promises of social justice and economic equality are not the reality of socialism. "Free stuff" is *never* free—the price of socialism is your freedom! Yet Americans are being propagandized to believe the never-ending Marxist socialist lies.

Americans carefully teach their children not to accept candy from strangers. This book shows how socialism is the political candy that is seducing unsuspecting Americans into surrendering their precious freedom and that of their children. Familiarity breeds acceptance, and socialism is no longer a stranger in America.

The managerial elite driving the Great Reset support an *end justifies the means* approach to achieve its goals. The methodology includes psychological conditioning and sociological pressures to conform to a new normal in the New World Order.

Propagandized education and the mainstream media are essential components for coordinating disinformation, censoring dissenting opinions, and non-stop echoing of the managerial elite message. The vehicle for transitioning the U.S. to the managerial state is COVID-19. The narrative of political medicine provided by the global predators is part of the asymmetric warfare and fear campaign designed to regress the public to childish compliance.

The globalists running the war on America have successfully infiltrated American institutions and corrupted them. Political institutions no longer protect American sovereignty. Judicial institutions no longer provide American justice. Educational institutions no longer provide American education. Military institutions no longer protect America's borders. Medical institutions no longer protect American public health.

This is classic asymmetric warfare—revolution without bullets. The shots fired in this war on America are coming from a needle. The coronavirus debacle has shattered family bonds and further bifurcated the country between "vaccinated" and "unvaccinated."

The fear and divisiveness within families reflects the fear and divisiveness in the nation. Divisiveness has left American families and America in disarray, vulnerable to the insatiable globalist elite appetite for planetary domination.

Without public awareness and political intervention by states' rights activists, history will trace American freedom from its birth in 1776, through its extraordinary growth nurtured and supported by American family bonding, to its collapse into socialism and 21st-century global bondage.

The Collapsing American Family: From Bonding to Bondage is dedicated to American sovereignty, and to those who continue to fight the good fight to preserve our precious American freedom.

CHAPTER 1

United We Stand, Divided We Fall

President Donald J. Trump was sworn into office on January 20, 2017, a time of enormous social upheaval in the United States of America. For seventy years, since the end of World War II, the enemies of American liberty had been assaulting established American norms and weakening America's national identity.

The country had just suffered through eight years of Barack Obama's anti-American policies that had seriously undermined the nation. Hillary Clinton, Obama's legacy candidate, was expected to be elected and complete Obama's cunning promise to Americans to "fundamentally transform America" into a socialist nation.

Instead, the American people elected President Trump to *Make America Great Again.*

Trump's restoration plan was to strengthen America's foundation by rebuilding American manufacturing, strengthening our military, and restoring the nuclear American family and thereby our national American family. President Trump planned to make *being* an American great again—and he did, against tremendous opposition from inside and outside his political party.

For four years President Trump championed Americanism and unapologetically put America first. Domestic and international policy decisions were based on American interests, and defined by a meritocracy indifferent to race, religion, and gender. America's economy was booming again with jobs, and there was a resurgence of American optimism and hope for the future.

American Judeo-Christian traditions were unapologetically observed. First lady Melania Trump made holidays at the White House spectacularly beautiful and festive again. Americans celebrated national holidays together, proud to be members of our American family.

Strengthening America and the American family made President Trump the existential enemy of globalism and its leftist foot soldiers here and abroad. The attacks on the president personally, professionally, and politically were unparalleled in the history of our nation. Yet Trump survived them all and continued to strengthen and unify the country with success after success.

Planetary governance requires the collapse of the United States, and President Trump was successfully reversing Obama's ruinous path to socialism. The enemies of America were desperate to defeat President Trump in the 2020 election, knowing that the robust American economy virtually guaranteed his reelection.

And then came COVID-19, the economic bioweapon unleashed in Wuhan, China, that disrupted Trump's economy, decimated the middle class, divided the country, empowered political medicine, and compromised Trump's presidency. The COVID-19 debacle exposed the details of globalism's tyrannical grand plan for the future and facilitated the greatest transfer of wealth in the history of the world to the scheming globalists.

The COVID-19 catastrophe is the product of corrupt political medicine, not medical science. It is the sinister vehicle for deliberately regressing the world population into childish submission, compliance, and the descent into planetary governance. It is the actualization of Henry Kissinger's infamous prediction at the 1992 Bilderberg meeting in Evian, France:

> Today Americans would be outraged if U.N. troops entered Los Angeles to restore order; tomorrow they will be grateful. This is especially true if they were told there was an outside threat from beyond, whether real or promulgated, that threatened our very existence. It is then that all peoples of the world will plead with world leaders to deliver them from this evil. The one thing every man fears is the unknown. When presented with this scenario, individual rights will be willingly relinquished for the guarantee of their well-being granted to them by their world government.

The Biden/Obama/Harris regime is exploiting the COVID-19 hysteria to impose restrictions on free speech, freedom of movement, and freedom of worship. They are enacting anti-American executive orders and unconstitutional mandates in a lawless power grab that is centralizing government control.

Medical tyranny at the corrupt Centers for Disease Control and Prevention (CDC) and National Institute of Allergy and Infectious Diseases (NIAID) is demanding experimental treatments mislabeled as "vaccines" for every American. Collaborating blue states are restricting travel, schooling, restaurants, and barring entry to public facilities without proof of "vaccination." They are imposing lawless mandates and severe restrictions that deny people's right to work, resulting in more dependence on the government.

America is now a house divided, in economic freefall, and being sucked into the vortex of the Great Reset. The "unvaccinated" are falsely vilified, blamed for illness, and segregated from society. Life is hurtling toward the Great Reset with the support of globalism's World Economic Forum, the United Nations, the Vatican, the International Monetary Fund, the British royal family, and the governments of the United States, the European Union, China, and India.

We are at a tipping point in our country, and *The Collapsing American Family: From Bonding to Bondage* explains how we got here. We cannot solve the COVID-19 "vaccine" problem without understanding its purpose in the war on America. The future is uncertain, but this I know is true: our future begins and ends with the American family.

United we stand, and divided we fall.

CHAPTER 2

America and the Family Business Rule

There is an old saying in family businesses: "The first generation starts a business. The second generation runs it. The third generation ruins it."

Metaphorically, our American family business is now in its third generation.

Our Founding Fathers rejected monarchy, oligarchy, aristocracy, and theocracy to form the United States of America as a constitutional republic—the greatest experiment in individual freedom and upward mobility the world has ever known. What happened?

To answer the question, we must examine the historical context of the three generations.

Our Founding Fathers lived at a time in history when *We the People* had little value. Societies throughout the world were structured along binary feudal lines and divided between the ruling elite and the enslaved population that served them. Slavery was a matter of degree— from physical chains and ownership of another human being, to caste systems that predetermined social position, to social structures where populations were subjugated by ruling monarchs, oligarchs, or the tyranny of religious theocratic rule.

Our Founding Fathers had a different vision. They decided to build a more perfect union, a representative democracy that valued individuals and entrusted them with the responsibility of elections to choose their own leaders. It was a radical experiment in social policy that represented a seismic shift in social attitudes.

A government of the people, by the people, and for the people offered unparalleled opportunities for upward mobility and the freedom to pursue one's dreams. Capitalism and a free-market economy allowed workers to keep the fruits of their labor and created a thriving middle class. What was the catch?

The freedom and opportunity that defined the American ideal required its citizens to become responsible, self-sufficient adults. Individual freedom, religious freedom, freedom of speech, freedom of assembly, freedom of the press, and freedom to petition the government were rights that required responsible adulthood.

Living free and dying free were not taken for granted in the 18th century. The success of the American ideal depended upon the shared American spirit of commitment to personal freedom by both the governed and the government. It was understood that the freedoms guaranteed by our Constitution and Bill of Rights were a promise of equal opportunity, not a guarantee of equal outcome, the war cry of today's socialists.

The 19th century was a period of enormous growth in America and marked a fundamental change to our metaphorical American family business—the second generation of the family business rule. The Industrial Revolution transformed America from an agrarian society of handmade goods to an industrial society of machine-made goods. The agrarian farm economy gave way to an industrial urban economy of wage labor, factories, trade unions, banking with an expanded credit system, and a railway system to move manufactured goods from factory to market.

The growth of America during the 19th and early 20th centuries was supported by the American spirit, the American ideal, and the <u>American dream</u>,[1] [endnotes listed at back of book] defined by Wikipedia as:

> The American Dream is a national ethos of the United States, the set of ideals (democracy, rights, liberty, opportunity, and equality) in which freedom includes the opportunity for prosperity and success, as well as an upward social mobility for the family and children, achieved through hard work in a society with few barriers. . . . The American Dream is rooted in the Declaration of Independence, which proclaims that "all men are created equal" with the right to "life, liberty and the pursuit of happiness."

The ethos of freedom and equal opportunity is what ended slavery in the United States with the Thirteenth Amendment in 1865 and gave women the right to vote in the United States with the Nineteenth Amendment in 1920. The early and mid-20th century in America were marked by world wars that threatened American freedom and strengthened the bonds of the American family in common cause.

There was a decade of calm and rebuilding at the end of World War II that ended with America's involvement in the disastrous Vietnam War from 1955 to 1975.

The third generation of America's family business began in the 1960s with the Cultural Revolution that continues to threaten the American ideal and the American dream. The anti-establishment generation began their assault on the vision of the Founding Fathers and rejected its intrinsic requirement to become fully functional emotional adults who accept the responsibilities of life in a free society. These emotional children disguised as chronological adults were determined to enjoy the benefits of freedom without accepting the responsibilities of freedom. They preferred the dependency model of collectivism and its seductive promises of "social justice" and "income equality."

The Declaration of Independence is an ideological document that proposed a limited government of the people, by the people, and for the people. The first generation created the document and started the American family business based on freedom, equal opportunity, and responsible adulthood. The second generation embraced the ideals of freedom, equal opportunity, and adult responsibility and successfully ran the family business. The third generation demands freedom, demands equal outcome, rejects adult responsibility, and is ruining the American family business. This is how it works.

The third generation of our American family identifies itself as *progressive* by demanding a centralized government that *frees* Americans from the burdensome responsibilities of freedom and guarantees equal outcome. "Progressive" is truly a misnomer because its infantile demands are entirely regressive. The regressives' demand is for eternal childhood where the government Mommy/Daddy takes care of its citizens from birth to death. Here is the problem.

Freedom is an adult enterprise, and freedom is never free. The cost of freedom is adult responsibility.

The regressives' demand for birth-to-death government control is a return to the binary feudal structure of the ruling elite and the enslaved population that served them. Mommy and Daddy provide for little Johnny but they also control every aspect of little Johnny's life. The cost of dependence is freedom.

Children are entitled to expect their parents to care for them until they are adults able to care for themselves—it is the cycle of life that supports an independent, adult, autonomous society. Chronological adults who demand that the government care for them as if they were children have perverted the cycle of life and will eventually collapse the society. The collectivist pledge of social justice and income equality promised by socialism and its deceitful leaders has been proven false in every society where it has been tried. Real-world socialism always debunks the promise of socialism.

The regressives and their identity politics form the base of the Democrat party in America today. Identity politics is a political perspective based on characteristics such as gender, religion, race, social background, class, and sexual orientation, that "identify" a particular group. The underlying assumptions of identity politics are that named groups are oppressed, need protection, and interconnect politically in their commonality. Their shared disadvantage and victim identity is called intersectionality, and their shared goal is to fundamentally transform America into a socialist nation.

The Democrat party is taking aim at capitalism, the free market, the Electoral College, the Supreme Court structure, and the Constitution itself by insisting that the Constitution is a *living* and therefore mutable document and not the solid infrastructure of a free America.

Collectivism, whether it is called socialism, communism, or globalism, is designed to benefit the leadership at the expense of the population. There is no private property, upward mobility, or middle class in collectivism because the government owns or otherwise controls all property, which includes the people themselves. There is only scarcity and servitude for the masses.

The third generation of America's family business, represented by the radical socialist Democrat party and the colluding mainstream media, has embraced the dependence of collectivism and is ruining America's family business. We the People are all shareholders in America's family business and must reassert our commitment to personal freedom, responsible adulthood, and life in a free society. We simply cannot allow the third generation to ruin America's family business.

CHAPTER 3

Selling Socialism to America

Socialism is a tough sell to Americans who evaluate ideas based on facts, and a remarkably easy sell to Americans who evaluate ideas based on feelings. The adult world of facts is a foreign land to the infantilized world of feelings where low-information millennials currently dwell. The heated political battle between Americanism and socialism parallels the ideological battle between parents and their children who refuse to grow up emotionally and leave the nest.

Becoming an emotional adult requires embracing a fact-based cause-and-effect view of the world that rejects the fantasies of childhood. "No, Johnny, you cannot fly like a bird even though you really, really, really want to." What happens if Johnny insists that he can fly and takes a confident leap from a tall building? Johnny dies.

Socialism and Johnny have a lot in common—both insist they can do what objective reality demonstrates they cannot do.

So, why is that a problem?

America is being challenged by a Peter Pan generation that refuses to grow up, living in a world of subjective reality where feelings rather than facts determine public policy. Their fragile selves require enforced political correctness and safe spaces to protect them from unwelcome facts and opposing ideas. Johnny climbs to the top of a tall building because he "feels" like a bird—he refuses to accept the fact that he is a human being and cannot fly. Human beings have limitations, just as socialism does.

The limitations of socialism make it impossible to provide the social justice and income equality that it promises. First, the principle of robbing the rich to pay the poor eventually leaves everyone penniless. Second, socialism is actually a binary political system with a very small wealthy ruling class and a very large population that serves them. There is no middle class in socialism because there is no private property and no upward mobility. The government confiscates or controls all goods and services. Ask the Venezuelans.

Socialism's free stuff is never free because you forfeit your freedom.

Low-information political leaders such as Alexandria Ocasio-Cortez (AOC) have emerged to sell socialism to America. Who is buying? AOC's supporters are millennial voters, children of the baby boom generation who, like AOC, have been indoctrinated to believe in collectivism by the leftist narrative that dominates public education K–12 and dictates university curricula. The Left's takeover of college campuses and its rejection of objective reality is discussed in chilling detail in Andrew Cunningham's March 8, 2019, American Thinker article, "Marxism, the Frankfurt School, and the Leftist Takeover of the College Campus."[2]

> While socialist and Marxist-influenced ideas have spread throughout the corridors of America and thus led to the election of such prominent democratic socialists as Alexandria Ocasio-Cortez and Rashida Tlaib, many Americans don't realize how deep an impact Marxist ideas have made culturally—namely, on college campuses.
>
> The Frankfurt School was a movement of far-left European philosophers who sought (among many other things) to apply the ideas of Marx in a social context. What developed from this school was Critical Theory, which is ultimately a re-envisioning of the way the world is seen. The Frankfurt School rejected objective truth and the historical records of humanity and objected to any form of objective knowledge. . . .
>
> The Frankfurt School's rejection of objective truth has led to the creation of leftist ideologies that demonize all forms of conservatism while praising intersectionality [the leftist descriptor of interconnecting social categories such as race, class, and gender regarded as interdependent systems of discrimination, disadvantage, and victimhood]. Once an idea is preached into impressionable minds, reiterated throughout the echo chambers of social media, and proselytized to the masses, these ideas became mainstays of mainstream culture.

The rejection of objective reality is foundational to the shift from facts to feelings that underlies millennial perspectives and policies.

It is painful to listen to AOC and hear the absurdity of the public policies she proposes. After reviewing her Green New Deal, one has to ask, "Did this woman really earn a degree in economics from Boston University?"

AOC is the disturbing outcome of the feeling-based education that intentionally values feelings over facts. Worthless degrees are awarded that celebrate the regressive, infantilized, subjective reality of children and not the fact-based world of adults. Education in America has reversed itself. Rather than teaching the foundational facts necessary to succeed in the adult world, American education's focus on student feelings has had a paralyzing effect and produced a Peter Pan generation of low-information, childlike, dependent voters.

The refrain from Peter Pan's signature song, "I Won't Grow Up,"[3] is socialism's millennial anthem:

> I won't grow up!
>
> I will stay a boy forever
>
> I'll never grow up, never never grow up
>
> Not me!

We do not live in never-never land. We live in the United States of America where freedom and opportunity require a commitment to living in the adult world of objective reality. Socialism demands a return to childhood dependence and the infantile world of subjective reality epitomized by the Green New Deal. We must grow up and embrace the fact that human beings are not birds—they cannot fly even when they really, really, really feel that they can.

Socialism will kill America as surely as Johnny trying to fly.

CHAPTER 4

The Relationship Charade: Walking on Eggshells Is Not Reconciliation

Many articles have been written exploring the trend of adult children choosing estrangement in American families. The alarming movement toward the dissolution of family bonds of love and loyalty has become an accepted alternative to reconciliation. What is the source of this dreadful shift? What happened to *honor thy father and thy mother?*

Sheri McGregor, MA, has written an important book titled *Done with the Crying* (2016) that explores the disturbing increase in families with adult children who disown their parents. There are, of course, appropriate conditions for estrangement, but the current national trend is baffling to the 9,000 confused and grieving parents McGregor surveyed, who cannot fathom why the children they have loved from birth are choosing to reject them. *Done with the Crying* attempts to help devastated parents accept their loss and move on with their lives. McGregor asks *What now?* I am asking *Why now?*

Generation gaps between parents and their adult children have traditionally been resolved with courtesy, respect, and humor. Adult children honored their parents even when they disagreed with them and chose a different path for their own lives. A fundamental level of gratitude for the parents' efforts, dedication, and sacrifice allowed the differences to be minimized and the family bonds maximized. What changed?

The bewildered parents in McGregor's study cannot accept the estrangement because they simply do not understand it. The staggering lack of respect, restraint, gratitude, and overarching sense of entitlement in their adult children's attitudes is confounding. The demand for parental conformity often includes outrageous restrictions on the parents' freedom of speech.

In the upside-down world of self-seeking millennials, parent/child roles have been reversed. Parents are expected to conform to their adult children's new norms. If the parent refuses, the adult child withdraws to a "safe space" seeking protection from the "toxic" ideas of his parents. Toxicity, like hate speech, has been redefined as anything the adult child opposes.

If grandchildren are involved, the adult children weaponize them to use against the grandparents. It is a particularly cruel choice because estrangement injures the grandchildren who are confused and must grieve the sudden loss of the love and attention of Grandma and Grandpa.

Respondents in McGregor's book expose the adverse participation of the mental health community, which continues to counsel disrespected parents to persevere and strive for reconciliation no matter how cruel and abusive their adult children's behavior becomes. It is shocking that any mental health professional would advocate unconditional love in adult relationships. Separating an individual from his/her behavior is pathological in adulthood. Any adult with self-respect recognizes the destructiveness of accepting the unacceptable. So, why has the mental health community abdicated its responsibility toward growth and maturity and instead embraced the regressive trend toward dependency that inappropriately demands unconditional love in adulthood?

To answer this question, it is necessary to review the growth process.

> Parents need to understand the growth process is twofold; it has a physical component and a psychological component. We all grow up physically because it takes no effort and is outside our control. Chronological age is an uncontested, biological accomplishment. Psychological growth is another matter entirely. The demands of responsible adults trying to draw us out of the state of narcissism rage against our natural, regressive desires to remain children. We resist psychological growth. We struggle with the wish to become powerful, independent adults and the longing to remain powerless, dependent children. We demand the freedom that belongs to responsible adults, yet we are nostalgic for a time of complete dependence when we were nurtured entirely. Psychological growth is the universal challenge of childhood. (*Dear America*, p. 14)[4]

Students of the '60s who rejected established cultural standards graduated and became the teachers and social science "experts" who enthusiastically embraced leftist politics and political correctness. They launched a seismic paradigm shift that steered American society away from adult responsibility toward valuing feelings and happiness above all else. Instead of encouraging children to strive for achievement and merit-based awards, parents were told that their children's self-esteem would suffer in competition. Effort alone became the criteria for awards. Teachers told children they were all butterflies, and all students received trophies for "trying."

Political correctness values feelings over facts. It is extremely destructive because the effort to avoid hurt feelings sacrifices objective reality. Effort and achievement are *not* equivalent. Historically, education at home and at school prepared children for adulthood in the adult world of facts, where it is necessary to achieve. Consider the consequences in everyday life when trying is considered equivalent to achieving. Workers try to complete tasks but don't. Students try to understand concepts but don't. Mothers try to get meals on the table but don't.

In the real world of objective reality, trying is not the same as accomplishing. Understanding this basic concept is foundational to understanding the conflict between objective and subjective reality that is the root of the collapse of the nuclear and national American families.

The war on America is a psychological war that deliberately exploits the inner conflict of growing up. It disrupts the growth process, encourages regression, intentionally blurs the boundaries between objective and subjective reality, and interferes with reality testing. The goal is to produce generations of dependent adults who function in the subjective reality of childhood where they are emotionally regressed and do not distinguish between fact and fiction. A regressed population that lacks a developed skill for testing reality is easily controlled because, like young children, it believes what it is told.

When three-year-old Johnny insists he can fly, his mother gently and protectively assures him he cannot. She is teaching Johnny the difference between objective reality/facts, and subjective reality/feelings. Johnny begins to learn the difference between facts and feelings, wanting and having, saying and doing, and trying and achieving. He is beginning to test reality.

At three years old, Johnny's insistence that he can fly comports with his chronological age. His blurring of facts and feelings are acceptable and age-appropriate at age three.

At thirty years old, Johnny's insistence that he can fly would be considered delusional in a sane society. His blurring of facts and feelings at thirty is completely out of touch with objective reality and entirely age-inappropriate. The logical and natural consequence of Johnny's delusion if he attempts flight at age thirty is death. Objective reality is unavoidable.

When thirty-year-old Johnny allows his inner child to make decisions, he has entered the realm of subjective reality; he is no longer functioning in objective reality. His demands will therefore be inappropriate, and the expectation that his parents meet those demands equally inappropriate.

The Cultural Revolution, fomented by the radical left, demands regression, incites rebellion, and fuels the infantile anger that drives the Culture War on America. The challenge of childhood to grow up emotionally is intentionally hindered, which necessarily creates conflict with parents who fully and appropriately expect their adult children to be emotional adults.

Instead of *honoring thy father and thy mother*, the millennial sense of infantile entitlement has frozen their generation in a world of feelings where only self and self-gratification exist. Instead of behaving like rational adults in their twenties, thirties, and forties, millennials have been encouraged to allow their narcissistic inner children to drive their buses and make inappropriate demands on their parents.

Thought precedes behavior. Millennials who have been indoctrinated toward entitlements, unconditional love, and eternal childhood rage when their dependency needs are unmet. Their anger is then exploited as they are groomed to become the useful-idiot soldiers necessary to topple the existing government with promises of cradle-to-grave care from a romanticized socialist government. The estranged child's loyalty shifts away from his nuclear family to his new family of choice. He converts, and embraces the new religion of liberalism where his rejection of traditional authority is applauded in an all-encompassing atmosphere of adolescent rebellion.

Fragile, disinformed snowflakes are too childish and too angry to examine the reality of life in actual socialist countries. They do not interview citizens of Venezuela or Cuba; instead, they just parrot socialist propaganda. When parents expose the glaring inconsistencies between leftist ideology and reality, the indoctrinated sons and daughters choose estrangement as an avoidance strategy to protect themselves from unwanted challenges to their idealized socialist narrative.

The bewilderment and shock of estrangement for parents is rivaled only by the stunning realization that the Left purposefully foments family estrangement in order to shatter the bonds of family loyalty and parental authority. Grieving parents cannot accept estrangement until they understand that their adult children are choosing ideology over genealogy. The courtesy, respect, and gratitude that characterized past generations are absent in the indoctrinated millennial generation.

The outcome of the politically correct paradigm shift from facts to feelings has been catastrophic. It has produced a generation of disrespectful, infantilized, intolerant chronological adults lacking an adult work ethic, work skills, and coping skills, too fragile to listen to anyone who disagrees with them. The outcome of their incompetence is anger and self-loathing. Even exceptional millennials who have managed to achieve remarkable things in their professional lives are kept fixated and angry by their infantilism and dependency needs.

Competence is the mother of self-esteem. Accomplishment creates genuine self-esteem and the marvelous sense of satisfaction that proficiency provides. Telling children they are all butterflies (subjective reality) is dishonest because children are not all the same and they know it. Encouraging a child to accomplish a task is far more productive of self-esteem than empty compliments, because encouragement supports growth, maturity, and the acquisition of skills. The crippling policies that created the paradigm shift toward feelings has yielded a crop of immature, fragile, angry snowflakes. Anger is an extremely powerful emotion that can be exploited for destruction—precisely the underlying strategy of the Left.

Only within the subjective reality of their politically correct social groups can underdeveloped millennials feel good about themselves. It explains why those on the Left tolerate people who look different but cannot tolerate anyone who thinks differently, including their own parents. Like any orthodoxy, leftism relies on absolute conformity to its tenets of political correctness, moral relativity, and historical revisionism in order to survive and recruit new members to its ideological identity politics. Those who disagree are maligned, shunned, and rejected—including parents.

There is no reconciliation with angry adult children who continue to reject their parents' objective reality. There is no respectful "agreeing to disagree" with adult children who demand that their parents surrender to subjective reality and accept the reimagined millennial version of the socialist nightmare.

If parents of adult children surrender to the madness of subjective reality, they become part of the psychological war on America. Asymmetric psychological warfare can be resisted only by understanding the goal of the war: a socialist America.

The answer to *Why now?* is entirely political. The psychological operation (PSYOP) that is destroying the American family is an insidious information/propaganda tactic designed to sell dependency, socialism, and globalism to an unaware American public. Educational indoctrination and media propaganda are its primary delivery systems. Your children and your children's children are the targets.

The future of America will be determined by the future of the American family. Parents must remain in objective reality in order to remain rational adult role models for life in a free society of ordered liberty.

Objective reality is the core of American life, liberty, and love.

Walking on eggshells with adult children is not reconciliation—it is a relationship charade. Parents have an obligation to remain in objective reality even when their adult children choose to leave, and even if they take beloved grandchildren with them.

CHAPTER 5

The Educational Battlefield:
the deliberate dumbing down of america

The 20th-century Cultural Revolution established a tactical shift from conventional warfare to asymmetric warfare by the enemies of America. They understood that America must be defeated from within. Nineteenth-century American poet William Wallace's famous poem praising motherhood provides the clue for why the nuclear family became the target and the educational system was used to foment family strife.

The Hand that Rocks the Cradle Rules the World[5]

by William Ross Wallace (1819–1881)

Blessings on the hand of women!
   Angels guard its strength and grace.
In the palace, cottage, hovel,
   Oh, no matter where the place;
Would that never storms assailed it,
   Rainbows ever gently curled,
For the hand that rocks the cradle
   Is the hand that rules the world.

Infancy's the tender fountain,
   Power may with beauty flow,
Mothers first to guide the streamlets,
   From them souls unresting grow —
Grow on for the good or evil,
   Sunshine streamed or evil hurled,
For the hand that rocks the cradle
   Is the hand that rules the world.

Woman, how divine your mission,
   Here upon our natal sod;

Keep—oh, keep the young heart open
   Always to the breath of God!
All true trophies of the ages
   Are from mother-love impearled,
For the hand that rocks the cradle
   Is the hand that rules the world.

Blessings on the hand of women!
   Fathers, sons, and daughters cry,
And the sacred song is mingled
   With the worship in the sky—
Mingles where no tempest darkens,
   Rainbows evermore are hurled;
For the hand that rocks the cradle
   Is the hand that rules the world.

Education is perpetual from generation to generation, and our Founding Fathers recognized that an educated population was necessary to protect and preserve our precious constitutional freedoms. The original source and responsibility for education belonged to the parents. Children were homeschooled at first and then parents established schools in their communities by hiring local teachers to teach their children as part of their parental responsibilities. Thus, education in America derived from the nuclear family and its values.

Education in totalitarian states is top-down and government-controlled in both form and content. Vladimir Lenin famously said, "Give me four years to teach the children and the seed I have sown will never be uprooted."

The shift in American education has been an inexorable march away from parental, local, and eventually state control toward federalized government-controlled education. It is the march away from the vision of our Founding Fathers toward the Marxist-Leninist vision of totalitarian government educational control.

Charlotte Thomson Iserbyt's explosive 1999 book, _the deliberate dumbing down of america_,[6] exposes the political perversion of American education as the vehicle for changing America "from a sovereign, constitutional republic with a free enterprise economic base to just one of many nations in an international socialist (collectivist) system (New

World Order)." (p. 7)

Iserbyt marks the early twentieth century as the "Turning of the Tides":[7]

> For a nation that had been able to point with pride to extraordinary advances in all areas of endeavor carried out by *individuals*, with no assistance whatsoever from the government, the early years of the twentieth century surely reflected a "Turning of the Tides." An alien collectivist (socialist) philosophy, much of which came from Europe, crashed onto the shores of our nation, bringing with it radical changes in economics, politics, and education, funded—surprisingly enough—by several wealthy American families and their tax-exempt foundations.

> The goal of these wealthy families and their foundations—a seamless non-competitive global system for commerce and trade—when stripped of flowery expressions of concern for minorities, the less fortunate, etc., represented the initial stage of what this author now refers to as *the deliberate dumbing down of america.* (p. 7)

The enemies of American freedom and sovereignty understood that the hand that rocks the cradle must be the government, not the parents. Educator Sam Blumenfeld's foreword to Charlotte Iserbyt's book is a marvelous overview:

> Charlotte Iserbyt is to be greatly commended for having put together the most formidable and practical compilation of documentation describing the "deliberate dumbing down" of American children by their education system. Anyone interested in the truth will be shocked by the way American social engineers have systematically gone about destroying the intellect of millions of American children for the purpose of leading the American people into a socialist world government controlled by behavioral and social scientists.

> Mrs. Iserbyt has also documented the gradual transformation of our once academically successful education system into one devoted to training children to become compliant human resources to be used by government and industry for their own purposes. This is how fascist-socialist societies train their children to become servants of their government masters. The

successful implementation of this new philosophy of education will spell the end of the American dream of individual freedom and opportunity. The government will plan your life for you, and unless you comply with government restrictions and regulations your ability to pursue a career of your own choice will be severely limited.

What is so mind boggling is that all of this is being financed by the American people themselves through their own taxes. In other words, the American people are underwriting the destruction of their own freedom and way of life by lavishly financing through federal grants the very social scientists who are undermining our national sovereignty and preparing our children to become the dumbed-down vassals of the new world order. It reminds one of how the Nazis charged their victims train fare to their own doom.

One of the interesting insights revealed by these documents is how the social engineers use a deliberately created education "crisis" to move their agenda forward by offering radical reforms that are sold to the public as fixing the crisis—which they never do. The new reforms simply set the stage for the next crisis, which provides the pretext for the next move forward. This is the dialectical process at work, a process our behavioral engineers have learned to use very effectively. Its success depends on the ability of the "change agents" to continually deceive the public, which tends to believe anything the experts tell them.

And so, our children continue to be at risk in America's schools. They are at risk academically because of such programs as whole language, mastery learning, direct instruction, Skinnerian operant conditioning, all of which have created huge learning problems that inevitably lead to what is commonly known as Attention Deficit Disorder, and the drugging of four million children with the powerful drug Ritalin. Mrs. Iserbyt has dealt extensively with the root causes of immorality in our society and the role of the public schools in the teaching of moral relativism (no right/no wrong ethics). She raises a red flag regarding the current efforts of left-wing liberals and right-wing conservatives (radical center) to come up with a new kid on the block, "common ground" character education—which will, under the microscope, turn out to be the same warmed-over values education alert parent groups have resisted for over fifty years. This is a perfect example of the Hegelian Dialectic at work.

The reader will find in this book a plethora of information that will leave no doubt in the mind of the serious researcher exactly where the American education system is headed. If we wish to stop this juggernaut toward a socialist-fascist system, then we must restore educational freedom to America. Americans forget that the present government education system started as a Prussian import in the 1840s–'50s. It was a system built on Hegel's belief that the state was "God" walking on earth. The only way to restore educational freedom, and put education back into the hands of parents where it belongs, is to get the federal government, with its coercive policies, out of education. The billions of dollars being spent by the federal government to destroy educational freedom must be halted, and that can only be done by getting American legislators to understand that the American people want to remain a free people, in charge of their own lives and the education of their children. (pp. xi–xii)[8]

Charlotte Iserbyt's extraordinary book exposes the shocking humanitarian hoax that uses public education to indoctrinate American children against America and the Judeo-Christian values taught to them by their parents. A humanitarian hoax is the deliberate and deceitful tactic of presenting a destructive policy as altruistic. Iserbyt documents the profound political corruption and malfeasance that have been deliberately destroying American education for decades. She reveals the overarching theory and practices used to politicize and centralize public education using federal monies to extort compliance.

I was moved by Mrs. Iserbyt's comprehensive research and her unwavering commitment to exposing the profound corruption and deceitful use of public education as a social engineering tool in America. Over twenty years ago, she warned the nation about the dangers of ceding local control of education to the federal government.

Mrs. Iserbyt's warnings are the nightmarish reality of the 2021 Biden administration's embrace of racist, anti-American critical race theory and highly inappropriate sex education in public schools today. Her work is a wake-up call for patriotic parents and grandparents to stand firm and resist federal takeover of our state and local school districts, because federalized education is the road to socialism and one-world government. Preserving the authority and autonomy of local schools is the responsibility of parents in the local school districts. Public education has become a battlefield for the minds/souls of our children.

In the preface, Mrs. Iserbyt speaks passionately about her reasons for writing the book:

> This resister's book, or collection of research in book form, was put together primarily to satisfy my own need to see the various components which led to the dumbing down of the United States of America assembled in chronological order—in writing. Even I, who had observed these weird activities taking place at all levels of government, was reluctant to accept a malicious intent behind each individual, chronological activity or innovation, unless I could connect it with other, similar activities taking place at other times. This book, which makes such connections, has provided for me a much-needed sense of closure.

> *the deliberate dumbing down of america* is also a book for my children, grandchildren, and great-grandchildren. I want them to know that there were thousands of Americans who may not have died or been shot at in overseas wars, but *were* shot at in small-town "wars" at school board meetings, at state legislative hearings on education, and, most importantly, in the media. I want my progeny to know that whatever intellectual and spiritual freedoms to which they may still lay claim were fought for— are a result of—the courageous work of incredible people who dared to tell the truth against all odds.

> I want them to know that there will always be hope for freedom if they follow in these people's footsteps; if they cherish the concept of "free will"; if they believe that human beings are special, not animals, and that they have intellects, souls, and consciences. I want them to know that if the government schools are allowed to teach children K–12 using Pavlovian/Skinnerian animal training methods—which provide tangible rewards only for correct answers—there can be no freedom. . . .

In 1971 when I returned to the United States after living abroad for 18 years, I was shocked to find public education had become a warm, fuzzy, soft, mushy, touchy-feely experience, with its purpose being socialization, not learning. From that time on, from the vantage point of having two young sons in the public schools, I became involved—as a member of a philosophy committee for a school, as an elected school board member, as co-founder of Guardians of Education for Maine (GEM), and finally as a senior policy advisor in the Office of Educational Research and Improvement (OERI) of the U.S. Department of Education during President Ronald Reagan's first term of office. OERI was, and is, the office from which *all* the controversial national and international educational restructuring has emanated.

Those ten years (1971–1981) changed my life. As an American who had spent many years working abroad, I had experienced traveling in and living in socialist countries. When I returned to the United States, I realized that America's transition from a sovereign constitutional republic to a socialist democracy would not come about through warfare (bullets and tanks) but through the implementation and installation of the "system" in *all* areas of government—federal, state and local. The brainwashing for acceptance of the "system's" control would take place in the school—through indoctrination and the use of behavior modification, which comes under so many labels: the most recent labels being Outcome-Based Education (OBE), Skinnerian Mastery Learning or Direct Instruction.[i] [footnotes listed at end of chapter] (pp. xiv–xv)[9]

Charlotte Iserbyt courageously dedicated her professional life to preserving American liberty by exposing the sinister scheme to transform America through educational indoctrination. Her odyssey began with a highly inappropriate handout given to her fourth-grade son:

In 1973 I started the long journey into becoming a "resister," placing the first incriminating piece of paper in my "education" files. That first piece of paper was a purple ditto sheet entitled "All About Me," next to which was a smiley face. It was an open-ended questionnaire beginning with: "My name is _____." My son brought it home from public school in fourth grade. The questions were highly personal; so much so that they encouraged my son to lie, since he didn't want to "spill the beans" about his mother, father and brother. The purpose of such a questionnaire was to find out the student's state of mind, how he felt, what he liked and disliked, and what his values were. With this knowledge it would be easier for the government school to modify his values and behavior at will—without, of course, the student's knowledge or parents' consent. . . .

After two failed attempts to get elected to the school board, I finally succeeded in 1976 on the third try. The votes were counted three times, even though I had won by a very healthy margin!

My experience on the school board taught me that when it comes to modern education, "the end justifies the means." Our change agent superintendent was more at home with a lie than he was with the truth. . . .

Another milestone on my journey was an in-service training session entitled "Innovations in Education." A retired teacher, who understood what was happening in education, paid for me to attend. This training program developed by Professor Ronald Havelock of the University of Michigan and funded by the United States Office of Education taught teachers and administrators how to "sneak in" controversial methods of teaching and "innovative" programs. These controversial, "innovative" programs included health education, sex education, drug and alcohol education, death education, critical thinking education, etc. Since then, I have always found it interesting that the controversial school programs are the only ones that have the word "education" attached to them! I don't recall—until recently—"math ed.," "reading ed.," "history ed.," or "science ed." A good rule of thumb for teachers, parents and school board members interested in academics and traditional values is to question any subject that has the word "education" attached to it.

This in-service training literally "blew my mind." I have never recovered from it. The presenter (change agent) taught us how

to "manipulate" the taxpayers/parents into accepting controversial programs. He explained how to identify the "resisters"
in the community and how to get around their resistance. He
instructed us in how to go to the highly respected members of
the community—those with the Chamber of Commerce, Rotary,
Junior League, Little League, YMCA, Historical Society, etc.—to
manipulate them into supporting the controversial/non-aca-
demic programs and into bad-mouthing the resisters. Advice was
also given as to how to get the media to support these programs.

I left this training—with my very valuable textbook, *The Change
Agent's Guide to Innovations in Education*, under my arm—
feeling *very* sick to my stomach and in complete denial over that
in which I had been involved. . . .

In retrospect, I had just found out that the United States was
engaged in war. People write important books about war: books
documenting the battles fought, the names of the generals involved, the names of those who fired the first shot. This book is
simply a history book about another kind of war:

> · one fought using psychological methods;
> · a one-hundred-year war;
> · a different, more deadly war than any in which our
> country has ever been involved;
> · a war about which the average American hasn't the
> foggiest idea.

The reason Americans do not understand this war is because *it
has been fought in secret*—in the schools of our nation, targeting *our children* who are captive in classrooms. The wagers
of this war are using very sophisticated and effective tools:

> · Hegelian Dialectic (common ground, consensus and
> compromise)
> · Gradualism (two steps forward; one step backward)
> · Semantic deception (redefining terms to get agree-
> ment without understanding). [Orwellian doublespeak]
> (pp. xv–xvii)[10]

Mrs. Iserbyt decodes the war on America as a war on American education. She documents the stealth battle plan that dumbs down America,

centralizes educational control, shifts the authority of the family to the state, and indoctrinates American children in anti-American collectivism.

Destroy the family, you destroy the country. —Vladimir Ilyich Lenin

the deliberate dumbing down of america documents the hidden purposes of weaponized American education using quotes from government documents:

- to use the schools to change America from a free, individual nation to a socialist, global "state," just one of many socialist states which will be subservient to the United Nations Charter, not the *United States Constitution*

- to brainwash our children, starting at birth, to reject individualism in favor of collectivism

- to reject high academic standards in favor of OBE/ISO 1400/90007 egalitarianism [outcomes-based education/International Standards of Operation]

- to reject truth and absolutes in favor of tolerance, situational ethics and consensus

- to reject American values in favor of internationalist values (globalism)

- to reject freedom to choose one's career in favor of the totalitarian K–12 school-to-work/OBE process, aptly named "limited learning for lifelong labor," coordinated through United Nations Educational, Scientific, and Cultural Organization.[ii] [footnotes listed at end of chapter]

Only when all children in public, private and home schools are robotized—and believe as one—will World Government be acceptable to citizens and able to be implemented without firing a shot. The attractive-sounding "choice" proposals will enable the globalist elite to achieve their goal: the robotization (brainwashing) of all Americans in order to gain their acceptance of lifelong education and workforce training—part of the world management system to achieve a new global feudalism. . . .

In order to win a battle, one must know who the "real" enemy is. Otherwise, one is shooting in the dark and often hitting those not the least bit responsible for the mayhem. This book, hopefully, identifies the "real" enemy and provides Americans involved in this war—be they plain, ordinary citizens, elected officials, or traditional teachers—with the ammunition to fight to obtain victory. (pp. xix–xxi)[11]

Charlotte Iserbyt's exceptional work is foundational for the discussions that follow. Every element of the stealth battle plan impacts the American family and demonstrates how American education, which was once the staunch ally of the American family, is now its existential enemy.

Footnotes from *the deliberate dumbing down of america*:

[i] OBE/ML/DI or outcomes-based education/mastery learning/direct instruction.

[ii] "Privatization or Socialization" by C. Weatherly, 1994. Delivered as part of a speech to a group in Minnesota and later published in *The Christian Conscience* magazine (Vol. 1, No. 2: February 1995, pp. 29–30).

CHAPTER 6

John Dewey:
The Father of Weaponized Education in America

John Dewey, American philosopher, psychologist, and educational reformer, provided the foundation for weaponized education in America. He led the *progressive* movement that changed the mission of American education from acquiring basic skills and foundational knowledge, to the mission of social engineering.

In 1899, John Dewey was elected president of the American Psychological Association and in 1905 became president of the American Philosophical Association. Dewey was professor of philosophy at Columbia University's Teachers College from 1904 until he retired in 1930. He returned to teach as professor emeritus until 1939. Teachers College, founded in 1887, endowed with $500,000 from the Rockefeller Foundation in 1902, is the oldest and largest graduate school of education in the United States.

Dewey also helped found the American Federation of Teachers (AFT) in 1916 and continued as its most notable member. Teacher training and teacher labor unions, financially connected to and supported by the Rockefeller Foundation, presented a conflict of interest in American education.

Students are an educational product. Curriculum are designed with specific goals, objectives, and student outcomes.

Traditional American education was designed to teach the skills and knowledge that encouraged individualism, critical thinking, and creativity—the foundation of American exceptionalism, ingenuity, and entrepreneurship that produced the freest, most powerful nation on earth.

John Dewey was an unapologetic globalist who advanced the elitist position that the purpose of education is social engineering with the goal of establishing a new social order. Dewey considered education a social process, and the school a social institution where social reform should take place. His formula eliminates the development of critical-thinking skills in children. Without critical-thinking skills, individuals are easily manipulated and indoctrinated; like children, they simply accept what they are told.

According to Dewey:

> The purpose of education should not revolve around the acquisition of a pre-determined set of skills, but rather the realization of one's full potential and the ability to use those skills for the greater good. (My Pedagogic Creed, 1897)

> The mere absorption of facts and truths is so exclusively an individual affair that it tends very naturally to pass into selfishness. There is no obvious social motive for the acquirement of mere learning, there is no clear social gain in success thereat. (The School and Society, 1899)

Dewey was a radical socialist who was contemptuous of any influence outside the controlled school environment. American educator Bruce Deitrick Price aptly describes Dewey's perspective as "The Dewey Deception":[12]

> Listening to John Dewey, you'd think that children have no families, homes, parents, siblings, friends, relatives, neighbors, communities, sports, religions, hobbies, no life outside the school. If they aren't socialized at his school his way, they'll be lost souls. Such arrogance. So, Dewey inverts the main reason for the school's existence, which is to provide the intellectual discipline and direction that might not be provided by all those other forces. Dewey wants to take schools out of the education business, as traditionally understood, and put them in the conditioning (or parenting) business.

In his October 1, 2012, American Thinker article, "John Dewey Is a Fraud,"[13] Price exposes Dewey's arrogant and deceitful scheme for social engineering:

> It is generally agreed that John Dewey (1859–1952) is the Father of American Education and the Greatest American Educator Ever.

The problem with the labels is that John Dewey, albeit a genius, was not an educator in the sense that most people use this word. He was not interested in teaching as most people understand that term, as for example in the statement "I teach French."

Dewey was not primarily concerned with teaching new information. He was concerned with inculcating new attitudes.

John Dewey was a social engineer—one might even say a community organizer. He believed that socialism is the future. His self-appointed mission was to implement the transition to this brave new world.

All of his grand theories, his scores of books, and his hundreds of articles can be summed up as a program for making America socialist.

There is one little problem at this point: almost nobody in America was asking for this transformation. So, Dewey was in the awkward position of redecorating your house when you didn't ask for it to be redecorated, or more precisely seducing your kids when you don't want your kids to be seduced.

Dewey basically had to ignore law, precedent, tradition, legislatures, voters, elections, expectations of families, and the needs of society. He attempted an end-run, and thus a conspiracy. . . .

Dewey and the hundreds of people in his immediate orbit serenely agreed that cooperation was the highest virtue, sociology was the future, psychology provided the essential truths of life, God was dead, religion was obsolete, family must be belittled, and patriotism, honor, and other old-fashioned virtues must be slowly ground down to nothing. . . .

Speaking roughly of the modern period 1950–2000, education's top people had to practice a delicate ingenuity. They wanted curricula that created leveling, not excellence. So, they had to come up with one cleverly designed-to-fail method after another, wrap each one in gaudy lingo, and sell them all to the poor benighted parents of America, two famous examples being Look-say and Reform Math. [Both terms are explained below.]

Always, these top educators were trapped in their lie, in Dewey's lie. They had to pretend they were interested in education when the real goals were psychological indoctrination and sociological transformation. The Education Establishment,[14] I would submit, exactly continues Dewey's dream today.

Ask teachers, and you will find that they must attend an endless array of Professional Development (PD) classes. They must constantly discard the wonderful new gimmicks from a few years ago and start all over with the latest new thing. But the old ideas and the new idea are all equally bad, because at bottom they are obsessed with indoctrination, not education.

Which brings us back to the main theme: John Dewey wasn't interested in education as you and I understand this term. Everything he did was in fact intended to subvert and diminish traditional education.

That is not too harsh. Excellence got in the way of cooperation. If Jackie knew the capital of France, but Albert did not, you have introduced a division into the classroom, and thus into society. John Dewey and the members of his cult did not give a damn about the capital of France if this bit of trivia got in the way of their social plans. See it from their point of view, and everything they did was logical.

John Dewey's secret scams are the reason why we have 50 million functional illiterates, why high school graduates can't multiply seven times eight, why most American kids can't find Japan on a map, why even simple knowledge like "what is a moon" is probably not part of the lives of most Americans.

The progressives who control education deified John Dewey and placed him on a pedestal, but that was a marketing tool. Then they could say, "We should do X because John Dewey says it's the best way, and he is our greatest educator." Parents and young teachers would wilt before the prestige of the great John Dewey.

The major problem in all of American education is dishonesty. Schools could be much better, at less cost. But few will tell the truth about any aspect of public education, ever since John Dewey launched his disingenuous crusade to transform America via the classroom.

> The Education Establishment today will not tell the truth about Whole Word, Reform Math, Constructivism, Cooperative Learning, self-esteem, Learning Styles, Common Core, or just about anything else they do in the public schools. There are many lies, but the big lie is that John Dewey is a great educator. He was a great socialist. He was a titan at articulating how we might implement social engineering, but he was not an educator as traditionally understood.

By far the most destructive legacy of John Dewey's progressive education is the Look-say teaching method, also known as the whole word method. Rather than breaking words down into individual letters or groups of letters, children are taught to read words as whole units. The children are repeatedly told the word name while shown the printed word. Eventually they are expected to *sight-read* the word.

Sight-Reading and Reform Math are the primary tactical weapons in a weaponized education, because they are the foundation of higher education.

The public was first alerted that something was seriously wrong with education in America over six decades ago. The reading crisis was ignited in America in 1955 with the publication of Dr Rudolph Flesch's stunning book, *Why Johnny Can't Read and What You Can Do About It.*

Educators have known for over six decades that English is a phonetic language and sight words are a failed strategy, yet they continue to use it. In 2017, Bruce Deitrick Price published an extraordinary book titled *Saving K-12: What Happened to Our Public Schools? How Do We Fix Them?*[15]

On pages 22–23 he presents an incontestable argument for anyone who does not understand why teaching sight words is so devastating. Price guides the adult reader through the experience of a child trying to learn to read with sight words. It is the most compelling argument against sight words imaginable. It dramatizes how insidious the deliberate, politically driven insistence on teaching reading with sight words really is. Price begins:

> Just for a moment, consider the silly theory that our top edu-

cators put forward. There should be no sounding out of letters and syllables; instead, children should memorize words as graphic designs or diagrams. Put yourself in the head of a kid showing up for first grade. The teacher points to a design like "**xhyld**" and instructs, "This means house. When you see this say *house*." So, can you memorize "**xhyld**"?

Probably. But will you be able to pick it out from similar designs, of which there are dozens, such as: **xhydd, xyhld, xhydl, xyyld, xhdyl, xyjkl, xkyht, xygld**, etc. of course, you'll need to be ready for variations such as **XHYDD, XYHLD, XHYDL, XYYLD, XHDYL, XYJKL, XKYHT, XYGLD**. Okay, maybe you have a photographic memory, so you might have a chance. But no ordinary person has even a tiny chance of being literate. You can probably feel the dyslexia creeping into your brain.

And you've just started on your first list of words. You'll need 5,000 words to be barely literate. But guess what the guru of this madcap theory said? "Children can acquire sight vocabularies of 50,000 words." Not without a chip implant. But it's even worse. College students probably need 100,000 words. (Total English vocabulary is over 500,000 words.)

The idea that reading has something to do with memorizing word shapes is nuts. There's no polite way to say it. English is a phonetic language, and you first need to learn the alphabet and then the sounds they represent.

Dewey's influence on American education is unprecedented. His *progressive* educational reform movement remains the foundation of American education. Its anti-American political goals have been wildly successful in transforming American education from a source of American strength and prosperity to a weapon of mass American destruction.

History validates Dewey's deception and its value as a weapon in the war on America. The coda[16] to Price's article reads:

John Dewey, the world-famous educator, was retained circa 1920 by the new Russian government to advise on the implementation of his *progressive* ideas throughout the USSR. Circa 1932, the communist government realized that Dewey's *progressive* education had created a generation of ignorant delinquents.

The communists in Russia banished Dewey's ideas from their country. Meanwhile, the communists et al in the United States celebrated Dewey and his policies.

In 1956, Morris Kline (1908–1992), chairman of the mathematics department at New York University, began publishing articles critical of teachers who blamed students for failing math. In 1974 he published his book, *Why Johnny Can't Add: The Failure of the New Math*. Kline argued that mathematics is a cumulative skill that requires a strong foundation. Teaching abstract concepts to children before the acquisition of basic computational skills is a failed strategy. New Math is the failed equivalent of Sight-Reading. Both have been renamed, relabeled, repackaged, reproduced, and reintroduced by educational "experts" as "new" solutions to the crises in education. The reading and math crises have led to staggering levels of illiteracy and mathematical incompetence in the United States.

The operative word for understanding the ongoing insistence on demonstrably failed strategies is *crisis*. It is the technique being used to implement educational social engineering. To understand the deception, we will examine in the next chapter the Hegelian dialectic and how it enables the politics of crisis.

CHAPTER 7

The Hegelian Dialectic

The Hegelian dialectic is a process for change developed by German philosopher Georg Wilhelm Hegel (1770–1831). The dialectic is based on Hegel's conviction that reality is fluid and nothing is constant. Since nothing is constant, there are no absolutes. Since there are no absolutes, there is no objective reality. Since there is no objective reality, everything is relative and exists in the fluidity of subjective reality. Political relativism, and the moral relativity it supports, found its philosophical home in Hegel's dialectic and its signature subjective reality.

Hegel's dialectic is foundational to Marxian socialism, and is the basis for the radical leftist politics convulsing America today. Karl Marx simplified the dialectic, "In the eyes of dialectical philosophy, nothing is established for all times, nothing is absolute or sacred."

Hegel rejected individualism in favor of collectivism, and denied objective reality in favor of ideology. His dialectic provided the infrastructure for Marx's utopian promise of *heaven on earth* when communism is firmly established worldwide. Since socialism was always the stepping-stone to communism, the words socialism and communism are used synonymously throughout this book.

What distinguishes the Hegelian dialectic from the Marxist dialectic is the subject of the dialectic. For Hegel it was ideas. For Marx it was economics and the means of production. In both cases the dialectal approach rejects any and all absolutes.

Hegel's dialectic is the operating *change* principle and tactical strategy for the war on America. Nothing is absolute or sacred for leftists and globalists, particularly the U.S. Constitution and the existence of the United States of America as a sovereign constitutional republic.

Hegel's dialectic presents a method of philosophical argument that attempts to resolve opposing ideas through a contradictory process: Thesis → Antithesis → Synthesis. It is basically a three-step problem-solving tool: Problem → Reaction → Solution.

Let's examine how political social engineers, the *change agents*, are using Hegel's dialectic to shatter the foundations of American education and collapse America from within. We begin with the example of teaching reading as a cumulative skill.

- *thesis* = reading taught with phonics

existing educational method strengthens America with foundational skills and basic knowledge

- *antithesis* = *change agents* introduce sight-reading

crisis of illiteracy deliberately created by Dewey "experts" insisting on sight-reading

- *synthesis* = teachers agree on a newer, "improved" version of sight words

thesis/phonics changes (consensus) from the first iteration of sight words to its next version of relabeled sight words moving farther away from phonics.

Former U.S. Secretary of Education T. H. Bell verbalized the process: "We need to create a crisis to get consensus in order to bring about change."

The deceit in Bell's statement reveals the flaw in Hegel's wholesale approach to reality. Hegel's dialectic assumes all ideas are the same—but not everything is an idea. For example, gravity is a force of nature, not an idea. Gravity exists in objective reality regardless of Johnny's subjective opinion on gravitational force. If, in Johnny's opinion, gravity does not exist and he attempts to fly off the rooftop of a tall building, we already know that Johnny will fall to his death.

The dialectical approach to reality rejects the concepts of absolutes such as gravity. There are certainly ideas in life that are relative and matters of opinion, but Hegel's dialectic regards *all* things as ideas and matters of opinion. If Johnny acts out the subjective reality of Hegel's relativism, Johnny dies.

Even the simple mathematical equation $2 + 2 = 4$ is rejected as an absolute. The problem, of course, is that numbers and equations are assignations of real things no matter what the symbol for the thing is. Similarly, the alphabet letters of languages are symbols. The Hegelian dialectic can reject a letter in a language as not being an absolute, but it cannot reject the objective reality of the real thing that letter represents.

The Hegelian dialectic is being applied politically to form as well as content in public education. Public education, constitutionally under state and local authority, is being targeted by the leftist/globalist movement for centralization and federalization.

Charlotte Iserbyt explains the practical application of Hegel's dialectic through property taxes:

> The internationalist change agents must abolish local control (the "Thesis") in order to restructure our schools from academics to global workforce training (the "Synthesis"). Funding of education with the property tax allows *local control*, but it also enables the change agents and teachers' unions to create higher and higher school budgets paid for with higher taxes, thus infuriating homeowners. Eventually, property owners *accept* the change agents' radical *proposal* (the "Anti-thesis") to reduce their property taxes by transferring education funding *from* the local property tax *to* the state income tax. Thus, the change agents accomplish their ultimate goal; the transfer of funding of education from the local level to the state level. When this transfer occurs, it increases state/federal control and funding, leading to the federal/internationalist goal of implementing global workforce training through the schools (the "Synthesis").[i] [footnote listed at end of chapter] (p. xviii)[17]

The relativism of Hegel's theory is its fatal philosophical flaw but its most useful political feature, because denying the existence of absolutes allows its adherents to deny any and all things they disagree with. An absolute is something that exists independently and not in relation to other things. It is not relative or comparative or a matter of opinion. It is an *is*.

Absolutes, particularly the existence of objective reality, is foundational to ordered liberty in a sane society. Reality testing is the infrastructure of a sane society. People can disagree on the merits of things and ideas, but not on the *existence* of those things and ideas. The Hegelian dialectic underwrites the equivalence of truth and lies, and of reality and unreality. Blurring the boundaries between truth, lies, reality, and unreality results in painful cognitive dissonance—the profound psychological stress of holding contradictory perceptions. Cognitive dissonance creates psychological instability, social divisiveness, and a crisis in the ability to test reality.

Crisis is the essential ingredient of Hegel's dialectic. The operating principle of the leftist/globalist attack on America is to create crises that are "resolved" using the relativism of the dialectic to impose predetermined solutions—syntheses. It is an extremely manipulative strategy that is deceitfully marketed as conflict resolution and/or crisis management.

Seismic social change happens incrementally, so one manufactured crisis after another after another is deliberately created to achieve a predetermined outcome. It is gradual, step-by-step social engineering, with each crisis weakening America and moving society closer to the political objective of socialism and eventually planetary governance.

The globalist elite will support any collectivist system that they can control, including socialism, communism, fascism, oligarchy, monarchy, theocracy, and technocracy, as long as they hold the power at the tip of the pyramid. Elitism is loyal only to itself.

The constitutional separation of powers and guarantee of individual citizen rights in the United States of America presented a singular obstacle to the globalist elite. Corrupt politicians were necessary, but they were not enough to assure peaceful takeover of the government. Dominating the United States required gradualism and an incremental march through American institutions in order to succeed.

The leftist/globalist war on America is an *end justifies the means* campaign that presents lies as truth and unreality as reality. Hegel's dialectic is the underlying process and rationalization for the echo chamber of disinformation relentlessly assaulting Americans and the censorship that accompanies it. Freedom of speech is always the first casualty of tyranny—and there is no freedom without freedom of speech.

Joseph Goebbels, Adolf Hitler's chief propagandist, described the efficacy of the lie:

> If you tell a lie big enough and keep repeating it, people will eventually come to believe it. The lie can be maintained only for such time as the State can shield the people from the political, economic and/or military consequences of the lie. It thus becomes vitally important for the State to use all of its powers to repress dissent, for *the truth is the mortal enemy* of the lie, and thus by extension, the truth is the greatest enemy of the State.

The power of Hegel's dialectic is that it frames the debate. Accepting Hegel's assumption that objective reality does not exist is like asking the question "How many times did you beat your wife?" The innocent husband is compelled to defend himself against the false assumption that he beats his wife.

It is essential that Americans recognize and reject the dialectical thinking that is seducing our children and collapsing the American family by pitting the objective reality of parents against the subjective reality of their indoctrinated children.

Footnote from *the deliberate dumbing down of america*:

[i] See Appendix XXII for an article by Tim Clem which explains this process in much more detail.

CHAPTER 8

The Mathematics of the Culture War on America

Kurt Lewin (1890–1947), a German-American psychologist, is recognized as the founder of social psychology—the study of how the personality, attitudes, motivations, and behavior of the individual influences and is influenced by the group.

Lewin studied group dynamics and organizational development and challenged the prevailing "nature vs. nurture" debate on behavior. Departing from conventional psychological theory, Lewin presented his mathematical equation of behavior, which claimed that an individual's immediate situation, not necessarily past influences, was a strong determinant of behavior. Lewin's 1947 three-stage theory of change is referred to as Unfreeze, Change, Refreeze. Rooted in the Hegelian dialectic,[18] Lewin's model is a mathematical formula for Marxist reeducation.

Hegel unapologetically described the process of social engineering: "The synthetic solution to these conflicts can't be introduced unless those being manipulated take a side that will advance the pre-determined agenda." Sometimes called the consensus process, the Hegelian dialectic is used to achieve collectivist groupthink.

Lewin's equation, $B = F\,(pe)$,[19] contends that behavior is a function of the person in his environment, what he called that person's "life space" or "field." Lewin theorized that neither nature nor nurture was enough to explain an individual's behavior—that it was the interaction between the individual and his constantly changing environment that produced the result.

There are fields and vectors in mathematics. Force-field analysis[20] examines all the factors/forces that influence a person or group's behavior. Lewin believed that a person's behavior exists as a function of his total field/environment (life space) which is dynamic and constantly changing. It is the psychological equivalent of the famous quote by Heraclitus that "No man steps in the same river twice."

Lewin introduced the concept of "genidentity,"[21] defined as identity through and over time. Since no two lives have the same life experiences, no two lives can be living in the same reality. This multiple-reality construct denies an objective reality and embraces reality as a subjective perceptual phenomenon.

Consider this example. A man is walking down the street. There are four people nearby. The first person says there is a man walking down the street. The second person says there is a person walking down the street. The third person says I'm not sure who is walking down the street. The fourth person says there is a woman walking down the street.

The objective reality is that a man is walking down the street regardless of what the observers' perceptions are. Objective reality is rooted in facts and exists independent of the perceptions of those facts. *Subjective* reality tolerates conflicting realities because it is rooted in perceptions and informed by opinions. The consequence, of course, is that societal acceptance of multiple realities ultimately creates social chaos because there is no agreement on what is real.

The Culture War on America embraces subjective reality. It is a weapon of destabilization in the information war and part of the Marxist strategic attack on objective reality.

In mathematics, topology is defined as the study of geometric properties and spatial relations that are unaffected by the continuous changes of shape or sizes of figures. A circle can be stretched into a triangle and still retain its properties. Topology is sometimes called rubber-sheet geometry[22] because it does not distinguish between a circle and a square. Topological spaces are the spaces studied in topology.

Lewin believed the individual's field can be expressed as a geometrical topological construct like the circle stretching into a triangle and then reshaping into a rectangle as that individual's environment changes. He developed a theory of behavior, topological psychology,[23] utilizing philosophical and mathematical concepts.

Topological psychology focuses on group communication, group dynamics, and social psychology rather than individual psychology. His work was foundational in the development of group psychology and what we now identify as Orwellian groupthink. His field theory of learning has had major educational implications in classrooms from K–12 through university.

Lewin's topological psychology is the foundation for his three-phase model of change that has been applied in business organizations to re-orient employees toward cohesiveness and solidarity. It is foundational to current Marxist indoctrination in corporate America and the U.S. military.

The three phases are simplified as Unfreeze → Change → Refreeze. The process can be visualized geometrically as

#1 a cube of ice that melts into

#2 a puddle of water that is reshaped and refrozen into

#3 a cone of ice.

Lewin's group-change theory has a lot in common with mind-altering methods and brainwashing techniques that break down an individual's defense mechanisms and established sense of identity. Conventional values are shattered and replaced with new standards and the desired mindset: the individual has been "reprogrammed."

It is not difficult to see why this works. Human beings seek homeo-stasis—balance—both physically and mentally. They are uncomfortable being destabilized and desire equilibrium. The leftist effort to reshape American culture is utilizing an expanded version of Lewin's three-stage change process to dismantle existing established cultural norms and replace them with socialism.

Unfreeze → Change → Refreeze = the Culture War on America.

To unfreeze the American mindset, every communication sphere has been targeted and weaponized.

The educational system, public and private, is indoctrinating and repro-gramming students with the anti-American leftist narrative of political correctness, moral relativism, and historical revisionism.

The media—including television, movies, radio, and the Internet—is indoctrinating and reprogramming audiences with repetitive leftist messaging in an echo chamber of collectivist propaganda, desensitizing violence, and degenerate sex.

The colleges and universities are graduating "experts" in the social sciences of sociology, psychology, communications, and political science who then indoctrinate and reprogram the next generation in the same woke leftist principles.

In every sphere the transfer of information is biased toward anti-American collectivism at the expense of established cultural norms of individualism and the meritocracy. The Culture War on America is an information war that seeks to destroy America from within by reprogramming the American mindset to reject individualism and embrace collectivism.

America has completed the initial unfreezing stage that required overcoming entrenched Judeo-Christian norms and dismantling existing attitudes. A comparison of American life and its reflection in television programming demonstrates the seismic shift and breakdown of established cultural norms of behavior. We are now fully engaged in the transitional second phase of change characterized by confusion.

People are shocked by the changing mores and standards of behavior. Parents are shocked by their children's disrespectful attitudes and behaviors. Employers are dismayed by insolent employee attitudes and behaviors. College campuses are being overrun by anarchists. There is an awareness that life is different and becoming very unfamiliar. Things seem out of control, chaotic, and incomprehensible.

Chaos is the deliberate change agent. Human beings seek equilibrium, and chaos causes extreme anxiety and confusion. If people become uncomfortable enough, they will accept anything that stabilizes society and ends the chaos. Society then enters the final stage of change, refreezing the culture into an entirely different shape and restoring a sense of social equilibrium.

Kurt Lewin's Unfreeze → Change → Refreeze model of change is the psychological warfare being used to manipulate Americans into accepting collectivism as the new normal. It is a sinister power grab by the Left in its Culture War on America.

The hippies of the '60s did not go quietly into the night when they graduated from college, and the enemies of America did not disappear after World War II. They reconstituted themselves as college professors, deans and administrators, teachers, sociologists, psychologists, political scientists, media executives, politicians, and Hollywood bosses, all cooperating in the Culture War on America that seeks to destroy American democracy and replace it with socialism.

We are at the tipping point in the war on America. If the war continues unopposed, one more generation of leftist indoctrination will assure a voting public eager to refreeze America into a cone. The cone is worth examining.

In 1945, British novelist George Orwell published *Animal Farm*, a political satire that ridicules the deceit of revolutionary leaders and the totalitarian regimes they create. Orwell tells the story of farm animals rebelling against the farmer who controls them. The animals join the revolution to establish a new society where all the animals are equal, free, and happy. They end up living in a dictatorship led by a ruthless pig named Napoleon. Orwell's Napoleon achieved dominance by focusing on early puppy education. Napoleon takes nine newborn puppies away from their mother and trains them to be his attack dogs. Just before the farm election, he signals the ferocious dogs to attack Snowball, his competitor, and the dogs drive Snowball off the farm.

Orwell's 1949 novel, *Nineteen Eighty-Four*, goes even further to describe the globalist dream as a dystopian nightmare. The novel is set in England, which has been transformed into the totalitarian superstate of Oceania. Orwell describes the horrors of globalist totalitarian rule in a surveillance society that eliminates privacy, freedom, and human rights; rewrites history; and eradicates objective reality. Oceania's government requires adulation and total submission from its citizens. Orwell's Oceania is the endgame of the political tyranny convulsing America today.

Collectivism, whether socialism or communism, is being marketed as the great equalizer. It is being falsely advertised to gullible young people as social justice and income equality. Young people imagine collectivism as everyone living the good life of happiness, equality, and individual freedom reflected in the lyrics of John Lennon's idealized song, "Imagine." Orwell understood the deceit and warned of the real-life tyranny of collectivism.

Song lyrics and fiction are no longer necessary. Real-time experiments in socialism and communism exist in Venezuela, Cuba, Russia, and

China today. The objective reality is that there is no income equality in these countries. Instead, there is widespread poverty, shortages of every kind, and rampant violence. Only the elite occupy the privileged tip of the cone in collectivism.

There is no individual freedom without private property. The objective reality is that when government owns or otherwise controls all property, citizens become employees of the state and do not own the fruits of their labor—the government does. It is up to the government to distribute or withhold all products. The elitist tip of the collectivist cone always takes care of itself.

We the People who live in objective reality must continue to expose the destructive leftist agenda. We cannot submit to its indoctrination and subjective reality. We must preserve free speech and the rights of citizens to own private property and enjoy the fruits of their labors. America can remain the land of the free and the home of the brave only if we refuse to be Unfrozen, Changed, and Refrozen.

CHAPTER 9

Sexual Predators Threaten the American Family

Judith A. Reisman, PhD (1935–2021), devoted her professional life to exposing sex researcher Alfred C. Kinsey (1894–1956) as a predatory fraud, and porn magnate Hugh Hefner (1926–2017) as his "pamphleteer" accomplice. Presenting perversion and pornography as normative and acceptable, the duo changed cultural norms that continue to threaten the American family today.

With particular focus on the sexual exploitation of children, Dr. Reisman demonstrates how the American family is being bombarded by multiple weapons of mass destruction. One of the most egregious and heart wrenching is the deliberate sexualization of innocent, impressionable young children. In schools, inappropriate sex education confuses them. In entertainment, explicit pornographic themes and images frighten them. On the Internet, interactive websites seduce them.

Shocking pornographic content is presented with blatant contempt for parental authority and established Judeo-Christian norms. The multiplex attack strategy is engineered to make its manipulating content familiar and acceptable. How could this happen in America?

Alex Newman, investigative journalist at The New American, interviewed Dr. Reisman on June 3, 2020. During the interview, published as "Exposing Sick Roots of 'Sex Ed'—Kinsey, CIA & Child Abuse,"[24] Dr. Reisman states:

> The Central Intelligence Agency (CIA) was involved in supporting "research" by pervert Alfred Kinsey involving massive amounts of child abuse. This criminal pseudo-science, also sponsored by the Rockefeller Foundation,[i] [footnotes listed at end of chapter] was the pretext needed to begin changing American laws and culture on marriage, rape, family, and more. Kinsey's research, involving rape and sexual abuse of children, also served as the foundation for sexualizing young students in public schools with

grotesque "sex education" programs that groom children for sexual exploitation and abuse.

Dr. Reisman's extensive research documents the crimes of Alfred Kinsey, patriarch of the "sexual revolution," and the staggering cultural carnage he caused. Dr. Reisman examined the "research" Kinsey provided for his two books, *Sexual Behavior in the Human Male* and *Sexual Behavior in the Human Female*, published in 1951 and 1953, respectively. Her appalling findings revealed that Kinsey sexually abused thousands of children, some as young as two months old, for his experiments, and he regarded their screaming as evidence of orgasm. Kinsey's perverse conclusion, that *children are sexual from birth*, became the foundation for subsequent changes in sex education and sex laws.

Kinsey, a sexual deviant himself, believed children needed to know how to have sex in order to be happy. In 1964, he hired Mary Calderone (1904–1998), medical director of Planned Parenthood, 1953–1964, and president and co-founder of the Sexuality Information and Education Council of the United States (SIECUS), 1964–1982. Calderone was recruited to develop sex education programs for American schools with outreach from the Kinsey Institute and support from Planned Parenthood and the Rockefeller Foundation. Planned Parenthood would provide sex education internationally. Kinsey said students needed to be taught about masturbation and intercourse, which relied on Kinsey's perverse experiments.

Kinsey claimed that 10 percent to 37 percent of adult males are homosexual, without disclosing that his "research" was done during World War II, when men and women serving their country in any capacity were forbidden to speak about their personal lives. Signs reading "Loose lips sink ships" were posted everywhere. Consequently, almost 87 percent of Kinsey's adult research population were prisoners and prostitutes.

Kinsey admits he had 1,400 sex offenders as his research population, yet falsely published his findings of their sexual behavior as "normal" male and female sexual behavior. In essence, Alfred Kinsey's two books presented the perverse behavior of prisoners and prostitutes as "normal" sexual behavior of adults, and the sexualization of children as normative.

When the Rockefeller Foundation's financial ties to Kinsey started being investigated in the mid 1950s, the Rockefeller Foundation shifted its money from sex research to creating the American Law Institute's Model Penal Code, adopted in 1962 and used subsequently to change all of our sex laws.

The American Law Institute[25] is a research and advocacy group of judges, lawyers, and legal scholars established in 1923 "to promote clarification and simplification of United States common law and its adaptation to changing social needs."

Dr. Reisman explains the history of sex laws in America and the seismic shift after Kinsey's horrifying conclusion that all children are sexual from birth and need sexual experiences to be happy. Before Kinsey, sex laws were protective and harsh; after Kinsey, sex laws became increasingly lax.

Once Kinsey's subjects were deemed "normal," aberrant behavior was legitimized; once it was legitimized, it was legalized. And once it was legalized, it was taught in the classroom. In a cascade of destruction, children went from being legally protected sexually to being legally exploited sexually.

Legitimizing and legalizing aberrant behavior also legitimized and legalized pornography. Hugh Hefner, Kinsey's "pamphleteer," launched *Playboy* magazine and the pornography revolution in 1953. Kinsey is the most-cited "expert" of the Lesbian Gay Bisexual Transgender (LGBT) and North American Man/Boy Love Association (NAMBLA) movements.

For years Dr. Reisman attempted to bring Alfred Kinsey to justice. The evidence of his crimes was irrefutable, yet Kinsey was being shielded from prosecution. Dr. Reisman was stonewalled, discouraged, and her professional reputation was smeared. Finally, she realized Kinsey was being protected because his work was foundational to the sexual revolution targeting American families. Kinsey was an essential part of the Culture War on America and America's children.

The entire sex education narrative is traumatizing to children. The damage to children, adults, and society is enormous, and it is all based on pedo-criminal quackery. Homosexual sex is now being taught in the classroom, and pedophilia is being promoted as an acceptable sexual orientation.

Mary Calderone's SIECUS unapologetically includes the tagline Sex Ed for Social Change. Dr. Reisman warns parents that it is legal to teach obscenity to children in schools because schools are exempt from obscenity laws. Parents must not relinquish their authority to the schools, because the grotesque sex education is grooming America's children for sexual exploitation and abuse.

As children lose their innocence through the teaching of obscene and inappropriate sex education in schools, there are individual and social consequences. Dr. Reisman reports that little children are now sexually abusing other little children. A 2017 AP report[ii] [footnotes listed at end of chapter] states there were 14,000 cases reported in one year.

She explains that it is impossible to raise healthy, independent, thinking children because exploitive sex education creates angry, out-of-control children. They will take their revenge because destruction begets destruction. They will burn churches, blow up buildings, and be easily controlled by the state. Sexual exploitation weaponizes children.

When Alex Newman asked her what can parents do, Dr. Reisman answered that parents must get their children out of the public school system and homeschool them if necessary. She says the Kinsey Institute is a tax-funded institution that still operates at Indiana University. Dr. Reisman, in conjunction with Rhonda Miller, president of the Indiana Liberty Coalition, have issued a "Call to Investigate Indiana University's 'Kinsey Institute'" (February 7, 2020).[iii] [footnotes listed at end of chapter] The Kinsey Institute received more than $20 million in federal funds from 1986-2012. The legal case and documented evidence against them are irrefutable, yet they are still being protected.

Parents need to demand that the Kinsey Institute be criminally investigated, because the root of the poisonous pedagogy must be exposed or the abuse will continue and expand under the rubric of education. There is even an app available, *The Kinsey Reporter*, inviting students to become "citizen scientists" and participate in sex research. It encourages anonymous self-reporting of sexual activity including sex abuse and rape, without consequence.

The Kinsey Institute will not be decommissioned or brought to justice unless the case is brought to court. Dr. Reisman won her 1994 court case against _Playboy_[26] in the Netherlands, accusing them of producing child pornography. She presented the results of her study done for the U.S. Department of Justice.

> The research was an investigative analysis of PLAYBOY, PENT-HOUSE and HUSTLER over the period of December 1953 to December 1984 to examine for nonviolent, violent, and criminal image portrayal and scenario involvement of children. The research reported the findings of 14,854 images of crime and violence and 6,004 images of children (with the predominate group being girls between ages 3 to 11 years) as part of the overall sexual and violent scenario. There were 989 sexual scenarios which included children actively involved with adults; and each magazine portrayed children as unharmed and/or benignly affected by the child/adult sex.
>
> —Role of Pornography and Media Violence in Family Violence, Sexual Abuse and Exploitation, and Juvenile Delinquency; NCJRS Abstract[27]

Dr. Reisman invites you to visit her website, The Reisman Institute,[28] for more information. She recommends reading Debra DeGroff's book, _Between the Covers: What's Inside a Children's Book?_ and viewing _Contraland_, a film released in 2020 that examines sexual abuse of children. Above all, do not allow your children to be indoctrinated by a school system that supports the perversion of Alfred Kinsey, a sexual predator, and normalizes the catastrophic, perverse sexualization of children.

Footnotes from "Exposing Sick Roots of 'Sex Ed'—Kinsey, CIA & Child Abuse":

[i] Rockefeller Foundation; https://rockfound.rockarch.org/kinsey-reports

[ii] AP report; https://www.ap.org/explore/schoolhouse-sex-assault/schools-face-vexing-test-which-kids-will-sexually-attack.html

[iii] Call to Investigate Indiana University's 'Kinsey Institute'; http://www.drjudithreisman.com/archives/2020/02/corruption_in_t.html

CHAPTER 10

The Scheme and the Schemers Determined to Reeducate America

A lex Newman continued to report on the sexualization of children in American schools in his stunning August 2, 2021, video, *Why the Deep State Is Sexualizing Kids*.[29] The summary reads:

> The Deep State is fiendishly working to sexualize children through government schools and so-called entertainment, and there is a very sinister agenda behind it, warns *The New American* magazine's Alex Newman in this episode of *Behind the Deep State*. Indeed, since Karl Marx, totalitarians have understood that undermining and destroying the family is critical to achieving their objectives. Sex education literally hurts children in horrifying ways, and yet it keeps getting more and more extreme with each passing year. Don't let your children become the next victims.

The reeducation of America was conceived decades ago. William Reich (1897–1957), an Austrian psychoanalyst, communist, and self-described Freudo-Marxist, famously coined the term *sexual revolution*. Reich stated that it is necessary to undermine the family for the purpose of undermining Western civilization. Reich believed that sex education would be key in accomplishing this goal because it would divest parents of their moral authority. He promoted sex education for that purpose and taught classes at The New School for Social Research (NSSR), originally named The New School, in New York from 1939 to 1941.

The New School was founded in 1919, with financial contributions from the Rockefeller Foundation, by a group of *progressive* intellectuals . . . among them John Dewey. The stated mission of the school was to explore and promote *global peace* and *global justice*.

The Sexuality Information and Education Council of the United States

(SIECUS), founded by Mary Calderone, is the institutional voice and architect of the Comprehensive Sex Education (CSE) program that advocates sex education for social change. CSE is the perverse educational curriculum indoctrinating your children in public schools across the country.

Monica Cline, former volunteer "comprehensive sex educator" at Planned Parenthood, is quoted in Newman's video. He references Cline's stunning interview with Virginia Allen and Lauren Evans in their August 20, 2020, *Daily Signal* article, "<u>Problematic Women: Planned Parenthood Ideology 'Killing the Family,' Ex-Volunteer Says</u>."[30]

In the article, Cline exposes the truth about sex education and explains how Planned Parenthood (PP) is actively attempting to break down communication between parents and their children.

At Cline's initial meeting with Planned Parenthood's director of sex education, she was told horrifying stories of little girls as young as ten years old coming to a PP clinic with sexually transmitted diseases, in need of having objects removed from their bodies, and for abortions. Cline assumed her job would be to teach these girls not to have sex.

She was shocked at the director's response: "No, dear. We're not here to teach them not to have sex. We're here to teach them how to do it safer. It would be judging for us to go against their choice, and so, we're just going to teach them how to do it safer by using condoms, lubrication, how to get tested and treated for STDs and have abortions."

So, regardless of whether children were sexually active or not, the job of the comprehensive sex educator is to introduce children to every possible sexual activity, whether it's multiple partners at once, whether it's the use of sex toys, whatever it may be. It doesn't matter how old they are.

The director said, "They're not going to tell you what they are doing. And so, it is your job to break down their inhibitions, basically."

Eventually, Monica Cline realized the children were being pressured and deliberately sexualized in school because no adult was offering them the alternative of abstinence. At one point she asks a group of thirteen- and fourteen-year-olds, "Guys, do you realize you don't have to have sex? You don't have to have oral sex, vaginal sex, or anal sex. And if you don't, you never have to come in contact with someone else's body fluids." A little girl raised her hand and said, "Ma'am, no one has ever told us that."

That was the turning point for Monica Cline. She finally and fully understood:

> There is a "huge movement to normalize childhood sex." The sex education program of Planned Parenthood is "encouraging children to dehumanize themselves and each other, making them sexually active at a young age, normalizing every sexual behavior. . . . By doing that those children become dependent on getting condoms and contraceptives and getting treated, and yes, even getting abortions. And so, once that dependency occurs, and the parent who is purposely left out of the picture, there's no one else who's really guiding those children. . . . They empathize with them and say, 'Oh, yeah. Your mom and dad would probably be really mad to know you are sexually active. But we know it is perfectly normal, and we're here to help you. . . . It sounds so positive. But what they are really doing is creating a barrier between a family and their child, the guidance of a parent.

Cline explains that parents have absolutely no input or control over the sex ed content. PP and other comprehensive sex education organizations consider parents a barrier to services. The goal is to mandate their sex education, which is really an ideology, and change the sexual attitudes of our entire nation by influencing our children. PP volunteers are not supposed to be in schools unless invited, but volunteers are sneaked into schools by sympathetic teachers and administrators.

Cline goes on to say:

> They believe that children are sexual from birth. And they use a little bit of truth, and then distort it completely. And just because we're born with sexual parts doesn't mean that we should be sexually active.

> According to Planned Parenthood and The Future of Sex Education [National Sex Education Standards (Second Edition)], they believe in the sexual rights of children. They do believe that children at any age, even infancy, have the right to sexual

pleasure. You can read that in their own mission statements. You can go to their websites and learn that. They're not hiding it anymore. And they believe it's normal, and so they're really trying to change the sexual attitudes of a whole nation and across the globe that this is true.

And so, you're going to see that they are now creating programs for parents, to start convincing parents that their children are sexual beings, and that they should be able to learn about their bodies and pleasure themselves, or with other children. . . . They use a lot of Alfred Kinsey's research, which is incredibly unethical and should have been illegal. But yet, Alfred Kinsey has influenced public health education and has influenced our laws in this nation as well. . . . Kinsey, they consider him a hero because he loosened the belt of people, of sexual repression, and gave people the spectrum of being from homosexual to straight and everything in between.

And now they are using that same "spectrum" for gender identity as well. So, I think parents need to be very concerned, because even if the curriculum is not in your school, I get phone calls from parents all over the country that progressive teachers are teaching their children this in class, even if it is history, or whatever it may be.

When Evans asked, "Why? What is their motivating factor to teach children this?" Cline answered:

A big piece of this, which for some people, it's something I think is hard for them to understand, is that there is a huge movement through socialism that really wants to do away with the nuclear family. They want to do away with anything that is of [one's own], whether it's private property, or private family.

And so, they believe that children do not necessarily belong to their parents, but that they can educate the children in the way that they want them to go. And sex education is a big piece of that, because when you teach children to dehumanize themselves, to take intimacy and family and marriage out of sex, even to the point of killing your own children through abortion, you are essentially killing the family. You're destroying the family.

And of all the tactics they are using—you can read any curriculum—not only is it going to be graphic, but they will not ever guide a child to talk to their own parent ever. You won't hear a word about the parent. A parent is completely eliminated from this education.

They want the children dependent on the government, or on public health, whatever it may be, but they do not want the children to be depending on the parent anymore. And so, all of this really is to break down the family. And they're essentially . . . we're watching it happen . . . they basically have been given words in school. And they go home and tell their parents, "You're just old fashioned, or you are worshipping a god of hate, or you're very conservative. You don't understand the culture."

And these kids are learning all this at school.

After a decade volunteering as a "comprehensive sex educator" for Planned Parenthood, Monica Cline became a specialist in avoiding sexual risk. She started an organization called It Takes a Family.[31] The organization advocates for the protection of families and children from graphic sex education and abortion. Her mission statement:

> *I want to equip and empower PARENTS to be their children's primary educators about sex and relationships. Because It Takes a Family to raise strong and confident children.*

CHAPTER 11

Pushback against Reeducating America

Monica Cline has strong support for her opposition to the sexualization of children and to the use of a *spectrum* for deconstructing the biological fact of binary gender identity.

Dr. Michelle Cretella, president of the American College of Pediatricians, states that "Comprehensive Sexuality Education (CSE) goes far beyond sex ed, and is a dangerous assault on the health and innocence of children." In a November 15, 2017, interview with John Ritchie, "Dr. Cretella on Transgenderism,"[32] she unapologetically and unequivocally states that "transgenderism is a mental illness, not a civil right." Quotes from her interview:

> Essentially, transgender ideology holds that people can be born into the wrong body: It's simply not true. We can demonstrate this by looking at twin studies. No one is born in the wrong body. So, to take that lie and essentially indoctrinate all of our children from preschool forward with that lie, we are destroying their ability for reality testing.
>
> This is cognitive and psychological abuse. I want to say just a little more about that. The reason it destroys reality testing is because most children at age three (pre-school age) can correctly identify themselves by saying "I am a boy" or "I am a girl" and most children will not understand that a boy grows into a man and stays a man and that a girl grows into a woman and stays a woman. So, when many seven-year-olds see a man get into a dress and put on makeup, they may believe that he just became a woman. The other side is not being honest and not acknowledging that. . . .
>
> So transgender ideology—yes, it's child abuse because we are gaslighting our children. And now that they're thoroughly confused, they will think that they really are the opposite sex and

will be sent down a medical pathway. As they approach puberty, they will be put on puberty blockers and then on cross-sex hormones. That combination will permanently sterilize most, if not all, of those children and also puts them at risk for heart disease, diabetes, and various cancers. If girls have been on testosterone, which is their sex change hormone, for a full year, by age 16 they can get a double mastectomy. So, gaslighting, pubertal castration and surgical mutilation: It's institutionalized child abuse. . . .

Gender as a term, prior to the 1950s:

#1. Did not refer to people;

#2. Was not in the medical literature.

Sexologists were PhDs and MDs in the '50s who were taking people who believed they were transsexuals (the term was transsexual at the time), mostly men who wanted to be women, and basically invented the so-called "sex reassignment surgery." Amongst themselves in the '50s, they said, "What are we treating? How are we going to justify this?" because they knew full well even then that sex is in the DNA and that mutilating the body does not change a person's sex. They basically looked at the word gender, which meant male and female referring to grammar.

So, in the 1950s, one of the sexologists at the time was Dr. John Money. And they said, "We're gonna take gender and say that for people it means 'the social expression of an internal sex identity.' That's what we're treating." They pulled it out of the air to justify lining their pockets to do mutilating surgeries. And this is the very same definition that the activists are using. It has no basis in reality. . . .

NO surgery will change the DNA which is imprinted in every single cell of the body. Again, this is a combination of reason and science. They meld. They go together. . . .

Transgenderism is a social construct. The "fluidity" of sexuality: That's a social construct. They have it exactly backwards. And the word gender, as I said earlier, is nothing more than a linguistic engineering term and should have no place in medicine. . . .

If my feelings alone determine who I am, then there really is no such thing as a man or a woman. . . . The error is to equate equality with sameness . . . they're not. Same does not mean equal. Because we're equal in human dignity, but being male or female, that is the ultimate diversity we should be celebrating. There is no greater diversity than female and male. That is our innate identity and it's written on every cell of our body at the level of our DNA. . . .

The natural family, meaning a loving marriage between a man and a woman, is the most pro-child institution we have. So, if you love children, nurture your marriage first of all. It's the greatest gift you can give a child. We must stand up for that, because our children are hurting. Decades, decades of social science demonstrates that this is the most important thing we can do in terms of children's physical, mental, emotional and spiritual health. It's the family . . . it's the family.

Stella Morabito, senior contributor to *The Federalist* and former intelligence analyst, wrote a scathing indictment of the movement to legalize sex with children.

The war on children that uses Kinsey's perversion to legitimize adult sex with children is examined in Morabito's February 21, 2019, article, "The Pedophile Project: Your 7-year-old Is Next on the Sexual Revolution's Hit Parade."[33] Quotes from her article:

Activists for normalizing pedophilia are on the move. Public acceptance of adult sex with children is the next domino poised to fall in identity politics. It's being sustained, among other things, by the rapid sexualization of children in the media and in K–12 education. . . .

As with any propaganda campaign that pushes outrageous changes on an unwary public, it's all about timing. Academics might refer to timing as the Overton Window[34] or the Availability Cascade.[35] But we should all be able to understand the process of conditioning the public to accept the unacceptable. . . .

We're already being desensitized to the sexualization of children and implanting gender confusion in them. Parents from Long Beach, California to Queens, New York[36] are taking their toddlers to drag queen story times[37] at local libraries. Some, like the mother of nine-year-old Lactatia,[38] now actually groom their boys to be drag queens and encourage them to get other children[39] to do the same. . . .

Your children have been defined by the left's sexual nihilists as totally sexual beings. So, what next? The logical answer: from sexual beings to sex objects. We may well see even more legalized exploitation of children unimaginable to many Americans today. Let's face it: pedophilia has been waiting in the wings, and is itching to come out. So, let's not be blindsided when it hits full force.

There are two main avenues to legalizing adult sexual relations with pre-pubescent children: 1) to designate it as a sexual orientation; and 2) to lower—or abolish—the age of consent for sexual activity. Both efforts are on track by pedophilia advocates, especially in academia and in the mass media. Take a look at this TED Talk[40] released last year, in which the speaker chides us: "Let's be mature about pedophilia." The speaker, Madeleine Van Der Bruggen, makes the case that pedophilia is simply a sexual orientation that can be neither chosen nor changed. . . .

Just as the American Psychiatric Association (APA) re-classified gender identity disorder to gender identity dysphoria, it also tinkered with classifying pedophilia in its fifth edition of the Diagnostic and Statistical Manual of Mental Disorders (DSM-V.) As the psycho-bible of mental disorders, the DSM has always been the go-to source for making the sexual revolution the law of the land. Its reclassifications of homosexuality and transgenderism are really just the beginning. There is no reason other than timing to think it won't do the same for pedophilia. . . .

Perhaps the biggest bombshell recently is that December 2018 article,[41] "Childhood 'Innocence' Is Not Ideal: Virtue Ethics and Child-Adult Sex" mentioned above, written by convicted child molester Tom O'Carroll in the peer reviewed journal *Sexuality and Culture*. . . .

O'Carroll's goal is to make the case that pedophilia is simply a sexual orientation that should have all the protections of anti-discrimination laws for other sexualities. He tries to appeal to the same litany of arguments that subjects children to early sexualization and to the transgender curriculum: that kids can decide for themselves how to express themselves and shouldn't be denied a choice in how they identify—no matter how young they are. . . .

So, get used to it: the goal is to frame pedophilia as a human right, redirecting your attention away from the adult and reframing it as a child's right to sexual expression. If the child claims to consent, who are you to get in his or her way? Hence, every child becomes fair game for child molesters, especially if the child can be persuaded and influenced to say he or she consented. . . .

Once pedophilia is classified as a sexual orientation, then it's protected under that umbrella, which covers all areas of life: employment, education, medicine, housing, business, military, even the parish life of churches, family life, and much more. . . .

There can be no doubt pedophilia will eventually be officially classified as a "sexual orientation" if more people don't grow some spine. You don't have to be a master of logic to understand that once that happens, then expressions of disapproval will be deemed illegal discrimination. . . .

Consider this: If pedophilia is ever normalized, what are the chances that the word "pedophobia" and the term "pedophobe" will be used as slurs against people who disapprove? Against churches that disapprove? Could they be used in the same way the terms "homophobia" and "transphobia" are used as slurs today?

Of course. In this scenario, if you express reservations about sexual activity between pre-pubescent children and adults, you will be publicly shamed and silenced as a "pedophobe" for doing so. A bigot. A hater. . . .

For those just waking up, we're not in Kansas anymore. We're on a speeding train through the Twilight Zone. And the hyper-suggestibility of most folks in this age of internet-induced mass delusion[42] will get us there even faster.

The movement to relabel pedophilia a sexual orientation and not a perversion is a disguised effort to legalize pedophilia. Parents in their 50s, 60s, and 70s who surrender to the subjective reality of their indoctrinated adult children are unwittingly aiding and abetting the abuse of their grandchildren. The grandchildren are the prime targets in this monstrous power grab by the political elite. Targeting young children as sexual objects with the fiction that children enjoy being sexualized is a descent into madness and the realm of irredeemable malevolence.

CSE is the instrument indoctrinating our children that facilitates social acceptance of sexual abuse as normative. It is monstrous. The Stop CSE[43] website was created to warn parents and policy makers of the serious harms of explicit comprehensive sexuality programs. It is a joint effort of Family Watch International, the UN Family Rights Caucus, the Stop the Kinsey Institute coalition, and concerned parents worldwide.

The film *The War on Children: Exposing the Comprehensive Sexuality Education Agenda*[44] is available on the Stop CSE website in ten-minute and thirty-five-minute versions. The website offers petitions to sign and other ways to get involved to stop the sexualization of our nation's precious children.

The breakdown of the family through education is a sinister, multi-pronged offensive. Traumatizing sex education, crippling dumbing down, and corrosive anti-American indoctrination are all parts of the social engineering being reinforced in your home by the colluding entertainment media.

Weaponized education is predatory conditioning for social engineering. In wartime, predatory conditioning is called brainwashing. We are at war inside America whether we acknowledge it or not, and our children are being brainwashed.

Reclaiming our schools needs to start at the local level. Parents across America must unite to replace their local school boards with men and women who will protect our precious children from Comprehensive Sexuality Education and its predatory sexualizing agenda.

CHAPTER 12

Political Predators Threaten America with Extinction

A predator is defined as an animal that naturally preys on other animals. Predation is a natural and accepted fact of life in the wild animal kingdom—eat or be eaten is a matter of survival.

A predator is also defined as a person or group who ruthlessly exploit other people. Predation is an unacceptable fact of life in the civilized world of ordered liberty and mutuality where predation is a matter of domination, not of survival.

Sexual predators live in this group. Sexual assaults including rape, childhood sexual abuse, sexualization of children, and abusive sex education are crimes of power, dominance, and subjugation.

Political predators are a variation on the same theme of power. Like sexual predators, political predators commit crimes of dominance and subjugation against unsuspecting members of society. Political predation is part of the war on family and the movement to destroy America from within.

Political predators need to disguise their motives. No stranger ever seduced a child with spinach, and socialism cannot be sold as power, dominance, and subjugation. The political candy offered to impressionable American students is "new" socialism. The predators promise a sweet, worry-free, humanitarian, fair, humane, superior life of social justice and income equality. Of course it is a lie, but children believe what they are told and get into the car for the candy.

The tactical strategy of the political left is built on "community organizing." They have taken over local school boards to promote Comprehensive Sexuality Education (CSE) and critical race theory (CRT). Leftist control has to be confronted and opposed at the local level to stop the destruction of our school system and the transforming of our children into Marxist collectivists.

Marxist political predators have been seducing American children with leftist anti-American indoctrination in public schools since 1979 when Jimmy Carter established the Department of Education. The propaganda campaign escalated with Common Core and its anti-American leftist narrative of moral relativism, historical revisionism, and political correctness.

The anti-American propaganda is now fully actuated with critical race theory indoctrination in schools. Beginning with preschool programs and extending through the university level, American students are taught to be self-loathing, anti-American racists.

Critical race theory is a binary theoretical framework rooted in Marxism that defines individuals as either oppressed or oppressors based on their skin color: all white people are oppressors and all people of color are oppressed. CRT is an obscene and entirely un-American doctrine because it views every individual through the prism of race rather than the prism of merit.

The critical race theory movement began at Harvard Law School under Professor Derrick Bell in the 1980s. It is the spawn of the Frankfurt School's Critical Theory, and has become the flashpoint of the Culture War in America today.

The entire narrative of CRT is racist. So, why is it being taught in American schools? Why is racist CRT considered enlightened and "woke"? Why did President Trump ban CRT, and why has the Biden/Obama/Harris regime resurrected it?

The goal of critical race theory devotees and their cancel-culture campaign is to foment race riots and a race war in the United States. I will repeat this crucial point. The goal of CRT devotees is to foment race riots and a race war in the United States of America. How would CRT accomplish do that?

Saul Alinsky[45] provides the answer in his infamous tactical primer, *Rules for Radicals: A Practical Primer for Realistic Radicals*,[46] the playbook of the American Left dedicated to Satan. Alinsky instructs radicals to "rub raw the resentments of the people . . . your function—to agitate to the point of conflict . . . all issues must be polarized if action is to follow." (p.

116, 117, 133 Vintage)

Race is the simplest issue to exploit because it is visible. Fomenting racial hostility is a very effective strategy for dividing and conquering a nation. The political predators use critical race theory to divide society by race and families by ideology. When Johnny comes home and announces he is a white, privileged, racist oppressor, the family conflicts begin.

The war on America promotes racism to divide and conquer America. Rule #13 from Alinsky's primer continues to guide the Democrat war on America and on America-first President Trump, because even out of office, the former president remains the existential enemy of Marxism and globalism.

Rule 13: *Pick the target, freeze it, personalize it, polarize it. Don't try to attack abstract corporations or bureaucracies. Identify a responsible individual. Ignore attempts to shift or spread the blame.* (p. 130)

Truth is entirely irrelevant for Alinsky and his radical Democrat followers. Alinsky writes, "The real and only question regarding the ethics of means and ends is and always has been, 'Does this particular end justify this particular means?'" (p.24) According to Alinsky, "the primary task of radicals is to cultivate, in people's hearts, a visceral revulsion to the mere sight of the target's face."

It does not matter that Trump is not and never was a racist, or that his policies were extremely beneficial to the black, Hispanic, and Asian communities in America. Trump and his entire conservative/populist movement must be portrayed as racist in order to foment race riots. Even President Trump's support of law enforcement and ordered liberty have been perverted by the radical Democrats into racist attacks on white police officers. Yet again, the leftist Democrats project their own racist policies onto their targeted enemy.

The Democrat outrage over the January 6, 2021, Capitol "insurrection" is pure Alinsky-style political theater. An excellent article by John Perazzo, published on the website Frontpage Magazine on July 15, 2020, titled "Why BLM Yawns at Police-Shooting Statistics,"[47] explains the performance.

Alinsky taught that in order to cast themselves as noble defenders of high moral principles, radical activists should take pains to react dramatically – with greatly exaggerated displays of "shock, horror, and moral outrage" – whenever their targeted enemy erred, or could be depicted as having erred, in any way at all.

Nancy Pelosi is the queen of Democrat hypocrisy and Alinsky-style outrage. Pelosi's insistence upon a military presence in Washington, D.C., after January 6, 2021 was designed to validate her own fabricated fearmongering narrative. The script disingenuously described what happened on January 6 as a "deadly insurrection" carried out by Trump supporters to prevent Congress from certifying the election, rather than a false flag operation to prevent the ongoing legitimate challenge to certification.

Around 26,000 National Guard troops were deployed to "secure" the Capitol and barbed wire fencing installed around the building to "protect" politicians from mostly white Trump supporters. Jamaal Bowman (D-NY) said on MSNBC on March 4, 2021, "We must do everything we can to protect ourselves." National Guard troops remained for 137 days. Meanwhile, our southern border was and remains completely open and unguarded. The reverse-racist messaging is that open borders to un-vetted, covid-infected migrants of color from foreign countries are less of a threat to the nation than white Trump supporters.

There were over 500 radical leftist violent riots in 2020. Well-funded through George Soros' Open Society Foundation (OSF), leftist rioters burned buildings, looted, destroyed businesses, attacked police officers, and took over police precincts. Antifa and Black Lives Matter thugs were treated as peaceful protestors.

A special December 6, 2018, Judicial Watch report documents that U.S. Subsidizes Soros Radical Leftist Agenda Worldwide:[48]

> The U.S. government subsidizes billionaire George Soros' radical leftist agenda dedicating hundreds of millions of dollars to his deeply politicized Open Society Foundations (OSF) worldwide, records uncovered by Judicial Watch show. In a special investigative report,[49] Judicial Watch documents the financial link between U.S.-funded entities and OSF affiliates to further the Hungarian-born philanthropist's agenda seeking to desta-

bilize legitimate governments, erase national borders, target conservative politicians, finance civil unrest, subvert institutions of higher education, and orchestrate refugee crises for political gain. The special report also illustrates the financial and staffing nexus between OSF and the U.S. government.

In 2018 OSF projected expending more than $530 million to promote Soros' radical globalist agenda in every corner of the world under the guise of supporting democratically elected governments, strengthening the rule of law and promoting fairness in political, legal and economic systems. The reality is far different, the report shows. Soros, with the help of American taxpayer dollars, bolsters a radical leftwing agenda that in the United States has included: promoting an open border with Mexico and fighting immigration enforcement efforts; fomenting racial disharmony by funding anti-capitalist racialist organizations; financing the Black Lives Matter movement and other organizations involved in the riots in Ferguson, Missouri; weakening the integrity of our electoral systems; promoting taxpayer funded abortion-on-demand; advocating a government-run health care system; opposing U.S. counterterrorism efforts; promoting dubious transnational climate change agreements that threaten American sovereignty; and working to advance gun control and erode Second Amendment protections. . . . The Soros operations are highly sophisticated and work across academia, the legal system, labor, agriculture and "social justice" organizations as well as religious and political groups.

Pelosi's Capitol Building political theater performance is unraveling. The _New York Times_[50] reported on Sunday, September 25, 2021, that it had obtained confidential records showing a member of the right-wing Proud Boys group was an FBI informant. As the informant marched to the Capitol Building, he was texting real-time updates to his FBI handler.

The Western Journal website reported on the stunning news, in a Kipp Jones article on September 25, 2021: "Report: FBI Handler Had Tap on Jan.6, Plant in Crowd Working for Him."[51]

He [informant] said he met with other members hours before the building was entered at the nearby Washington Monument at 10 a.m. that day. The FBI's reported mole recounted that Proud Boys members did not organize an attempt to enter the Capitol. He said, rather, that they went in when others did so as doors were opened.

The doors were opened! Yet Pelosi's boundless, Alinsky-style outrage continued. The Western Journal reported on July 11, 2021: "Attorneys: Jan.6 Detainee Held in Confinement 23 Hours a Day, Conditions Violate 'Every Single Basic Human Right'":[52]

> Lawyers John Pierce and Steven Metcalf II say that at least one of the people arrested on charges related to the events of that day is being held in solitary confinement for 23 hours a day and has inadequate access to clean water and legal counsel. . . .
>
> Of the nearly 500 people who have been arrested on charges relating to the Capitol incursion,[53] Pierce said there "are about 50, plus or minus, that are being detained, that have been in prison for months and will likely remain in prison for many more months until their day in court."
>
> He explained that these accused individuals are being held under the pretense of the 1984 Bail Reform Act, which authorizes the pretrial detention of those deemed a flight risk or threat to the public.
>
> One Ned Lang said his son Jake is being held in an area of a Washington, D.C., prison nicknamed "the hole," while Metcalf said the younger Lang doesn't even have access to clean drinking water.
>
> "I'm being told the water is black. He has to filter the water through a sock in order to even drink water," Metcalf said, adding that Jake Lang is sometimes unable to shower or shave for "days and days on end."
>
> "The conditions in the D.C. jail in particular are getting to a point of not only being unconstitutional and violating every single basic human right, but they're getting to a point where people have to speak out, and they have to know about what's going on," Metcalf said, adding that prisoners are being instilled with a "level of fear." . . .

It goes without saying that while those accused of participating in the Jan. 6 incursion have been doggedly pursued[54] by law enforcement and reportedly subjected to inhumane conditions in prison, those involved in the 2020 riots[55] following the death of George Floyd have been handled with kid gloves and even glorified by the left.

American citizens attending the January 6 rally were detained and denied due process, with many still held in solitary confinement for simply attending the rally and not even entering the Capitol. It is an unconscionable, unprecedented, lawless abuse of power. These American citizens are political prisoners being held in solitary confinement in violation of the Mandela Rules.

The Mandela Rules are a minimum standard of United Nations rules that define solitary confinement as "the confinement of prisoners for 22 hours or more a day without meaningful human contact." Solitary confinement, according to the Mandela Rules, can be used only in exceptional circumstances, and *prolonged* solitary confinement of more than fifteen days is considered torture.

Jonathan Mellis, a January 6 detainee, held without bond since his arrest in February 2021 and held in solitary confinement for over thirty days in direct violation of the Mandela Rules, remains in custody. According to a September 23, 2021, report on the website The Gateway Pundit,[56] other detainees have been held in solitary confinement for periods of up to six months since January 6.

Defense attorney Joseph McBride appealed to the American Civil Liberties Union and Amnesty International, calling the District of Columbia jail "DC–Gitmo."

"If the United States Government is going to argue for the indefinite pretrial detention of American Citizens and frame them as terrorists, then the US Government should be subject to and constrained by international law (specifically The Nelson Mandela Rules)[57] which prohibits prolonged solitary confinement and deems it torture," said McBride.

Body cam footage of police officers involved in the death of Rosanne Boyland on January 6 is being withheld by the government. Citizens involved claim they were acting in defense of Ms. Boyland, who ultimately died at the hands of the U.S. Capitol Police. Mellis maintains the reason he was defensive with police was because he witnessed police brutalizing females and heard people screaming for help. One of those people being brutalized was Rosanne Boyland.

Consider the Alinsky-style sequence and its Lewin-style tactical purpose.

Identify Trump as the target → attack him as a white supremacist → continue the attacks on Trump even after he is out of office → spread the attacks to his supporters → support reverse racism → target white police officers → support a violent black supremacist/Marxist movement (BLM) → involve corporate America in the attacks and the support for BLM → indoctrinate adults to support reverse racism with MSM echo chamber of CRT → support defunding the police → indoctrinate children in CRT with educational curricula that supports reverse racism → foment CRT with governmental policies that create intolerable cognitive dissonance until the fury breaks out into the streets → incite violence → blame the violence on white supremacists → race war is manifest → quell the Democrat CRT-incited violence with government violence (federalized police, military, or National Guard) → present Democrats as saving the country from Trump's white supremacists.

The sinister political purpose of fomenting race wars in America is the elimination of constitutional conservatism, the collapse of civil society, and the imposition of one-world government. This colossal humanitarian hoax is being sold to a regressed and frightened American public as deliverance. If the plan succeeds, our constitutional republic will be surrendered to globalism's planetary rule. It is the uber-wealthy globalists who fund the politicians, who support the radical Democrats, who support CRT, who support the fiction of a January 6 *insurrection* by white supremacists, who foment the racial divisiveness and coming race wars. Follow the money, always follow the money.

The radical socialist Democrat war on America that begins in early childhood education ends in anarchy on the streets of America today. Political predators are exploiting indoctrinated young Americans, supplying them with financing, bricks, and Molotov cocktails to riot and burn neighborhoods to the ground. The entire January 6 insurrectionist narrative, including American political prisoners in DC jails, is pure political theater scripted to support the globalist agenda of the political predators.

We have arrived at a time in our history when we are threatened with the extinction of America, of our sovereignty and our constitutional freedoms. Political predators do not acknowledge America's right to exist. The enemies of America are aligned in common cause to fundamentally transform the nation and extinguish the United States of America.

CHAPTER 13

The Collapsing American Family: Macrocosm and Microcosm

Political predators attacking the cohesion of our national American family are a macrocosm. The simultaneous radical leftist attack on the cohesion of America's nuclear family is the microcosm. The destruction of the nuclear family is foundational to the attack on America's national identity and America's cultural identity.

It is important to understand the combatants in terms of competing ideologies. Leftism is rooted in Marxist collectivism and loyalty to the state. Americanism is rooted in individualism and loyalty to the family. Consider the Chinese communist revolution, 1946–1949. Thousands of years of family veneration were extinguished and replaced with loyalty to the newly established People's Republic of China (PRC).

Chairman Mao Tse-tung led the bloody revolution and the Cultural Revolution that followed, 1966–1976. Mao claimed the people's revolution alone could not wipe out bourgeois ideology since class struggle continues during socialism—so bourgeois ideology and its roots in traditionalism had to be defeated.

Chairman Mao instituted a national cancel-culture campaign that burned books, demolished statues, erased history, destroyed culture, and eradicated cultural norms in a comprehensive reeducation campaign that replaced traditional Chinese culture with Maoism—the Chinese communist variety of Marxist-Leninism.

Maoism's defining theory, ironically called *New Democracy*, maintained that socialism could be achieved only through popular, democratic, and anti-imperialist activity with the communists in charge.

In contemporary America, radical leftist Democrats are imitating the Maoist cancel-culture model. They target the three supporting pillars of Americanism: family, faith, and freedom. Cancel culture is asymmetric warfare used by the advancing leftist army to prepare America for socialist replacement ideology.

The nuclear American family is cancel culture's primary target because family provides continuity and cultural commitment to faith and freedom generation after generation. The enemies of freedom understand that destroying the nuclear family destabilizes the foundation of America and is the key to collapsing America from within.

How is this possible in the United States of America? History is an exceptional teacher.

Hitler experimented in Germany by removing children from their parents and indoctrinating them with Nazi reeducation lessons that demanded loyalty to the state. The move proved very effective. Hitler Youth children actually turned in parents who rejected Nazism.

Marxist cancel culture is ripping families apart to root out the ideological foundation of America's constitutional republic that guarantees decentralized government, individual rights, and states' rights.

It is leftist preparation for a Marxist-style centralized, federalized, collectivist replacement ideology. According to Karl Marx, the father of Soviet communism, an ideal communist society would have centralized banking, centralized education, and centralized labor. All infrastructure facilities, all agriculture, and all industries would be government owned. There would be no private property, no inheritance rights, and the government would levy high taxes on everyone so it could support its programs.

The problem with communism is the same problem with socialism. Margaret Thatcher described it best: "The problem with socialism is that eventually you run out of other people's money." It is the fundamental problem China faced in its communist revolution. So, while Nixon and Kissinger bragged about opening trade with China in 1973, and arrogant American globalist/industrialists smirked about exploiting cheap Chinese labor for their goods, the smiling Chinese communists quietly solved their cash-flow problems. Western currency would finance the communists' 100-Year Plan to take over the world.

The money poured into China as one globalist corporation after another moved its manufacturing out of the United States and into China.

Eventually the smiling Chinese communists used their massive wealth to go on a buying spree. They bought American high tech and dual use companies while they continued to steal our technology. They established hundreds of Confucius Institutes and chairs at universities across America. They exported Chinese communist culture and spread its weaponized cancel-culture tactics throughout the U.S.

Black Lives Matter (BLM) founders are unapologetic Marxist communists. Their organization is dedicated to critical race theory (CRT), the racist narrative that applies critical theory, the Marxist divide between oppressed and oppressor in society, to race. BLM spews its racist propaganda and the mainstream media validate the fiction. The propaganda machine relentlessly presents the false narrative that America is an irredeemably racist nation of white oppressors and oppressed people of color, and only communism can rescue us.

Author Stella Morabito exposes CRT as a "Classic Communist Divide-and-Conquer Tactic"[58] in her September 29, 2020, Federalist article. Morabito describes CRT as "the insidious ideology being used to promote estrangement rather than friendship, and hostility rather than goodwill. Indeed, the tactics used by proponents of critical race theory share many parallels with old tactics used by the Bolsheviks."

CRT not only foments racial tension it also creates family tension. Conservative parents who reject the racism inherent in CRT are scorned by their propagandized children. Educational indoctrination toward Marxism/communism and racist CRT in schools across America is an attack on the conservative American family that begins in K–12 and extends through the university level.

Impressionable children not only reject their parents' conservative values, they reject their parents and rupture the family. Rupture has become a socially acceptable form of protest. The radical left calls itself *progressive*. Progress toward what? A communist society where there is absolute conformity and zero individual freedom? Zero individual property rights? Zero states' rights? Zero freedom of speech?? What they offer is a tyrannical, anti-American absolutism.

The *progressive* choice for rupture reveals a stunningly *regressive* lack of maturity—an infantile inability to agree to disagree. The *progressive* narrative is a childish, emotional insistence on absolute conformity.

Progressives don't care what you LOOK like. Progressives demand that you THINK the way they do. Children are now demanding that their conservative parents conform to this regressive ideology or suffer family estrangement.

The collapsing American family is a microcosm of the collapsing American democracy. The Biden/Obama/Harris regime supports BLM and CRT, both of which unapologetically attack the nuclear American family. Additionally, the current administration has demonstrated its commitment to canceling the foundational American principle of free speech.

Without free speech there is no freedom. Radical leftists are restricting free speech by censoring conservative voices on the Internet, at work, at home, in schools, and in the mainstream and entertainment media. Freedom of speech is no longer a part of many American families. Leftist censorship has infiltrated American family life. Children are now demanding that their conservative parents censor themselves. No political discussions allowed.

When parents surrender to emotional extortion and conform to their children's ideological indoctrination and demands, the parents no longer pose a threat to the Marxist movement. Even when parents embrace a competing ideology or are a source of factual information, capitulation renders them irrelevant.

CHAPTER 14

Leftist Socialism:
The Toothfish of Modern Politics

Patagonian <u>toothfish</u>,[59] a rejected, ugly, oily bottom-dwelling fish, was rebranded Chilean sea bass and became an expensive delicacy for gullible millennials.

Socialism, a rejected, ugly, oily, bottom-dwelling ideology that enriched the elite and enslaved the masses, was rebranded social democracy and became a rallying cry for naïve 21st-century millennials.

It is often useful to look backward in order to move forward, so let's review. Karl Marx, author of *The Communist Manifesto* (1848), stated unequivocally, "Democracy is the road to socialism." <u>Social democracy</u>[60] began in the late 19th as a political ideology advocating an evolutionary and peaceful transition from capitalism to socialism using established political processes to facilitate the transition, rather than the violent revolutionary process of Marxism. The Russian Social Democrat Labour Party began in 1898. In 1903 the party split in two and the Bolshevik majority, led by Vladimir Lenin, seized power in the October Revolution of 1917. In 1918, Lenin changed the name of the party from the Russian Social Democratic Labour Party to the Russian Communist Party. It was a decision that emphasized Lenin's return to the violent revolutionary road to socialism, and his conviction that the goal of socialism is communism.

The Socialist Party of America had been unable to field a successful presidential candidate since its formation in 1901. So, in 1972 the Socialist Party of America officially rebranded itself as <u>Social Democrats, USA</u>.[61] The name was changed because many Americans still associated the word *socialism* with Soviet Communism. Rebranding was necessary to eliminate the name's negative image and conceal the party's actual goals.

The thing about rebranding is that it does not change the product itself; only the name changes, along with its psychological associations. Lyman Tower Sargent, American professor of political science and utopian studies explains, "socialism refers to *social* theories rather than to theories oriented to the individual. Because many communists now call themselves *democratic socialists*, it is sometimes difficult to know what a political label really means."

Rebranding <u>toothfish as Chilean sea bass</u>[62] was a successful marketing strategy designed to sell a rejected fish in the food industry. Similarly, rebranding the Socialist Party of America as Social Democrats was a successful marketing strategy designed to sell a rejected ideology in the political sphere. Both marketing strategies were highly successful.

The democratic socialism currently embraced by the leftist radicals that dominate the Democrat party in America has embraced identity politics to increase its membership with inclusive promises of *social justice* and *income equality*. These slogan promises disguise the reality of socialism.

Millennials would be well advised to ignore the slick Madison Avenue marketing campaigns of hypocritical political elites like Bernie Sanders, Elizabeth Warren, Barack Obama, Joe Biden, and Kamala Harris, and actually investigate real-life socialism in real-life countries like Cuba and Venezuela. Instead of accepting the fake news provided by the colluding mainstream media and their paid political pundits, millennials should listen to real people who have escaped the tyranny of real-world socialism. Perhaps millennials have not noticed that people are not drowning on freedom rafts sailing *from* Miami to Cuba—they are risking their lives to sail from Cuba *to* Miami.

The Socialist Party of America's dream to transition America from capitalism to socialism to communism is a long-term Marxist-Leninist project. It began with *The Communist Manifesto* in 1848, survived the Cold War tensions that almost exposed its communist influence in America during the 1950s McCarthy era, became the Social Democrats, USA in 1972, and survived the fall of the Berlin wall in 1989.

On Jan. 10, 1963, Congressman Albert S. Herlong Jr. of Florida read a list of forty-five communist goals into the Congressional Record. The list originated in Dr. Cleon Skousen's 1958 book, <u>*The Naked Communist*</u>.[63] Dr. Skousen (1913–2006), a Canadian-American author, speaker, lawyer, and teacher, lectured across the country and around the world warning of the unremitting communist threat.

The goals that articulate and expose the thinking and strategies of the political elite sixty-three years ago are the same goals and policies being implemented by today's radical leftist Democrat party, its radical leftist leaders, and the globalists pulling their strings. Some of the familiar names are Barack Obama, Nancy Pelosi, Bernie Sanders, Elizabeth Warren, Chuck Schumer, Alexandria Ocasio-Cortez, George Soros, and Bill Gates.

Today's Democrat party is the captured political party that fulfills goal 15 below: Capture one or both of the political parties in the United States.

Here is what Congressman/Rep. Herlong read into the Congressional Record in 1963:

Congressional Record—Appendix, pp. A34–A35 Current Communist Goals

EXTENSION OF REMARKS OF HON. A. S. HERLONG, JR. OF FLORIDA IN THE HOUSE OF REPRESENTATIVES

Thursday, January 10, 1963

Mr. HERLONG. Mr. Speaker, Mrs. Patricia Nordman of De Land, Fla., is an ardent and articulate opponent of communism, and until recently published the De Land Courier, which she dedicated to the purpose of alerting the public to the dangers of communism in America.

At Mrs. Nordman's request, I include in the RECORD, under unanimous consent, the following "Current Communist Goals," which she identifies as an excerpt from "The Naked Communist," by Cleon Skousen:

CURRENT COMMUNIST GOALS

1. *U.S. acceptance of coexistence as the only alternative to atomic war.*

2. *U.S. willingness to capitulate in preference to engaging in atomic war.*

3. *Develop the illusion that total disarmament [by] the United States would be a demonstration of moral strength.*

4. *Permit free trade between all nations regardless of Communist affiliation and regardless of whether or not items could be used for war.*

5. *Extension of long-term loans to Russia and Soviet satellites.*

6. *Provide American aid to all nations regardless of Communist domination.*

7. *Grant recognition of Red China. Admission of Red China to the U.N.*

8. *Set up East and West Germany as separate states in spite of Khrushchev's promise in 1955 to settle the German question by free elections under supervision of the U.N.*

9. *Prolong the conferences to ban atomic tests because the United States has agreed to suspend tests as long as negotiations are in progress.*

10. *Allow all Soviet satellites individual representation in the U.N.*

11. *Promote the U.N. as the only hope for mankind. If its charter is rewritten, demand that it be set up as a one-world government with its own independent armed forces. (Some Communist leaders believe the world can be taken over as easily by the U.N. as by Moscow. Sometimes these two centers compete with each other as they are now doing in the Congo.)*

12. *Resist any attempt to outlaw the Communist Party.*

13. *Do away with all loyalty oaths.*

14. *Continue giving Russia access to the U.S. Patent Office.*

15. *Capture one or both of the political parties in the United States.*

16. *Use technical decisions of the courts to weaken basic American institutions by claiming their activities violate civil rights.*

17. *Get control of the schools. Use them as transmission belts for socialism and current Communist propaganda. Soften the curriculum. Get control of teachers' associations. Put the party line in textbooks.*

18. *Gain control of all student newspapers.*

19. *Use student riots to foment public protests against programs or organizations which are under Communist attack.*

20. *Infiltrate the press. Get control of book-review assignments, editorial writing, and policymaking positions.*

21. *Gain control of key positions in radio, TV, and motion pictures.*

22. *Continue discrediting American culture by degrading all forms of artistic expression. An American Communist cell was told to "eliminate all good sculpture from parks and buildings, substitute shapeless, awkward and meaningless forms."*

23. *Control art critics and directors of art museums. "Our plan is to promote ugliness, repulsive, meaningless art."*

24. *Eliminate all laws governing obscenity by calling them "censorship" and a violation of free speech and free press.*

25. *Break down cultural standards of morality by promoting pornography and obscenity in books, magazines, motion pictures, radio, and TV.*

26. *Present homosexuality, degeneracy and promiscuity as "normal, natural, and healthy."*

27. *Infiltrate the churches and replace revealed religion with "social" religion. Discredit the Bible and emphasize the need for intellectual maturity which does not need a "religious crutch."*

28. *Eliminate prayer or any phase of religious expression in the schools on the ground that it violates the principle of "separation of church and state." (Remember these goals were published to expose them in 1958)   Coincidence?*

29. *Discredit the American Constitution by calling it inadequate, old-fashioned, out of step with modern needs, a hindrance to cooperation between nations on a worldwide basis.*

30. *Discredit the American Founding Fathers. Present them as selfish aristocrats who had no concern for the "common man."*

31. *Belittle all forms of American culture and discourage the teaching*

of American history on the ground that it was only a minor part of the "big picture." Give more emphasis to Russian history since the Communists took over.

32. *Support any socialist movement to give centralized control over any part of the culture–education, social agencies, welfare programs, mental health clinics, etc.*

33. *Eliminate all laws or procedures, which interfere with the operation of the Communist apparatus.*

34. *Eliminate the House Committee on Un-American Activities.*

35. *Discredit and eventually dismantle the FBI.*

36. *Infiltrate and gain control of more unions.*

37. *Infiltrate and gain control of big business.*

38. *Transfer some of the powers of arrest from the police to social agencies. Treat all behavioral problems as psychiatric disorders which no one but psychiatrists can understand [or treat].*

39. *Dominate the psychiatric profession and use mental health laws as a means of gaining coercive control over those who oppose Communist goals.*

40. *Discredit the family as an institution. Encourage promiscuity and easy divorce.*

41. *Emphasize the need to raise children away from the negative influence of parents. Attribute prejudices, mental blocks and retarding of children to suppressive influence of parents.*

42. *Create the impression that violence and insurrection are legitimate aspects of the American tradition; that students and special-interest groups should rise up and use ["] united force ["] to solve economic, political or social problems.*

43. *Overthrow all colonial governments before native populations are ready for self-government.*

44. *Internationalize the Panama Canal.*

45. *Repeal the Connally reservation so the United States cannot prevent the World Court from seizing jurisdiction over domestic prob-*

lems. Give the World Court jurisdiction over nations and individuals alike.

A shocking proportion of these forty-five communist goals have become policy in the United States. The Obama presidency exponentially increased the pressure toward their acceptance and accelerated the pace toward implementation. The election of President Donald Trump abruptly interrupted Obama's march toward communism, halting its progression for four years.

President Trump's America-first nationalism was diametrically opposed to Obama's campaign to transform America into socialism and ultimate surrender to one-world government. Obama's policies were immediately restored when Biden took office on January 20, 2021, and have been intensified to unprecedented and lawless levels.

CHAPTER 15

Obama's Grand Plan: Fundamental Transformation

The Obama years, January 2009–January 2017, saw an unprecedented politicization of government institutions. Barack Obama used his presidential office to move America closer to socialism by staffing government positions with radical leftist ideologues.

Obama's Grand Plan followed Marxist community organizer Saul Alinsky's infamous 1971 manual for activists, *Rules for Radicals*,[64] with religious fidelity. "True revolutionaries do not flaunt their radicalism. They cut their hair, put on suits and infiltrate the system from within," wrote Alinsky. Saul Alinsky followed Italian communist party chief Antonin Gramsci, who understood that in America it was necessary to penetrate existing institutions including churches, unions, and political parties.

Alinsky taught that change comes from power, and power comes from organization. (*Rules for Radicals*, p. 113)

> Therefore, if your function is to attack apathy and get people to participate it is necessary to attack the prevailing patterns of organized living in the community. The first step in *community organization* is *community disorganization*. The disruption of the present organization is the first step toward community organization. Present arrangements must be disorganized if they are to be displaced by new patterns that provide the opportunities and means for citizen participation. *All change means disorganization of the old and organization of the new.* (p. 116)

Obama cut his hair, put on a suit, blended in, became a "community organizer," and disguised his subversive intentions. Barack Hussein Obama became Alinsky's most successful student, with Hillary Clinton taking second place.

Obama's socialist agenda took aim at the nuclear American family and its support of American idealism and moral values. Like Napoleon the pig in Orwell's *Animal Farm*, Obama focused on educational indoctrination. Obama launched his assault on the American family through Common Core and its anti-American, anti-family, collectivist propaganda. It is a sinister campaign to undermine established American Judeo-Christian cultural norms celebrating patriotism, the meritocracy, and American sovereignty.

The Common Core State Standards (CCSS) launched under Obama in 2009 were deceptively marketed by a propaganda campaign emphasizing the positive benefits of national standards and uniformity in curriculum guidelines with measurable effectiveness for American public education K–12. Common Core State Standards (CCSS) are mistakenly understood to be a derivative of the No Child Left Behind Act, the law that held schools accountable for how kids learned and achieved. They aren't.

Obama's 2009 Race to the Top[65] program was introduced as a competitive grant program that awarded points to states for satisfying performance-based evaluations of teachers and principals based on measurable educator effectiveness. Sound familiar? It should, because measurable effectiveness = student test scores. Even though Race to the Top did not mandate adoption of Common Core, in order to receive federal stimulus money states had to commit to adopting Common Core standards. Initially, forty-six states adopted CCSS for public and private education. Virginia, Texas, Alaska, and Nebraska never adopted them. Five states subsequently withdrew from the standards, and twelve have adopted legislation to repeal the standards outright.

Currently, forty-one states, the District of Columbia, four territories, and the Department of Defense Education Activity (DoDEA) have adopted the Common Core State Standards. Nine states, Alaska, Hawaii, Texas, Florida, South Carolina, Virginia, Indiana, Minnesota, Nebraska, and Puerto Rico have not.

Common Core Standards Mission Statement:[66]

> The Common Core State Standards provide a consistent, clear understanding of what students are expected to learn, so teachers and parents know what they need to do to help them. The standards are designed to be robust and relevant to the real world,

reflecting the knowledge and skills that our young people need for success in college and careers. With American students fully prepared for the future, our communities will be best positioned to compete successfully in the global economy. . . . These Standards do not dictate curriculum or teach methods.

Sounds great. The problem is the deceptive language referring to the "real world," the "global economy," and the misleading statement that the Standards do not dictate curriculum or teaching methods. This is how it works.

Common Core State Standards are not a derivative of America's No Child Left Behind Act. Common Core State Standards are a derivative of the United Nations' Global Education First Initiative[67] (GEFI). The 3 Priorities[68] of GEFI:

Priority 1: Put Every Child in School

Priority 2: Improve the Quality of Learning

Priority 3: Foster Global Citizenship

Common Core is not teaching American children about the world and how to be effective and competitive in a global marketplace. The deceitful Common Core initiative is propagandizing American children toward collectivism, globalism, and one-world government with its anti-American, anti-Judeo-Christian, pro-Islamic bias. American education, both public and private, no longer advocates American patriotism, the meritocracy, American exceptionalism, or American sovereignty. America is no longer in control of American education, and the educational curriculum challenges the authority of the nuclear family. The contrast between what children learn in school and what their parents are attempting to teach them at home creates enormous conflict in the family.

Obama's infamous Cairo speech launched an eight-year initiative to Connect All Schools,[69] fraudulently presented as a program to help students in different countries, who believe different things be able to communicate and understand one another.

Obama's Common Core originates from the One World Education concept, a global goal orchestrated by the Connect All Schools program to globalize instruction.

World Net Daily[70] reported that in 2011 Qatar Foundation International (QFI) "partnered with the Department of State and the U.S. Department of Education to facilitate matchmaking between classrooms in the U.S. and international schools through . . . the 'Connect All Schools' project." QFI proudly states on its website that the initiative was founded in response to Obama's 2009 Cairo speech with the Muslim Brotherhood prominently seated in the front row.

The conspiracy of the leftist/Islamist axis to reeducate American children away from America-first patriotism toward collectivism and global governance is well under way and well-funded.

Most parents have no idea what their children are learning in school unless their child asks for help with homework or relates an experience at school. Parents in any of the states that have adopted Common Core State Standards need to start reading their children's textbooks immediately. It is up to parents to decide whether they support American sovereignty and fair trade in the global marketplace or global citizenship[71] and a globalized curriculum[72] promoting one-world government. It is a matter of informed consent.

This brings us to United Nations (UN) Agenda 21,[73] initiated in 1992 and described in a lengthy report titled United Nations Sustainable Development.[74] The entire document can be summarized in one sentence:

United Nations Agenda 21 is a plan for a New World Order that internationalizes the entire world into a global society under its own UN global governance.

Its lofty preamble reads like the lyrics of John Lennon's song "Imagine." In the old days, those who sought world domination were not so soft spoken—Hitler, Stalin, and Mussolini did not sing lullabies of peace. But the 21st century requires a different approach. We have "Imagine" and the updated 2030 Agenda for Sustainable Development.[75]

The Culture War is an insidious information war being waged on America through the political correctness, moral relativism, and historical revisionism embodied in the informational materials supplied by the pro-globalism enemies of national sovereignty at the United Nations. Educational jihad does not require bullets or bombs; it is quietly fought in classrooms with the educational propaganda of the World Core Curriculum.[76]

In 1989 the United Nations Educational, Scientific and Cultural Organization (UNESCO) awarded its Prize for Peace Education to Robert Muller for creating a World Core Curriculum (WCC). He said in accepting his award, "I dream that UNESCO will study and recommend by the year 2000 a world core curriculum for adoption by all nations."

Why is a world core curriculum desirable? Most people understand the mission of the United Nations to be promotion of the Westphalian state system[77] of mutual respect and cooperation among sovereign nations that honors cultural differences among nations. Were we misled? Was the goal of the UN always universal citizenship? Muller says, "In the final analysis . . . the main function of education is to make children happy, fulfilled, and universal human beings." *Universal* human beings?? I don't think so!

In November 2010 Obama's secretary of education, Arne Duncan, addressed UNESCO[78] and praised universal education without ever mentioning educational content. Educating the world's children is a laudable goal. Putting every child in school and improving the quality of learning is a marvelous undertaking. The problem is that most people naïvely assume that universal education advances literacy; they do not realize that it is a propaganda tool designed to advance global governance.

In a world of technology where hard-copy books are increasingly being replaced with software and lessons taught on computers, it is incredibly simple to alter, censor, and manipulate original texts. Having the world's children literate and able to read about the world, in order to better understand other cultures and live together in peace, is not the same thing as having the children of the world literate in order to be propagandized by manipulated curriculum content.

It is essential that curriculum content for American educational materials be developed *by* Americans *for* Americans, with an unapologetic America-first foundation. Parents endorsing the Common Core State Standards are unwittingly endorsing anti-American, anti-family, pro-Islam, globalized educational products designed by British publishing giant Pearson Education.[79] Pearson Education supplies educational materials[80] to Connect All Schools. Today, the educational indoctrination is fully engaged in teaching anti-American critical race theory.

Words matter. It is important for Americans to understand what one-world government means to the globalist elite. One-world government is not the fulfillment of John Lennon's iconic song "Imagine." It is a regressive return to the binary feudal structure of rulers and ruled. The United Nations is the instrument for imposing and managing planetary governance.

The value of educational propaganda in the globalist campaign is described in chilling detail by English aristocrat Lord Bertrand Russell in his 1953 classic, *The Impact of Science on Society*.[81] Educational indoctrination is the primary instrument for eliminating objective reality, dismissing the American family, subverting American culture, and destroying America from within. Russell unapologetically explained the process that drives a society to madness:

> *It may be hoped that in time anybody will be able to persuade anybody of anything if he can catch the patient young and is provided by the State with money and equipment.*
>
> *Education should aim at destroying free will so that pupils thus schooled, will be incapable throughout the rest of their lives of thinking or acting otherwise than as their schoolmasters would have wished. . . . Influences of the home are obstructive; not much can be done unless indoctrination begins before the age of ten; in order to condition students, verses set to music and repeatedly intoned are very effective. . . . It is for a future scientist to make these maxims precise and to discover exactly how much it costs per head to make children believe that snow is black. When the technique has been perfected, every government that has been in charge of education for more than one generation will be able to control its subjects securely without the need of armies or policemen.* (pp. 27–28, Routledge Classics, 2016 edition)

Russell echoed Lenin's statement: "Give me four years to teach the children and the seed I have sown will never be uprooted."

If American parents do not become actively involved in discovering what their children are learning in school, they will be unable to oppose the radical education initiative currently transforming the children of the world into *green* or *global citizens* prepared for the New

World Order. Common Core will successfully propagandize American children to reject American citizenship and become citizens of a world dictated and governed by the United Nations.

CHAPTER 16

Nationalism Is NOT a Dirty Word!

When did American nationalism become a dirty word? Under Obama, of course! Obama's leftist war against America is a war against American nationalism. America emerged from World War II as the most economically powerful nation on earth and invincible militarily. Enemies of the United States would need an alternate strategy in order to defeat her.

Aesop's 6th-century BC fable "<u>The Four Oxen and the Lion</u>"[82] provided that strategy.

> A lion used to prowl about a field in which four oxen used to dwell. Many a time he tried to attack them; but whenever he came near, they turned their tails to one another, so that whichever way he approached them he was met by the horns of one of them. At last, however, they fell a-quarrelling among themselves, and each went off to pasture alone in a separate corner of the field. Then the lion attacked them one by one and soon made an end of all four. United we stand, divided we fall.

American nationalism is the common denominator that unifies Americans as one national family. It explains why the war on America specifically targets American nationalism. Obama's leftist strategy is one of creating divisiveness inside America because divided we fall. This is how it works.

The overarching conflict in the world today is between nationalism and internationalism. Nationalism supports the national sovereignty of independent countries trading fairly in the global marketplace. Internationalism supports globalism—a globalized one-world nation with a one-world economy, one-world language, one-world currency, one-world flag, one-world educational curriculum, one-world court, one-world police force, one-world army, and most significantly, one-world government.

United Nations Agenda 2030 was announced the weekend of September 25–27, 2015, at the UN headquarters in New York City. The plan, "Transforming Our World: the 2030 Agenda for Sustainable Development," updates United Nations Agenda 21[83] which originated at the 1992 United Nations Earth Summit.

Agenda 2030's[84] fundamental-transformation plan is introduced with these sublime words in its preamble:

> This Agenda is a plan of action for people, planet and prosperity. It also seeks to strengthen universal peace in larger freedom. We recognise that eradicating poverty in all its forms and dimensions, including extreme poverty, is the greatest global challenge and an indispensable requirement for sustainable development. All countries and all stakeholders, acting in collaborative partnership, will implement this plan. We are resolved to free the human race from the tyranny of poverty and want and to heal and secure our planet. We are determined to take the bold and transformative steps which are urgently needed to shift the world onto a sustainable and resilient path. As we embark on this collective journey, we pledge that no one will be left behind. The 17 Sustainable Development Goals and 169 targets which we are announcing today demonstrate the scale and ambition of this new universal Agenda. They seek to build on the Millennium Development Goals and complete what these did not achieve. They seek to realize the human rights of all and to achieve gender equality and the empowerment of all women and girls. They are integrated and indivisible and balance the three dimensions of sustainable development: the economic, social and environmental.
>
> The Goals and targets will stimulate action over the next fifteen years in areas of critical importance for humanity and the planet.

Agenda 2030 and its 17 sustainable goals are marketed as deliverance from global poverty, disease, injustice, and overpopulation. "Sustainable development" is code for globalism's solution to the Malthusian dilemma of increasing population and decreasing natural resources. Let's review the goals:

Sustainable Development Goals

- Goal 1. End poverty in all its forms everywhere

- Goal 2. End hunger, achieve food security and improved nutrition and promote sustainable agriculture

- Goal 3. Ensure healthy lives and promote well-being for all at all ages

- Goal 4. Ensure inclusive and equitable quality education and promote lifelong learning opportunities for all

- Goal 5. Achieve gender equality and empower all women and girls

- Goal 6. Ensure availability and sustainable management of water and sanitation for all

- Goal 7. Ensure access to affordable, reliable, sustainable and modern energy for all

- Goal 8. Promote sustained, inclusive and sustainable economic growth, full and productive employment and decent work for all

- Goal 9. Build resilient infrastructure, promote inclusive and sustainable industrialization and foster innovation

- Goal 10. Reduce inequality within and among countries

- Goal 11. Make cities and human settlements inclusive, safe, resilient and sustainable

- Goal 12. Ensure sustainable consumption and production patterns

- Goal 13. Take urgent action to combat climate change and its impacts*

- Goal 14. Conserve and sustainably use the oceans, seas and marine resources for sustainable development

- Goal 15. Protect, restore and promote sustainable use of terrestrial ecosystems, sustainably manage forests, combat desertification, and halt and reverse land degradation and halt biodiversity loss

- Goal 16. Promote peaceful and inclusive societies for sustainable development, provide access to justice for all and build effective, accountable and inclusive institutions at all levels

- Goal 17. Strengthen the means of implementation and revitalize the global partnership for sustainable development

WOW! Sounds great! So, what's the problem?

Implementation. The implementation of Agenda 2030 and all of its sustainable goals requires a "New" World Order of planetary governance administered under the auspices of the United Nations.

The "New" World Order marketed by the globalist elite as the universal system for social justice and income equality is actually not new at all; it is a return to the very Old World feudal system of masters and slaves. There is nothing new about a binary socio-political system with the elite rulers at the top of the social pyramid and the enslaved masses occupying the base. Agenda 2030 declares the lethally corrupt United Nations to be the world body entrusted with making and enforcing the laws that rule the world.

This means the world population becomes the base of the internationalized world pyramid. There is no national sovereignty, separation of powers, or individual rights or freedoms articulated in Agenda 2030—only lofty words and political candy offered to seduce the free world into willingly becoming slaves of the globalist elite.

The globalists had a problem. They knew they could not succeed in establishing their "New" World Order without the participation of the United States. Barack Obama was very helpful.

American nationalism is the bulwark against internationalism: united we stand, divided we fall. Nationalism transcends individual differences among Americans and strengthens America by providing the common denominator that binds us one to the other to protect and preserve our country. Like Aesop's four oxen we stand together, united in common cause to fend off the globalist enemy.

American nationalism is diametrically opposed to supranational globalism. America-first President Donald Trump remains the symbol of American nationalism and explains the international effort to overthrow him during his four-year term, and the ongoing effort to prevent his return to office. Media sound bites deceitfully associate President Trump's patriotic American nationalism with despicable Nazi supremacy. They are an attack on our exceptional cultural identity designed to produce self-loathing and make nationalism a dirty word.

Nationalism is defined by Merriam-Webster[85] as "loyalty or devotion to a nation; especially a sense of national consciousness exalting one nation above all others and placing primary emphasis on promotion of its culture and interests as opposed to those of other nations or supranational groups." Supranational means transcending national boundaries, authority, or interests. Globalism is supranational and Barack Obama is a globalist.

Barack Hussein Obama[86] served the UN globalist agenda during his two terms, and continues to drive the divisive anti-American *resistance* movement against former President Trump. Let's examine the four oxen of American cultural identity that Obama's policies and divisive resistance movement relentlessly attack.

1. Constitution. The single greatest document in history, written by our Founding Fathers and guaranteeing individual liberty, separation of powers, and individual rights. The Constitution establishes ordered liberty, supports individualism and national sovereignty, and rejects collectivism and supranational globalism. Obama's activist judges seek to shred the clarity of the Constitution to make it a "living" document for their political purposes.

2. Family. The nuclear family has been under attack since the Culture War began in the '60s. The stability of the family, including its moral commitment to the Judeo-Christian Ten Commandments, was shattered by Obama and replaced with a religious loyalty to leftism. The new "family of choice" lives by the leftist credo of political correctness, moral relativism, and historical revisionism. It welcomes diversity of color and sexual orientation but completely rejects diversity of *thought.* The leftist demand for ideological conformity is tyrannical in its orthodoxy and commitment to UN goals.

3. Education. The reeducation of America through anti-American, pro-Islamist, pro-globalist educational curriculum content; Internet censorship; manipulative television advertising and program content; the staggering bias of mainstream media editorial reporting—all pressure America toward collectivism and one-world governance. Foundational to the leftist narrative is United Nations Agenda 2030, "the comprehensive blueprint for the reorganization of human society," and its 17 sustainable goals. Obama's Common Core sponsored universal education to prepare our children for global citizenship.

4. Military. Obama's administration weakened the U.S. military and national defense with the same leftist narrative of political correctness, moral relativism, and historical revisionism. His pro-Islamist embrace of the Muslim Brotherhood deliberately disinformed the military about the ideological foundation for jihad and terrorism. He weakened military morale, under-financed and under-supplied the troops, and allowed foreign governments to control strategic Port Canaveral and the Port of Wilmington.[87]

The United States military has the singular goal of protecting the sovereignty of America and its people. Obama's goal continues to be the weakening of our national defense to make way for supranational globalism. While China built its military might, Obama insisted our soldiers have sensitivity training and walk in high heels to feel how women feel.

The meritocracy is the foundation of all four elements of our cultural identity and national pride. The meritocracy provides unparalleled upward mobility in America, which incentivizes excellence in all fields. The meritocracy supports individualism, rejects collectivism, and evaluates actions based on the WHAT of behavior, not the WHO exhibiting that behavior. Obama's leftism abolished the blind justice of the meritocracy in favor of leftist tribalism that exclusively values the WHO, and hypocritically defends lawless members of their tribe. He politicized the FBI, DOJ, CIA, NSA, IRS, and State Department, and seeded the courts with activist judges—all determined to weaken America and impose one-world government.

The current Biden/Obama/Harris regime has seriously escalated the globalist effort to weaken the U.S. military and leave the nation defenseless. Obama bailed out Iran's failing terrorist regime with pallets of cash in the infamous Iran Deal. Biden's catastrophic withdrawal from

Afghanistan provided $58 billion in military equipment to our enemies.

Collectivism, whether it is socialism, communism, or globalism, is predatory. It does not provide social justice or income equality for the people—collectivism benefits only the ruling elite.

CHAPTER 17

Obama: The Leftist Toothfish of Modern Politics

Alexander G. Markovsky, an American citizen born and educated in the former Soviet Union, holds degrees in economics and political science from the University of Marxism-Leninism, and an engineering degree from Moscow University. Markovsky, who emigrated to the United States as a young man, has lived his life both in freedom and under tyranny. His two books, *Anatomy of a Bolshevik: How Marx & Lenin Explain Obama's Grand Plan* (2012) and *Liberal Bolshevism: America Did Not Defeat Communism, She Adopted It* (2016), were written to warn Americans that Obama's progressivism is literally Marxism in disguise.

In the preamble to *Anatomy of a Bolshevik*[88] Markovsky writes:

> The purpose of this book is to factually deconstruct President Obama and answer the question "Why?" Why is a President leading an assault on American values, the economy and our way of life? What is the ultimate strategic objective and what tactics is he using to accomplish it?

Markovsky explains that Marxists are dogmatic and predictable, and how life in the Soviet Union enabled him to see life through the prism of red communist glasses, not America's rose-colored glasses.

> Obama's agenda is not about business, it's about social justice; it's not about wealth creation, it's about wealth redistribution; it's not about the law, it's about fairness; it's not about individualism, it's about collectivism; it's not about self-reliance, it's about dependency; and, finally, it's not about capitalism, it is about socialism. (*Anatomy of a Bolshevik*, p. 77)

In summary:

> Obama's long-term strategy for the implementation of the socialist dream can be elucidated based on a preponderance of

the evidence and the application of the theories of Marxism and Leninism. In his quest to re-engineer the free-market economy and replace American self-reliance with government dependency, the President is using methods developed by the Russian Bolsheviks during the early stages of the Bolshevik revolution in Russia. His strategy rests on three pillars, which are fundamentally interrelated and interdependent: (*Anatomy of a Bolshevik*, pp.61–76)

1. Destruction of wealth
2. Replacing American self-reliance with government dependence
3. Replacement of a capitalist market-oriented economy with a government-controlled political economy

Markovsky explains the Bolshevik strategy of government taking control of the economy to dominate everyday life and make its citizens dependent on the government. But America is not the former Soviet Union. How is it possible for socialists to achieve their goals in a society of wealth, idealism, and pluralism?

The answer is Barack Obama, former president of the United States and current promoter of Marxist critical race theory in America. Barack Obama was groomed by the communists, rebranded by the globalists, protected by the Democrat party, and sold to America by the mainstream media. Barack Hussein Obama is the leftist toothfish of modern politics.

Obama denies he is a socialist: "Contrary to the claims of some of my critics and some of the editorial pages, I am an ardent believer in the free market." Markovsky decodes Obama's denial:

There is a simple explanation for the President's actions: our president lives in a different world; the world of Marxist Dialectical materialism, where change is the product of a constant conflict between opposites arising from the internal contradictions inherent in all events, ideas, and movements. So, as long as he sees the world as a conflict of opposing forces, Obama will seek conflict as the process leading to achieving his strategic objectives. (*Anatomy of a Bolshevik*, p. 42)

Markovsky's concluding chapter, "The Power of Demagoguery and Lies," answers his own question:

> "How did a man with no experience at anything, who is intellectually shallow, and has no record of accomplishment in any field, propel himself in so short a time, into the Presidency of the United States?"

> For the last 50 years, the progressives have been waging all-out war against American institutions such as education, religion, and family values. Their tireless efforts have paid off. Early on, they realized there is no better way to subvert America than to have a degraded education system. . . . The American educational system has been a disgrace for many years, producing an illiterate electorate that gravely endangers our democracy. (*Anatomy of a Bolshevik*, pp. 217–219)

Markovsky warns, "To understand the President one has to get into the mind of a Bolshevik." We must remember the Democrats' partnership with the media and recall Lenin's rule, "A lie told often enough becomes the truth." Markovsky says we must recognize that:

> The strategy of class warfare and the use of dependency that the President is engaging in, worked for the Bolsheviks in the past; there is no reason to believe it will not work this time.

In his epilogue, Markovsky reflects:

> Very often contemporaries miss the turning points of history. The depth and historical importance of events is often not fully recognized in its time. The election of a black President was certainly a historic event. The obvious was recognized and widely celebrated, but the important had been missed. History was not made by the color of the President's skin; it was made by the color of his ideas. In the euphoria of the celebration, the ideology of this new President has not been recognized.

> Contrary to universal acumen, the Presidency of the United States is not the final destination of Obama's political journey. It is an inflection point to the final destination: the egalitarian dream. Millions of Bolsheviks gave their lives for that dream. Obama is getting there without firing a single shot, making

Lenin a historical pygmy.

If Obama's Grand Plan succeeds, this great tragedy will run its predictable course: high taxation, hyperinflation, depleted savings, and the devaluation of the dollar; prolonged economic stagnation and the destruction of our democracy, all culminating in one party rule for all Americans in a social-democratic Obama era. . . .

The issue we face is: What kind of country are we going to be? Whether we remain "one nation under God, indivisible, with liberty and justice for all" or are we going to be "one nation under debt with equality in poverty for all." Whether we are the "Land of the Free" or the "Land of the Voting Herd."

The enemies are at the gates and the fifth column is already inside ready to open the gates to welcome the Marxist socialist future. (*Anatomy of a Bolshevik*, pp. 235–236)

Obama was reelected in 2012. The election of America-first President Donald J. Trump interrupted Obama's Marxist movement in 2016, but it resumed after the 2020 election steal installed front man Joe Biden in the White House to serve Obama's third term.

Alexander Markovsky views a socialist America as the end game of Obama's Grand Plan. A socialist America may be Obama's political goal, but Obama is the historical pygmy for the globalist elite who fund the Marxist movement in America.

Planetary governance is the objective of globalism, and globalism cannot succeed without the collapse of America into socialism. The Biden/Obama/Harris regime is in the White House to deliver a socialist America to the globalists.

CHAPTER 18

The Fractal Wrongness of Leftist Ideology

What is fractal wrongness? Let's begin with a <u>fractal</u>.[89] A fractal is a geometric pattern that repeats itself at every level of magnification. Mathematician <u>Benoit Mandelbrot</u>[90] introduced fractal geometry in 1975 and defined a fractal as "a geometric shape that can be separated into parts, each of which is a reduced-scale version of the whole."

The famous <u>Menger sponge</u>[91] is a math fractal. Fractals abound in nature. Ice crystals and snowflakes form in fractal shapes, leaves and trees grow according to fractal laws, even lightning bolts are examples of fractals in nature. In computer science fractals are images that are the same at any level of scale, which means that it is impossible to determine how much the image is magnified by simply looking at it.

<u>Fractal wrongness</u>[92] is the state of being wrong at every conceivable scale of resolution—the person's entire worldview is wrong. The political left has decided that anyone who disagrees with its platform of political correctness, moral relativism, and historical revisionism is fractally wrong. Fractal wrongness explains why the Left views the entire worldview of conservatives as deplorable and contemptible.

Leftism, like any other orthodoxy, has embraced its tenets with religious zealotry and a tyrannical demand for conformity that ignores obvious contradictions in its own narrative. Leftists, who pride themselves on being tolerant, are hypocritically intolerant of anyone who embraces a worldview that differs from their own. They solve this philosophical inconsistency with leftist Newspeak, the official language of the Left.

Newspeak is the language of George Orwell's dystopian superstate, Oceania, in his novel *1984*. It is the language of official propaganda that was created to replace Oldspeak—Standard English. Newspeak replaces meanings of familiar words with their opposite meanings. The key to translating Newspeak is to think in opposites.

Leftist Newspeak imitates *taqiyyah*—deliberately lying or obfuscating to further Islam. The non-Islamic world understands the word *peace* to mean pluralism, tolerance, and the absence of conflict. The Islamic world understands the word *peace* to mean the time when all the world will be Islamic. Leftist Newspeak interprets *peace* as manifest when all the Western world will embrace leftism. *Taqiyyah* and leftist Newspeak share the intentional replacement of one set of meanings with another. They are languages of contronyms.

A contronym is a word with two opposite meanings. The word *sanction* is a contronym that can mean either to ratify or its opposite, to penalize. The word *oversight* can mean either to supervise or its opposite, to overlook. Speaking the ambiguous language of opposites can be very misleading politically, because words matter.

Barack Obama deliberately transformed Standard English to Newspeak and made leftist Newspeak the official language in America during his eight-year anti-American, pro-Islamist, pro-socialist tenure. The years of Obama's administration were years of language ambiguity. Americans are still bewildered by the use of language that no longer means what it used to mean. Leftist "tolerance" means *intolerance* toward any opposing ideas. To leftists "free speech" is *hate speech* if it counters their narrative.

The confusion, divisiveness, and chaos created by ambiguous leftist Newspeak is itself a fractal.

Let's review. Fractals are self-similar complex patterns that are created by repeating a simple process over and over in an ongoing feedback loop. Self-similarity is the essence of fractals and the foundation of Ben Rhodes' infamous echo chamber used to market Obama's anti-American, pro-Islamist Iran deal. Rhodes, Obama's Deputy National Security Advisor for Strategic Communications and Speechwriting, mastered the art of political fractals. The mainstream media deliberately advanced Obama's deceitful deal in a never-ending pattern that repeated itself on television, radio, and the Internet in an ongoing feedback loop. Obama's leftist echo chamber is a fractal in politics that continues in the Biden/Obama/Harris regime.

The bifurcation of America along political lines has been advocated by the regime's fractal socialist politics and the insistence that any opposition to its leftist narrative is fractally wrong. The irony, of course, is that acceptance of the leftist narrative requires acceptance of the presuppositions of leftist Newspeak—the language of contronyms and dialectical processes. This is how it works.

Obama's 2008 campaign promise for *hope* and *change* was not spoken in the familiar language of Oldspeak to mean the American dream. Obama's *hope and change* were Newspeak words for the radical socialism codified in Saul Alinsky's *Rules for Radicals.* Obama's leftist intention to destroy the capitalist infrastructure of American democracy and replace it with socialism requires acceptance of the leftist assumption that the current capitalist infrastructure needs to be replaced.

If conservatives allow the Left to continue to frame the debate, then conservatives are always playing defense because they have been snared by Alinsky's Rule #12:

> *Pick the target, freeze it, personalize it, and polarize it.*

President Donald Trump was the chosen target for Obama's resistance movement, begun after Trump won the 2016 election, that took coordinated action to destroy his presidency. It failed.

Undaunted, the radical leftist Democrats pursued impeachment. They hoped congressional action would embarrass, discredit, and delegitimize Trump because they knew there were no legitimate grounds for impeachment. They failed.

The war on America-first Trump, even post-presidency, is the globalist war on American sovereignty, which currently features Marxist-inspired critical race theory.

Patriots cannot allow Obama's minions to continue to frame the debate, because the leftist assumptions are fractally wrong. Our Founding Fathers demanded the separation of church and state to prevent religious discrimination. The Founding Fathers defined church and state as distinctly separate entities. It was inconceivable in 1776 that a political ideology could ever or would ever be embraced as a religion. But leftist socialism has rejected the authority of traditional Judeo-Christian beliefs and substituted its own political ideology as the new religion and source of authority for millennials in America.

Once leftism was embraced as a religious ideology, there was no longer any requirement for facts or objective reality because religion is faith based and not discredited by factual inconsistencies, glaring ambiguities, or the absence of verifiable proof. Leftism had freed itself from the confines of rational scrutiny and could unapologetically proselytize its tenets of political correctness, moral relativism, and historical revisionism, including critical race theory.

Leftism is a religion disguised as a socio-political movement. Islam is a socio-political movement disguised as a religion. Both are tyrannical totalitarian movements demanding cultish conformity to their tenets. Both use the language of contronyms to solidify their bases and confuse the opposition. Both are determined to destroy America from within and take control of the country. Both are tools of the globalists who finance them. More on that later.

The pluralism envisioned by our Founding Fathers embraced differing thoughts, ideas, and behaviors within the legal confines and freedoms guaranteed by the Constitution. American pluralism rejected the fractal wrongness of leftist socialism, Islamic supremacism, Chinese communism, and any other competing ideology designed to destroy America from within.

Leftist Newspeak and Islamic *taqiyyah* are attempts to disguise the seditious leftist/Islamist/globalist goal of overthrowing our constitutional republic. President Trump was aware of both deceitful languages and intentionally used his Twitter account to bypass the mainstream media and speak directly to the American people in the clarity of Oldspeak. He was the target of vicious personal attacks for using Twitter, because the frantic leftist mainstream media were unable to control the political narrative. It is the reason why Twitter deplatformed a sitting president of the United States in a staggering display of political censorship.

The Biden/Obama/Harris regime has escalated the combined efforts and attacks of the leftist/Islamist/globalist axis. If the axis partners succeed in collapsing America from within, they will create a power vacuum. Since the axis is an alliance of convenience made up of competing supremacist ideologies, they will eventually battle each other to fill the vacuum.

Slavery has many faces. Whether a secular Orwellian society ruled by the leftist political elite, a religious theocracy ruled by imams and

Islamic supremacist sharia law, a Chinese communist surveillance state, an oligarchical technocracy, or a monarchy ruled by dynastic divine right of kings, surrender to any supremacist ideology ends in the binary socio-political system of rulers and ruled. Whatever its name, New World Order, One World Order, or Great Reset, it is enslavement on a planetary scale.

America rejected the fractal wrongness of supremacist ideologies 246 years ago. We are the United States of America, bound by the ideals and fractal rightness of the American dream. *One nation, indivisible, with liberty and justice for all.*

CHAPTER 19

Dialectical Speech:
The Language of Leftist Deception

P olitical language . . . is designed to make lies sound truthful and murder respectable, and to give an appearance of solidity to pure wind."[93]
(George Orwell, *Politics and the English Language*, 1946)

Dialectical speech is the political language of doublespeak and double meanings. Words matter. Doublespeak is language deliberately constructed to disguise or distort its actual meaning. The words used in doublespeak are ambiguous, often have two different meanings, and are deliberately spoken to confuse the listener. *Taqiyya* and Newspeak are both examples of doublespeak.

The word doublespeak derives from two Orwellian words, "doublethink" and "Newspeak." Doublethink is when a person accepts two mutually contradictory thoughts as correct without being aware of or troubled by the glaring contradiction between them. Doublethink eliminates cognitive dissonance—the anxiety ordinarily generated by conflicting thoughts. "War is peace," "freedom is slavery," and "ignorance is strength" are examples of doublethink.

Newspeak controls thought through language. Doublespeak combines doublethink and Newspeak in language that deliberately obscures, distorts, disguises, or reverses the actual meaning of words. It is semantic deception designed to manipulate public opinion in a mass social engineering campaign. Doublespeak is the language of fake news, and the language of the leftist coup against Western democracies and national sovereignty.

Twenty-first-century leftists use doublespeak to advance their "progressive" narrative. The regressive infantile impulses and temper tantrums exhibited by leftists today cannot seriously be called "progressive" except by double-speaking leftists who believe that going backward is going forward. REGRESSIVE is the accurate word for the infantile behavior and impulses that inform the "progressive" Left. Safe spaces, Play-Doh, counseling for disappointment, and segregated black-only lounges are all regressive demands of an increasingly regressed population.

To understand why regressives use doublespeak, what their goals are, who benefits, and the purpose of relabeling up as down and down as up, it is necessary to translate doublespeak into colloquial English (Oldspeak).

A glossary is helpful to decode the disingenuous doublespeak of leftist regressives that is broadcast incessantly by the colluding mainstream media, taught in propagandized educational curricula, and dramatized by Hollywood glitterati and television programming. If American democracy is to be preserved, it is essential that an informed citizenry understand how they are being indoctrinated toward socialism by a deliberate program of leftist propaganda and doublespeak.

GLOSSARY OF LEFTIST DOUBLESPEAK:

1. Build back better = slogan of Great Reset

Build back better follows Alinsky's social demolition model, discussed in Chapter 15: *All change means disorganization of the old and organization of the new.* The Great Reset requires destruction of the existing economic structure of private property, and rebuilding with a new economic structure in which: "You'll own nothing, and you'll be happy about it."

2. Comprehensive immigration reform = Open borders

"Comprehensive immigration reform" advocates open borders, sanctuary policies, and mainstreaming illegal aliens into American life at taxpayer expense in order to collapse the economy and surrender American sovereignty to the globalist elite.

2. Consensus = Unanimity of thought

In doublespeak, consensus means unequivocally accepting the leftist narrative in science, economics, social policy, and medicine. There is no consideration of dissenting opinions.

3. Diversity = Differences in appearance but not in thought

Diversity means "variety." Leftist diversity includes only appearances; it does not tolerate any variety of opinions. Leftism is tyrannical in its demand for conformity to its politically correct left-wing narrative of moral relativism and historical revisionism.

4. Domestic terrorists = Trump supporters

5. Education = Indoctrination

What was once a traditional American education of core subjects and pride in American democratic ideals has been transformed into an echo chamber of leftist propaganda promoting globalism, socialism, America loathing, political correctness, moral relativism, historical revisionism, and critical race theory.

6. Extremist = Trump supporter

Political opposition has been reclassified as a national security threat under the Biden regime, no longer protected by free-speech guarantees.

7. Freedom of speech = Approved speech

Leftists in America are determined to eliminate freedom of speech by enforcing their own code of political correctness, which labels any opposing speech as hate speech. Speakers with conservative points of view are disinvited, censored, or intimidated through organized boycotts and violent protests.

8. Global warming/climate change = Redistribution of wealth

In 1992 UN scientists on the Intergovernmental Panel on Climate Change (IPCC) stated: "It is extremely likely that human influence has been the dominant cause of the observed warming since the mid-20th century." But as Greenpeace founder Patrick Moore testified before the Senate Environment and Public Works Committee on June 24, 2014:

> Extremely likely is not a scientific term but rather a judgment, as in a court of law. The IPCC defines "extremely likely" as a "95–100% probability." But upon further examination it is clear that these numbers are not the result of any mathematical

calculation or statistical analysis. They have been "invented" as a construct within the IPCC report to express "expert judgment," as determined by the IPCC contributors.

Man-made climate change, among the greatest hoaxes ever perpetrated on industrialized countries, is designed to transfer their wealth to non-industrialized countries. The United Nations is committed to globalization and one-world government, and is supported worldwide by leftists with the same objective.

9. Globalism = One-world government

Leftists are not using the word globalism to mean global trade. When leftists say globalism, they mean one-world government. Their intention is to eliminate national boundaries and impose one-world rule.

10. Great Reset = New World Order = One World Order

In doublespeak, the Great Reset is the rebranded globalist New World Order of planetary governance. The Great Reset is also a reference to United Nations Agenda 21, United Nations Agenda 2030, and the Fourth Industrial Revolution.

11. Greater good = Collectivism

Government-mandated sacrifice by the individual for the group.

12. Human infrastructure

This is a new term coined by the Biden/Obama/Harris regime so that welfare payments and assistance checks can be included in the infrastructure spending bill.

13. Income equality = Redistribution of wealth

Income equality in a democracy is achieved through equal *opportunity*—there is no guarantee of equal *outcome*. When leftists speak of income equality, they mean compulsory income redistribution that guarantees equal outcome.

14. Ingsoc = English socialism (*1984*)

The political philosophy of the ruling class in Orwell's *1984* using Newspeak, doublethink, and constant historical revision to make people think they are voluntarily supporting a system that depends on unthinking obedience.

15. **Irregular migrant** = **Illegal alien**

16. **Literacy** = **Illiteracy**

The goal of "progressive" leftist education is compliant universal human beings prepared for life in the New World Order. Molding requires children who are dumbed down and lacking foundational skills (reading and math) and foundational knowledge.

17. **Progressive** = **Regressive**

The word progressive has a positive connotation and is commonly understood to mean something that happens or develops gradually or in stages. Synonyms for progressive include continuing, continuous, increasing, growing, developing, ongoing, accelerating, escalating, gradual, step-by-step, and cumulative. Progress leads to a society of growth and independence, which entails rational adulthood and maturity.

In doublespeak, progressive is synonymous with regressive—the opposite of progressive. In the upside-down world of doublespeak, steps toward socialism's cradle-to-grave dependence are considered progress.

18. **Resistance** = **Overthrow of the government**

Resistance is the refusal to accept or comply with something. In a democracy there are laws and elections designed for citizens to legally and peacefully express their discontent at the voting booth. When leftists speak of resistance, they are fomenting the overthrow of the government.

19. **Science** = **Scientism**

Scientism is an exaggerated trust in the efficacy of the methods of natural science applied to all areas of investigation (as in philosophy, the social sciences, and the humanities). It has replaced traditional religion as the moral and ethical authority for many members of society.

20. **Social justice** = **Reverse discrimination**

Social justice in a democracy is achieved through laws and constitutional protections that guarantee equal rights, equal opportunity, and equal protection under the law. When leftists speak of social justice, they mean reverse discrimination and a two-tier system of justice. White people are openly and institutionally discriminated against, sanctuary cities protecting illegal alien felons are endorsed, and anarchy and violence are fomented to effect social change.

21. Socialism = Communism

The goal of socialism is communism. Socialism is the soft sell.

22. Sustainable = Supports UN Agenda 2030 goals and one-world government

The goal of the man-made climate change/global warming narrative is the redistribution of wealth from industrialized to non-industrialized nations. It is socialism on a planetary scale.

In doublespeak, sustainable is the code word for anything supportive of the United Nations movement toward planetary governance.

23. Teacher = Change agent

Leftism views education as the vehicle for social change. Teachers are seen as facilitators who promote social change and student acceptance of planetary governance in the New World Order.

24. Tolerance = Intolerance

Leftism tolerates differences in race, religion, gender, ethnicity, and socio-economic status, but not differences of opinion.

25. Undocumented immigrant = Illegal alien

26. "Vaccine" = experimental mRNA Covid-19 treatments

Covid-19 "vaccines" are distinctly different from legitimate vaccines which provide immunity, prevent transmission, and have been rigorously safety tested on animals. Covid-19 jabs are experimental gene-altering mRNA treatments which neither provide immunity nor prevent transmission. Safety tests on animals were halted due to adverse reactions—humans are the test cohort for Covid-19 jabs.

CHAPTER 20

Collectivism: Persuading the Individual to Stop Being an Individual

I f students understood the *reality* of collectivism rather than its promise, their support for it would vanish. The globalist leaders selling collectivism know this to be true, and so they have had to rebrand collectivism as globalism. Magical songs are written about globalism; John Lennon's classic song "Imagine" is the globalist anthem.

The successful marketing of collectivism requires its names to change from previously rejected brands. Communism was promoted in America as socialism. When socialism began to falter as a brand (think Venezuela), it was promoted as hope and change for a New World Order. Its planetary ambition is its name: *globalism.*

Globalists are wielding the same old marketing lie used to sell any form of collectivism—that surrendering individual rights, property rights, and national sovereignty will deliver social justice and income equality.

Russian-American philosopher and writer Ayn Rand understood the sinister nature of collectivism and wrote extensively about socialism/communism and how it persuades the individual to stop being an individual:

> Socialism is the doctrine that man has no right to exist for his own sake, that his life and his work do not belong to him, but belong to society, that the only justification of his existence is his service to society, and that society may dispose of him in any way it pleases for the sake of whatever it deems to be its own tribal, collective good.[94]

Mass social indoctrination toward collectivism leads to cultural suicide and the death of the individual. Ayn Rand continues:

> When you consider socialism, do not fool yourself about its

nature. Remember that there is no such dichotomy as "human rights" versus "property rights." No human rights can exist without property rights. Since material goods are produced by the mind and effort of individual men, and are needed to sustain their lives, if the producer does not own the result of his effort, he does not own his life. To deny property rights means to turn men into property owned by the state. Whoever claims the "right" to "redistribute" the wealth produced by others is claiming the "right" to treat human beings as chattel.[95]

Europe's surrender of its national sovereignty began after World War II with the 1957 Treaty of Rome that created the European Economic Community (EEC), which eventually became the European Union (EU) of today. Internationalizing Europe's sovereign nations into the EU left the United States the single greatest obstacle to globalist planetary governance.

National sovereignty is to a country what individual sovereignty is to a human being. The leftist agenda seeks to destroy the socio-political capitalist infrastructure of America and transform it into a dependent European-style socialist state with cradle-to-grave control by the government.

The globalists' social indoctrination strategy targets the American institutions of family, religion, and education that promote independence, adulthood, individualism, and critical thinking—the qualities that made America great.

Ayn Rand warns us:

> Socialism is not a movement of the people. It is a movement of the intellectuals, originated, led and controlled by the intellectuals, carried by them out of their stuffy ivory towers into those bloody fields of practice where they unite with their allies and executors: the thugs.[96]

Capitalism is foundational to upward mobility, the middle class, ordered liberty, and the extraordinary individual freedoms guaranteed by our Constitution.

Capitalism is driven factually by supply and demand but artificially by the marketing and advertising industries that hawk its products. So, if a particular business or industry is suffering from lack of sales, it can hire a marketing firm to create an artificial demand for its products. Those products may or may not be beneficial to the public.

For decades tobacco was marketed and advertised as elegant, sophisticated, and desirable even though it was a known cancer-causing killer. *Buyer beware* is the operating principle in a market economy.

Billions of dollars are spent annually marketing, lobbying, and advertising products because marketing, lobbying, and advertising are extremely effective. Products are ordinarily considered to be goods and services, but what if the product is ideology?

Alexander Solzhenitsyn's novel *The Gulag Archipelago* (1973) destroyed any Western fantasies about collectivist ideology and life under communism/socialism when individual liberties are surrendered to the state. Socialism needed a new image if it was going to sell. How was the Left going to market collectivism?

In Matthew Continetti's brilliant lecture titled "The Problem of Identity Politics and Its Solution"[97] given on October 24, 2017, at Hillsdale College, he explores the challenge for the Left:

> How to carry on the fight against capitalism when its major ideological alternative was no longer viable? The Left found its answer in an identity politics that grew out of anti-colonialism. Marx's class struggle was reformulated into an ethno-racial struggle—a ceaseless competition between colonizer and colonized, victimizer and victim, oppressor and oppressed. Instead of presenting collectivism and central planning as the gateway to the realization of genuine freedom, the new multiculturalist Left turned to unmasking the supposed power relations that subordinated minorities and exploited third world nations.

The Left had a new marketing, lobbying, and advertising strategy that targeted first American universities and then K–12. American education was chosen as the vulnerable soft target for revolution—no bullets required. The long-term strategy was that two generations of leftist educational indoctrination would transform America from a capitalist constitutional republic into the socialist state required for internationalized one-world government.

The radical leftists on campus in the '60s did not go quietly into the night after Woodstock. They graduated and became the teachers, professors, textbook writers, psychologists, sociologists, politicians, doctors, lawyers, and decision makers in charge of public education, including curriculum content, that reflected their anti-American bias and globalist views. Gradually the individualism and critical-thinking skills that had created the vibrant, independent, upwardly mobile middle class and supported the American dream were deliberately dumbed down to encourage dependence, collectivism, groupthink, and a victim mentality.

In a sweeping effort that eventually transformed public education, collectivism was repackaged, marketed, lobbied, advertised, and sold to an unsuspecting American public. The former pro-American curricula that proudly promoted individualism, the meritocracy, capitalism, and the middle class was replaced. The revised curricula teach American students to be anti-American, self-loathing, dependent, fragile collectivists, unapologetically preaching global citizenship in a New World Order.

Many people take public education for granted and do not realize that public education made the American dream possible. Public education supported American freedom and distinguished America from societies across the globe where centralized governments, including monarchies, caste systems, and despotic regimes of communism and socialism, defined their citizens' futures.

The American dream reflected the possibilities and potentials for upward mobility in America. Legal immigrants who came to America seeking a better life understood that public education was the gateway to success in America. Those immigrants worked, assimilated, and sent their children to school to learn English and have a chance to realize the American dream.

It is essential to remember that the transformation of public education was in service to the political ideology of the Left that embraced collectivism and rejected capitalism. In order to destroy capitalism, the Left took aim at the economy of the existing middle class. This effort reached a crescendo during Obama's eight-year promise to fundamentally transform America. His crushing economic policies

· sent jobs and manufacturing overseas;

- created massive unemployment;

- bloated the welfare rolls;

- created more and more dependence upon the government;

- moved the country further toward collectivism.

Buyer beware is the operating principle in a market economy. Collectivism is being marketed and advertised as elegant, sophisticated, and desirable even though it is a known economy killer and freedom killer. It is Solzhenitsyn's Gulag renamed and marketed as identity politics.

The leftist movement was repackaged, marketed, and advertised as a multicultural religion. A religious zealot cannot be separated from his religious beliefs, which is why the identity politics of the Left are so effective.

The stunning hypocrisy of the Left is completely ignored because the overarching and unifying principle of their shared victim identity is hatred for America.

Forensic psychiatrist Lyle H. Rossiter, Jr., M.D. described the leftist movement to transform America as political madness. From *The Liberal Mind; The Psychological Causes of Political Madness*:[98]

> Any meaningful conception of freedom demands responsibility and assumption of risk by all competent citizens, not a childlike insistence that arbitrary others make one whole. If freedom is in fact disconnected from responsibility, as it is in the liberal agenda, then we have a society of literally care-free persons, each of whom is falsely held to be responsible for everyone else, and none of whom is properly held to be responsible for himself. (pp. 320-321)

> They bear no responsibility for their problems. None of their agonies are attributable to faults or failings of their own: not to poor choices, bad habits, faulty judgment, wishful thinking, lack of ambition, low frustration tolerance, mental illness, or defects in character. None of the victims' plight is caused by failure to plan for the future or learn from experience. (p. 329)

The liberal cure for this endless malaise is a very large authoritarian government that regulates and manages society through a cradle to grave agenda of redistributive caretaking. It is a government everywhere doing everything for everyone. The liberal motto is "In Government We Trust." To rescue us from our troubled lives, the liberal agenda recommends denial of personal responsibility, encourages self-pity and other-pity, fosters government dependency, promotes sexual indulgence, rationalizes violence, excuses financial obligation, justifies theft, ignores rudeness, prescribes complaining and blaming, denigrates marriage and the family, legalizes all abortion, defies religious and social tradition, declares inequality unjust, and rebels against the duties of citizenship. Through multiple entitlements to unearned goods, services and social status, the liberal politician promises to ensure everyone's material welfare, provide for everyone's health care, protect everyone's self-esteem, correct everyone's social and political disadvantage, educate every citizen, and eliminate all class distinctions. (pp. 329-330)

Radical liberalism thus assaults the foundations of civilized freedom. Given its irrational goals, coercive methods and historical failures, and given its perverse effects on character development, there can be no question of the radical agenda's madness. Only an irrational agenda would advocate a systematic destruction of the foundations on which ordered liberty depends. Only an irrational man would want the state to run his life for him rather than create secure conditions in which he can run his own life. Only an irrational agenda would deliberately undermine the citizen's growth to competence by having the state adopt him. Only irrational thinking would trade individual liberty for government coercion, sacrificing the pride of self-reliance for welfare dependency. Only a madman would look at a community of free people cooperating by choice and see a society of victims exploited by villains. (p. 374)

German philosopher Josef Pieper described the methodology for the descent into political madness in his 1992 book, *Abuse of Language— Abuse of Power*.[99] Pieper applies Plato's disdain for sophists to the late 20th century.

Sophists were teachers in ancient Greece who excelled in the use of fallacious arguments, especially with the intention of deceiving. Sophistry, like Orwellian doublespeak and the Hegelian dialectic, rely on the perversion of language and pseudorealities to succeed. Pieper writes:

> Plato's literary activity extended over fifty years, and time and again he asked himself anew: What makes the sophists so dangerous? Toward the end he [Plato] wrote one more dialogue, the *Sophist*, in which he adds a new element to his answer. "The sophists", he says, "fabricate a fictitious reality."
>
> That the existential realm of man could be taken over by pseudorealities whose fictitious nature threatens to become indiscernible is truly a depressing thought. And yet this Platonic nightmare, I hold, possesses an alarming contemporary relevance. For the general public is being reduced to a state where people not only are unable to find out about the truth but also become unable to even search for the truth because they are satisfied with the deception and trickery that have determined their convictions, satisfied with a fictitious reality created by design through the abuse of language. This, says Plato, is the worst thing that sophists are capable of wreaking upon mankind by their corruption of the word. (pp. 34–35)

Words matter. The leftist/globalist narrative using Orwellian doublespeak, the Hegelian dialectic, and sophistry is driving society into the madness of pseudoreality where the individual willingly stops being an individual and surrenders his selfness to the collectivist state.

CHAPTER 21

American Family or Marxist Village?

Amerca is a divided nation and supports two distinct narratives, with two distinct outcomes. One is the narrative of survivors and the other the narrative of victims. The narrative of survivors supports adult self-sufficiency, objective reality, and the independent American family. The narrative of victims supports childish irresponsibility, subjective reality, and dependence on the government in an authoritarian Marxist village.

The survivor mentality created America and is defined by its core values of personal autonomy and freedom. It is supported by institutions promoting personal growth, independence, individual sovereignty, and the common denominator of American nationalism. The survivor narrative is the narrative of American nationalism and the individualism that supports it.

Individualism acknowledges the critical biological reality that each human being is a separate and distinct entity from the moment of birth until death. Dr. Lyle Rossiter explains the psychodynamics of separateness and its political consequences:

> The fact that I am separate from everything else imposes fundamental limitations on any ideas that I might entertain about being merged with, continuous with, fused with, or in any other way combined with other persons or things in some collectivist conception of the world. The biological basis for autonomy lies in a simple reality: the body and self of each person remain forever discontinuous from the bodies and selves of all other persons and from the substance of all other things. This reality remains true regardless of how strongly we may yearn for magical fusion with others, and how determined we may be to achieve that fusion through religious, mystical, sexual or political rituals. Denial of these limitations, either for political purposes or for

psychological defensive purposes, has been the cause of much wishful thinking and profound political mischief among liberal intellectuals of the last two centuries. More specifically, in its denial of the separateness, agency, autonomy and sovereignty of the individual, the liberal agenda can also deny that the individual, and only the individual, must be regarded as the ultimate economic, social and political unit, not some arbitrary group or collective. The importance of this cannot be overstated. It is only by means of such denial that the liberties and lives of millions of individuals have been sacrificed on collectivist altars.

It is precisely the sovereignty of the individual that is scorned by the liberal's creed of collectivism. In denying the physical, biological and psychological nature of human beings, the liberal mind denies the basis of human freedom. (*The Liberal Mind*, pp. 135-136)

The regressive victim mentality was designed to deconstruct America and is defined by its core values of dependence, denial of the separateness of the individual, and escape from freedom's personal responsibilities. Intersectionality, the politicized version of the victim identity, is supported by institutions promoting regression, dependence, internationalism, and globalism. The victim mentality is the narrative of leftism—America's newest religion. Nationalists and globalists have irreconcilable differences because their fundamental premises are diametrically opposed to one another. Americans must choose between them.

Leftism, like any orthodoxy, is tyrannical in its demand for conformity. Its adherents pursue leftism's tenets of political correctness, moral relativism, historical revisionism, and intersectionality with religious zeal and self-righteous fanaticism.

Leftism's intolerance explains its inability to debate or discuss opposing ideas; it demands censorship and childish safe spaces instead. Leftism's intolerance explains its inability to withstand rational adult scrutiny; it provides the echo chamber of fake news instead. Leftism's intolerance explains its inability to have civilized discourse or follow the rule of law; it foments anarchy instead.

Intersectionality, leftism's collective victimhood, is a political designation. It is a descriptor for self-defined group victimhood based on childish feelings, not adult facts. If you feel life is not fair, you are a victim. If you feel you have been marginalized in any way, you are a victim. If you feel your maleness or femaleness is threatened in any way, you are a victim. If someone says something you don't like, you are a victim. It is a child's view of the world that denies adult responsibility.

Victimhood by definition lacks power. Identifying oneself as a powerless entity is a self-sabotaging, catastrophic strategy that leads only to more powerlessness. Childish whining about victimhood perpetuates the status of childish powerlessness.

Self-actualization and a survivor attitude are the strategies for growth and empowerment. Achievement is the mother of self-esteem, actual achievement in objective reality, not the fiction of "trying is the same as achieving" that is promoted in the subjective reality of intersectionality.

The escape from victimhood and powerlessness comes from individual growth, achievement, and adult responsibility. Lowering standards is not equivalent to achievement—it is just lowering standards.

Intersectionality demands are the demands of children that the environment change to meet their needs. It is the wrong answer to the right problem. Achievement is what propels a child toward adulthood. Consider the child who first feeds himself with his fingers and feels empowered. Then he wants to feed himself with a fork. Then he wants to drink from a cup. Achievement encourages success as surely as enabling dependence encourages failure.

Intersectionality says "I feel victimized because my sister can feed herself with her fingers and I cannot." "Don't feel bad," says the enabling mother. "I will always feed you."

Intersectionality says "I feel victimized because my sister can feed herself with a fork and I cannot." "Don't feel bad," says the enabling mother. "I will always feed you with a fork."

Intersectionality says "I feel victimized because my sister can drink from a cup and I cannot." "Don't feel bad," says the enabling mother. "I will always hold your cup for you."

The enabling mother is co-dependent and destructive. She presents herself as the child's advocate. In reality, she is keeping the child dependent upon her for her own selfish needs. She is a destroyer. So it is with governments. Governments that incentivize their citizens to remain dependent do so for their own benefit—the votes that will keep them in power. The victimhood and dependence that intersectionality incentivizes is extremely destructive. Just as the enabling mother cripples her child, so does the enabling government cripple its citizens.

Intersectionality and the culture of victimhood is the disabling strategy of dependence, collectivism, and death because when Mama dies there is no one there to feed the baby. A society of children will necessarily extinguish itself.

Social policy based on the self-defined group victimhood of intersectionality cannot succeed in the real world because the cycle of life requires achievement. Eventually the child must grow up. The noisy cry-bullies on campuses who graduate with useless degrees in fields of "feelings," not facts, will find themselves unemployable. What can they do? They have learned nothing useful for work in the real world and their attitudes make them unemployable. Universities may tolerate student tantrums while their mommies and daddies or the government pay their tuition, but employers are not going to pay for the privilege of childish outbursts from unqualified employees.

Restraint, discipline, and self-control are hallmarks of adulthood. Effort and achievement are not synonyms in the workplace. If colleges and universities are supposed to be preparing young people for life as adults, they have failed their mission—unless of course their 21st-century mission under leftism is to deliberately graduate unproductive, dependent, angry individuals.

Governments that incentivize the growth and independence of their citizens are builders. They incentivize jobs, self-respect, and the self-esteem that gainful employment provides. Former president Donald Trump was a builder. His America-first narrative continues to be that of the survivor, and his message is to be an empowered, independent, patriotic adult. Ex-president Obama was a destroyer. His America-last "resistance" narrative continues to be that of a victim, and his message is to be a powerless, dependent, Marxist child.

It takes an American family to raise a patriot. It takes a village to raise a

Marxist. The question Americans must answer is this: "Do I want to live as an empowered adult in a constitutional republic, or a dependent, powerless child in a socialist state?"

CHAPTER 22

Leftism's Assault on Parenthood Is an Assault on Adulthood

Mammals have a cycle of life with a beginning, a middle, and an end. The survival of the species requires that adult members of the group help newborns survive and develop into reproducing adults, who then help their own newborns develop into reproducing adults so that the cycle of life continues. The growth process from the smallest to the largest mammals demands food, water, shelter, and a transfer of information from the knowledgeable adult to the uninformed young. The adults in each community teach their young how to survive. What happens when that process is impeded?

The United States of America and its social order were founded upon principles of adulthood. The powers entrusted to adult family members gradually transferred to their children as the children became mature adults, preparing to have families of their own. Parents taught children survival skills and imbued them with their family's personal, moral, and religious values. The nuclear family identity and national family identity were assured. What happened?

There has been a gradual shift in the established social order of America. Institutional *experts* pressure society toward regression, dependence, and mediocrity rather than growth, independence, and individual achievement. This inversion has eroded parental authority and tilted young people away from independence and adulthood toward collectivism and mediocrity, both personally and professionally. The social order of adulthood is under attack.

Let's begin at the beginning. Traditionally, new mothers turn toward their own mothers for guidance—grandmothers have standing in the transfer of knowledge about raising children. Grandma's successes as well as her failures are a rich source of information for new moms. Not anymore.

Authors Ari Brown, M.D. and Denise Fields have written an overbearing and incredibly dismissive book titled *Baby 411: Clear Answers & Smart Advice for Your Baby's First Year*. On the acknowledgements page of the 2014 edition, the authors arrogantly state, "It's sad but true: any parenting book written before 2013 is already outdated." REALLY?

An equally pompous promotion on Dr. Brown's website <u>411 Pediatrics</u>[100] states, "We give you the 4-1-1. Ours is the ONLY parenting book series in the market that updates with new editions every two to three years, giving our readers the most current, scientific-evidence based advice." Ahhh—the exalted *scientific* advice of scientism!

Twenty-first-century parents are persuaded by anything claiming to be *scientific*. It is the foundation of their world. They willingly surrender their common sense and critical thinking skills to the *experts* who gladly tell them how to do anything and everything *scientifically*. A generation of American parents have surrendered their adult authority, common sense, and independence to the self-proclaimed experts who offer them self-assured advice and online communities for support.

Today's parents ruminate and obsess over whether they are doing the right thing and whether they are being good parents. Most of all they worry about whether their children are happy. They see happiness as the objective, not the consequence of a successful childhood. The goal of childhood is adult competence. Parents who confuse these issues and see *happiness* as the objective of childhood, have embraced a crippling perspective that interferes with achieving adult competence and the happiness that self-sufficiency brings.

Rather than having confidence in their own parenting instincts and the generational advice of trusted family, today's parents trust the routinely corrupt *scientific-evidence based* advice of designated *experts*.

Most parents are completely unaware of the ideological agenda of the *experts* in charge of the education and medical establishments in America. Their children are being indoctrinated away from independence and traditional Judeo-Christian values toward collectivism and global citizenship, and the parents are oblivious.

In a disturbing *Renew America* article, "<u>Memo to K–12 students: Resist</u>,"[101] educational reformer Bruce Deitrick Price exposes the psychological warfare being waged against K–12 students to prepare them for global citizenship in a restructured world of planetary governance:

> You are a participant in a vast psychological war. Believe it or
> not, you are the enemy in this war. *You* are the primary target.
> Yes, they want you, your unformed personality, your uninformed
> mind. They want to shape you and make you so that finally
> you're indistinguishable from other kids. You're not supposed
> to know much or think much. In <u>*Brave New World*</u>[102] you would
> be a Gamma or maybe a Delta. According to Wikipedia, "these
> people are deliberately limited in their cognitive and physical
> abilities, as well as the scope of their ambitions and the com-
> plexity of their desires, thus rendering them easier to control."

Limited cognitive abilities have been the undisputed consequence of
decades of debilitating educational systems that subvert learning basic
skills—reading, writing, and arithmetic—and impede acquiring foundational knowledge.

Parents today are extremely stressed. They lack confidence in their own
competence and ability to problem solve and are constantly in search of
experts who will soothe their fragile selves and absolve them of personal
responsibility. It's easier to believe the experts than trust themselves.
Why are these parents so fragile and uncertain?

Adulthood requires assuming personal responsibility for one's decisions
and taking responsibility for the consequences of those decisions. Today's parents are so other directed, they cannot achieve the self-confidence enjoyed by their parents and grandparents. Their search for vali-
dation by the *experts* deprives them of the empowerment that assuming
responsibility for their own choices provides.

When an individual surrenders his/her adult authority and independence, that individual is resuming the position of childhood instead of
assuming the position of adulthood. It takes an adult to raise a child to
maturity. The assault on family deprives parents of their authority and
transfers that authority to the politicized *experts* advancing their rival,
other-directed, collectivist agenda. Competence is the mother of self-esteem. In an other-directed society, consensus is substituted for competence. This means that groupthink, not meritocracy, determines the
value of an individual.

Consensus may sound like compassionate consideration, but in doublespeak consensus means political agreement and does not require a foundation in objective reality. It is simply a matter of people agreeing on something. So, if the political consensus is that children are better served in government daycare centers than at home with their mothers, the government moves to impose policies based on that consensus, not on behavioral science or established law.

Every incremental step that reduces individual personal authority awards the government more authority and control over the individual. The government's politicized institutions are advancing a globalist agenda that relies on scientism's consensus to give it power and authority.

Scientism is an exaggerated trust in the efficacy of the methods of natural science applied to all areas of investigation, including philosophy, the social sciences, and the humanities. Science, like every other force in nature, can be used for either construction or destruction. Scientism is the political perversion of honest science, used as a tool for social engineering.

Scientism ignores the *facts* of science and demands faith in the gurus of politicized science. *Trust the science* is leftism's mantra demanding adherence to this new religion.

Scientism is foundational to the politicized parenting advice in *Baby 411*, politicized dumbing down of America in schools, the insistence on sight words, new math, and politicized curriculum content. Scientism replaces honest scientific inquiry with politicized pseudo-science for mass social engineering.

CHAPTER 23

The Reeducation of America

Kurt Lewin's model of change (described in Chapter 8) requires the reeducation of America. It is revolution without bullets—an information war that derives its authority from scientism. The tactical strategy establishes a closed informational system to melt traditional cultural norms, replace them with leftist collectivism, and then refreeze society into socialism.

Leftist educational curricula in schools and anti-establishment messaging via television programming and all streaming devices deliver the dogmatic ideology of the leftist revolution. The Cultural Revolution is purging capitalism and traditional culture from American society.

The reeducation programming begins long before college. Preschool educational programs with fanciful characters and talking animals are not benign. Sesame Street creatures are not advocating individual growth, independence, critical thinking skills, excellence, and the merit system which support capitalism and democracy. They are advocating groupthink, dependence, passivity, mediocrity, and collectivism, preparing your children for living under socialism.

Students already indoctrinated toward collectivism enter the university passive, unaware, compliant, and primed for reeducation. The socialist reeducation curriculum at the university reinforces their passivity, and students graduate uninformed, disinformed, and misinformed, with degrees in the orthodoxy of leftism and its tyrannical demands for conformity.

The graduates are now credentialed *authorities* and *experts* who become zealous members of the leftist echo chamber that dominates the media and reinforces collectivism. The sons and daughters of conservative parents are now the political pundits, teachers, professors, administrators, policy advisors, doctors, nurses, psychologists, psychiatrists, engineers, politicians, bankers, lawyers, corporatists, athletes, writers, actors—every conceivable field of interest, all singing the same leftist tune.

Their narrative of political correctness, moral relativism, and historical revisionism is reflected in the programming and commercials being streamed into your household and mobile devices twenty-four hours a day. Media programming and advertising are in the business of social engineering. As they purge capitalism and traditional culture, they sell socialism and want you to buy their ideology.

The sales strategy pits subjective reality against objective reality, and children against their parents.

Leftist reeducation programming presents subjective reality in televised commercials. In the real world of objective reality most families are not intermarried and every play group, luncheon, dinner table, and family picnic does not include one Asian, one white person, one black person, and one Hispanic. In the real world most couples are not homosexual, white men and women are not all idiots, and black men and women are not all judges, doctors, and lawyers. Why do television programming and commercials portray contrived fabricated scenes and plots of subjective reality instead of factual scenes and plots of objective reality to sell their products? Because they are not selling products, they are reeducation America.

They are reeducating Americans on television just as the schools are reeducating Americans in the classroom. The unreal subjective reality of the programming is intentionally confusing and creates cognitive dissonance. Cognitive dissonance is the destabilizing state of having inconsistent thoughts, beliefs, or attitudes, especially relating to behavioral decisions and attitude changes.

Cognitive dissonance creates extreme stress because people seek psychological stability and consistency. The contradictory images being televised do not comport with objective reality, so they threaten and destabilize the viewer's sense of what is real. Cognitive dissonance is the psychological equivalent of physical pain, and people will do anything to stop it.

When parents point out the obvious inconsistencies in news/entertainment media commercials and programming, they are accused of being racist, sexist, homophobic, etc. The family conflict is between parents trying to pull their children back into the world of objective reality and children insisting that their parents live in subjective reality.

Democracy lives in the adult world of objective reality and facts. It embraces diversity that includes differences of opinion, protects freedom of speech, and insists upon individual personal responsibility. Socialism lives in the childish world of make-believe, subjective reality, diversity that rejects differences of opinion, restricts freedom of speech, and denies personal responsibility. The Left seeks to destroy objective reality and create social chaos. Why?

Social chaos is the prerequisite for seismic social change, and the leftists seek to destroy American democracy and replace it with socialism. This is how it works.

The medium is the message. In 1964 Marshall McLuhan explained that the medium is separate from the message and has a separate social effect upon the recipient. Television is the greatest vehicle for social engineering and mass psychological indoctrination ever invented. The images on the screen become familiar, and familiarity brings acceptance. The separate social effect of television and all screening devices is that the images are accepted as reality.

For children, talking animals and cartoon characters acquire authority. For older kids, adolescents, and adults the characters in the plots become reality and their fictitious lives, no matter how anti-establishment, become normative and acceptable. The breakdown of rules, restrictions, and cultural norms appears progressive to an adolescent, but is, in fact, extremely regressive to an adult.

The anti-establishment strategy is to present television commercials and programming that attack established cultural norms of American family, faith, and freedom with destabilizing images and messages creating cognitive dissonance. By destroying the three pillars of society, the Left hopes to advance its agenda of socialism.

Leftism advertises socialism as the structure that will provide social justice, income equality, and escape from cognitive dissonance. Socialism is presented as the stabilizing equalizing answer to your problems. Anyone who watches television commercials knows that there is little truth in advertising. Wiping a rag across the shower door does not remove the soap scum.

The truth about leftist diversity is that it excludes anyone who thinks differently. There are no conservatives invited to the luncheon or sitting at the picnic table. There is no diversity of thought. American democracy was founded on principles of equality, freedom of speech (thought), and individual rights.

Socialism is collectivism and values the group over the individual. There is no social justice or income equality in socialism. Winston Churchill observed, "Socialism is like a dream. Sooner or later you wake up to reality."

The Castro brothers lived in splendor while the Cuban people lived and continue to live in poverty. The self-righteous reeducated students are too arrogant, regressed, and indoctrinated to understand that socialism is the stepping-stone toward globalized one-world government. One-world government is the goal and underlying motive of the globalist elite who are financing the Cultural Revolution in America and fomenting the anti-establishment reeducation campaign.

Socialism, with its complete government control, is the prerequisite social structure for the globalist elite to internationalize sovereign countries, globalize the police force, and impose one-world government upon the world population.

One-world government is a binary socio-political system of masters and slaves. There is no social justice in one-world government, no income equality, no leftists, environmentalists, diversity, contrived television commercials, or political agitators of any kind in one-world government—only a passive, compliant population of slaves ruled by their globalist-elite masters.

Reeducation is the strategy that replaces objective reality with subjective reality in order to sell socialism to America. Reeducation is the medium and the message of the Cultural Revolution, and the globalist vehicle for imposing feudal planetary governance.

Parents who surrender to the subjective reality of their adult children are also surrendering America to globalist planetary governance.

CHAPTER 24

A Cautionary Tale: And Not a Shot Is Fired

A blueprint for planetary governance was discovered by the British in 1961. It is the manifesto written by Jan Kozak, a member of the Czechoslovak Communist Party Central Committee. He wrote an internal strategy paper detailing the overthrow of the Czech government, titled "How Parliament Can Play a Revolutionary Part in the Transition to Socialism and the Role of the Popular Masses." Two chapters of the manifesto were published as *And Not a Shot Is Fired*[103] and distributed worldwide.

These two chapters are a playbook for the globalist elite to fundamentally transform America into socialism using Marxist ideologues to prepare the public for global planetary governance.

The American edition, distributed by Long House publishers, includes an introduction by John Howland Snow, who describes Kozak's manifesto as "a blueprint for how a representative government can be made authoritarian, legally, piece by piece. The form remains an empty shell . . . and not a shot is fired."

Excerpts from the Robert Welch University Press, 1999 introduction by Thomas R. Eddlem explain the value of the Kozak document for contemporary America. It is a shocking cautionary tale:

> ONE MIGHT ask today, years after the fall of the Berlin Wall: "Why would anyone want to read a report by a communist about the revolutionary takeover of Czechoslovakia—a country that no longer exists? . . .

> Most Americans are falsely conditioned to believe today that elective governments are permanently established and practically invincible to destruction, so long as elections are free from fraud and consumers can buy Big Mac hamburgers in the market. *And Not a Shot Is Fired* authoritatively disproves that

myth. This document is a "how-to" manual for totalitarian take-over of an elected parliamentary system of government through mainly legal and constitutional means. . . . Kozak's manual is especially important for contemporary Americans because most of the same methods described in this book are at work in the United States today, although those methods are not being fol-lowed directly under communist ideological auspices. . . .

Most of what Kozak describes had been theorized a generation earlier by Italian Communist Party chief Antonio Gramsci. But only Kozak has demonstrated how such a takeover actually was accomplished. *And Not a Shot Is Fired* has enduring value for several reasons, not the least of which is that the brief treatise is sufficiently straightforward—and comparatively free of com-munistic dialectical jargon—that it can be profitably read by the casual reader. . . .

Ideology as a Tactic, Not a Belief

The one, overriding goal stressed by Kozak was the objective of seizing total power. There is no concern for the lot of the poor, or the conditions of the laborer, or even the wealth of the industri-alist evident in this manuscript; power is the one and only goal:

The overall character of the participation in this government was: not to lose sight, even for a moment, the carrying out of a complete socialist coup. (p.12) By using these methods, this principle was fulfilled in practice: not to lose sight for a single moment of the aim of a complete socialist overthrow (p.18). . . .

To power-hungry conspirators like Kozak, Communist ideology was mainly a useful cover for the organizational undertaking of a coup d'état—a tactic, not a belief system. . . .

Co-opting Ideological Language

The Communists adapted the language of socialist ideology and the political policies of socialist regimes for their own internal use on several fronts. Many socialist terms were given double meanings—sometimes called "dialectics"—among Communist revolutionaries for furtherance of their coup. . . .

The use of dialectic meaning in words was and remains a necessary part of any plan to overthrow free governments. Outright announcement of the goals and motivations of revolutionaries would arouse too much alarm among the people and create too much resistance, resulting in the defeat of the conspirators. . . .

Tactical "Ideology" for Would-Be Dictators: Socialism

To a Communist conspirator like Kozak, socialist ideology offered advantages beyond mere discreet communication with fellow revolutionaries. Revolutionaries frequently promote socialism because a socialist economy—even socialism under a parliamentary system of government—heavily concentrates power in the hands of the few people who run the state. Concentration of power in the hands of a few government leaders makes the state easier to seize by a determined conspiracy. To conspirators, socialism serves as a control-the-wealth program, not a share-the-wealth program. Thus, none should be surprised that Hitler and Mussolini took over freely-elected parliaments in their countries—legally and constitutionally, as Kozak and his co-conspirators later accomplished—only after posing as socialist ideologues of one form or another.

Some may contest the assertion that Hitler and Mussolini arose out of socialism because of popular notions that these dictators stem from the "right" wing of the ideological spectrum. Such illusions have no basis in fact. The very name "Nazi" was almost never used by the Nazis themselves; it was merely an acronym for Hitler's "National Socialist Party." . . .

Pressure from Above, Pressure from Below

Kozak outlined the main thesis of a giant pincer's strategy for transforming a parliamentary system of government into a totalitarian dictatorship—the strategy of combining "pressure from above" with "pressure from below" to effect revolutionary change. . . .

The theory for using "pressure from above" and "pressure from below" in order to acquire power, explained in this manual by Kozak, first emerged in the writings of an obscure Italian communist thinker named Antonio Gramsci. Gramsci had plenty of time for contemplating the reasons why his Communist Party had lost Italy to Benito Mussolini, since he spent the last years of his life in Mussolini's jails. Gramsci concluded that in order to capture the power in a state, one must first capture the culture. By culture, Gramsci meant the powerful non-governmental institutions of great influence throughout the nation, specifically: churches, unions, mass media, political parties, universities and educational centers, business organizations, foundations, etc. . . .

In the West, Gramsci explained, family loyalties, faith in God, and lawful limits on governmental power were thoroughly represented in the cultural institutions. Gramsci wrote that "there can and must be a 'political hegemony' even before assuming government power, and in order to exercise political leadership or hegemony one must not count solely on the power and material force that is given by government. . . ."[i] [footnotes listed at end of chapter]

Belief in God, family, and limited government in the developed nations of the West constitutes a cultural system of "fortresses and earthworks" against revolution, according to Gramsci. A coup d'état, without having first subverted these "fortresses and earthworks" through the acquisition of political/cultural hegemony, would only be temporary and result in a quick and successful counter revolution. The revolutionaries of today are well aware that their struggle for control of the culture cannot be won overnight. Gramsci follower and Frankfurt School of socialism apostle Rudi Dutschke explained the Gramscian struggle as a "long march through the institutions"[ii] [footnotes listed at end of chapter] to win Gramsci's "war of position" over any cultural institutions which would stand in the way of a coup d'état by a conspiratorial faction. . . .

The U.S. Constitution—a formidable "earthwork"

The U.S. Constitution—by way of contrast with parliamentary socialism/fascism—offers a formidable series of barriers to would-be dictators, with its separation of powers, system of checks and balances, reserved rights, delegated powers, and free enterprise-based economy. James Madison explained in The Federalist, #47, that the division of powers in the U.S. Constitution was devised with the following guiding principle of politics constantly in mind: "The accumulation of all powers, legislative, executive, and judiciary, in the same hands, whether of one, a few, or many, and whether hereditary, self-appointed, or elective, may justly be pronounced the very definition of tyranny. . . ."

What Can Be Done?

To a large extent, many of our cultural and governmental institutions have already been captured by forces in favor of the centralization of government power and, opposed to limited government and the traditional morality of the churches. Few Americans are even aware that an invasion of our institutions has been ongoing—or that the invaders have won several engagements. Author and political commentator John T. Flynn has already been proven partly right in his 1941 warning that "We will not recognize [American totalitarianism] as it rises. It will wear no black shirts here. It will probably have no marching songs. It will rise out of a congealing of a group of elements that exist here and that are the essential components of Fascism. . . . It will be at first decorous, humane, glowing with homely American sentiment."[iii] [footnotes listed at end of chapter]

Footnotes from the introduction to *And Not a Shot Is Fired*:

[i] Antonio Gramsci, Prison Notebooks, Volume I (New York: Columbia University Press, 1992), p.137.

[ii] Richard Grenier, Capturing the Culture (Washington, DC: Ethics and Public Policy Center, 1991), p. xlv.

[iii] John T. Flynn, "Coming: A Totalitarian America" (originally appearing in the February 1941 American Mercury), in Forgotten Lessons (Irvington-on-Hudson, NY: Foundation for Economic Education, 1996), pp. 142–143.

Published by Robert Welch University Press P.O. Box 8050
Appleton, Wisconsin 54913

Printed in the United States of America
Library of Congress Catalog Card Number: 99-071272 ISBN: 1-892647-01-X

CHAPTER 25

The Merit of the Meritocracy

deology is a tactic, not a belief is the essential lesson in Jan Kozak's strategy manifesto. Socialism is the tactic being used to collapse America from within. Its march through American institutions is based on Gramsci's theory of cultural hegemony.

Gramsci's theory posits that the state and ruling class (the bourgeoisie in Italy) use cultural institutions to maintain power in capitalist societies. Hegemony is just another word for dominance. The ruling class uses ideology rather than military force to achieve compliance with its cultural norms. The idea is that lessons of accepted normative behavior are repeated and reinforced at home, at school, and at worship. The cultural norms become codified into laws that further enforce the cultural norms, and thus cultural hegemony, rather than force, is used to maintain power.

Leftists simply substituted *white* for *bourgeoisie* and posited that the white ruling class uses cultural institutions to maintain their power in capitalist America. They replaced the economics of Marxist critical theory with race and created critical race theory (CRT) to insist that America is systemically racist. CRT identifies the white population as oppressor and the black population as oppressed. Victim and victimizer are identified solely by race.

It is essential to remember that ideology is a tactic, not a belief. The false narrative of critical race theory views every facet of life through a manipulative racial lens. Reverse racism is the ideology being used to divide, conquer, and fundamentally transform America into socialism.

Gramsci theorized that pressure from above (political) and pressure from below (public) could change cultural norms and have them codified into new laws. It is Gramsci's step-by-step march through American institutions that unfreezes, changes, and refreezes America into socialism as the "new normal." This is how it works.

Politicized educational indoctrination from above is used to dismantle established American norms. Reeducation with critical race theory replaces the norm of equal opportunity and the meritocracy responsible for American greatness with socialism's promise of *equity*—equal *outcome.*

In a stunning display of reverse discrimination, Columbia University's Teachers College organized a conference called "The Reimagining Education Summer Institute,"[104] exploring the "problem of whiteness" and how to combat whiteness. The description of the July 2017 conference states:

> We will challenge Eurocentric pedagogical approaches that not only under-prepare students for the realities of our increasingly multiethnic, multilingual, globalized society, but are also rooted in colonial and racist ideologies that stifle the voices, identities, and realities of students of color.

Three hundred participants, mostly K–12 teachers and principals, were "reeducated" to frame being white as the primary social problem to be addressed in elementary schools. Workshops and presentations titled "Whiteness in Schools," "Three Ways to Face White Privilege in the Classroom," and "Teaching for Social Justice" are representative of the blatant prejudice and reverse discrimination intrinsic in the conference designed to "reimagine education."

Similarly, at a diversity conference for employees at Jesuit colleges Dr. Kris Sealey, associate professor of philosophy at predominantly white Fairfield University, spoke about race in the university classroom and urged students to devote time to solving the "problem that is whiteness." Sealey has taught race-based courses such as "Black Lives Matter" and "Critical Race Theory."

> So more and more, the courses that I teach on race have become courses in which I expect my students to engage in [resist] the hegemonic power of whiteness. . . . To be white in the U.S. is to be a perpetrator of the power apparatus unless one actively and consistently resists.

The assumption in critical race theory is that everything is a matter of race. But not all issues are racial. It is the same fundamental flaw in Hegel's dialectic that assumes all ideas are the same—but not all things are ideas.

Critical race theory uses Hegel's dialectic to *prove* that any disparity between black Americans and white Americans is a matter of race. Remember, the Hegelian dialectic is the process used to guide our thoughts and actions into conflicts that lead us to a predetermined *solution.*

Dr. Sealey and the presenters at Teachers College criticize cultural hegemony as the evil method used for maintaining white power. The hypocritical solution they offer is to reformat American cultural institutions with reverse discrimination to establish cultural hegemony and establish black power. Reverse discrimination is still discrimination and cannot remedy the problem of discrimination; it can only exacerbate it.

If the white population surrenders to the black supremacist narrative of Marxist Black Lives Matter (BLM), critical race theory will be codified into law and our constitutional republic will be transformed into Marxist socialism, the predetermined solution Gramsci promised.

If the white population refuses to submit to black supremacy without a fight, there will be a race war. The social chaos of a race war will not end well for America. The police force will be nationalized, the federal government will declare martial law, and all individual freedoms will be suspended. Centralized government is the requirement of socialist control.

But a third alternative exists.

America's judicial system was created with the dream of blind justice. This meant that the judicial system would focus exclusively on the WHAT of behavior and ignore the WHO. To realize the dream of fairness requires a commitment to the ideal of the meritocracy, not a campaign to institutionalize reverse racism. Racism and reverse racism are the opposite of fairness because they focus on the WHO of behavior not on the WHAT of behavior.

Consider the blind auditions for orchestras. They are the fairest system and yield the most talented artists for positions in the orchestra. Musicians sitting behind a screen play for judges. There is only the music—it does not matter if the musician is white, black, Hispanic, Asian, old, young, Jewish, Christian, or Muslim. Only the music matters. The competence and achievement of the musician are what matters, not the color of his or her skin.

The meritocracy is the structure of fairness that supports the American dream of upward mobility and a robust middle class. The meritocracy focuses exclusively on the WHAT of behavior and ignores the WHO.

Fairness is a stabilizing principle. People will stand in line quietly and peacefully for hours until someone cuts in line. The unfairness of someone cutting in line provokes anger that can quickly escalate into violence. Fairness is the organizing principle we need to recommit ourselves to. Racism is entirely unfair regardless of the color of victim or victimizer.

So, why is there a movement to completely dismantle the meritocracy rather than a commitment to abide by it to make America truly egalitarian? Why are elementary schools, universities, and race hustlers attempting to destroy the meritocracy of our educational system and replace it with an institutionalized curriculum that indoctrinates American youth toward reverse racism in schools?

The answer can be found in Dr. Shelby Steele's extraordinary book *White Guilt*.[105] Steele explores the emotional power of white guilt being exploited by black political race hustlers in the United States hoping to transform America into socialism. Steel argues that the primary focus of the civil rights movement was the legitimate undertaking to remove racial barriers and achieve equality through equal opportunity. Without racial barriers the black community would become equal and active participants in the American meritocracy, and Martin Luther King Jr.'s dreams for racial equality would come true. America would finally be color blind and function like blind auditions for orchestras.

That was not to be the case. Instead, the counterculture movement of the '60s merged with the civil rights movement and instead of empowering the black community through the avenues of personal responsibility and the meritocracy, the black power movement embraced an angry narrative of blame, insuring perpetual victimhood for the black community. Rather than creating a climate of equality among races based on equal rights, equal opportunity, and equal protections under the law, white guilt was exploited to reverse racial discrimination and blame white privilege for the black community's condition and create an industry for race hustlers.

Steele affirms that being a victim is a position of powerlessness. The net effect of the intersectionality of race hustlers, the black power movement, and the counterculture selling permanent victim status has been fifty more years of hardship for the black community and increasing dependence on the government.

The breakdown of the black family is arguably the most devastating consequence of the social programs launched by President Johnson's 1964–1965 Great Society initiative. In 1965, the out-of-wedlock birth rate in the black community was 21 percent. By 2017 the rate was 77%. Economist and social theorist Thomas Sowell reflects on the carnage:

> The black family, which had survived centuries of slavery and discrimination, began rapidly disintegrating in the liberal welfare state that subsidized unwed pregnancy and changed welfare from an emergency rescue to a way of life.

Steele agrees and identifies the breakdown of marriage and the family as the biggest barrier to success for black communities. In a June 9, 2020 interview with Fox News reporter, Martha MacCallum, he states unequivocally that racism in America is over:

> It breaks my heart to see young people, Black Lives Matter, angry and still going over this victimization as though that is the truth of who we are as a people. . . .

> Our central problem is the breakdown of the family. Seventy-five percent of all black children are born out of wedlock. They don't have a father. There are very few men around in the community. When I was growing up, men were everywhere. Everybody had a dad. A good one or a bad one, but they had one. They perform a great service, they're irreplaceable. There is no social program, government intervention that is going to take the place of that. We, as black people, need to put more focus and use our imagination to reinforce the institution of marriage and family.

Dr. Steele argues that the black community has exchanged their freedom for free stuff—a very bad trade. A commitment to the meritocracy is the pathway for survival and upward mobility. Competence

elevates the black community. A color-blind education fostering competence, skills, and achievement is necessary for success, not indoctrination in blame, permanent victimhood, and powerlessness.

Critical race theory is being used to deny the merit of the meritocracy,
tear the nation apart, and collapse America into socialism. Socialism
is the thief that steals individual freedom while selling the fiction that
freedom is free.

The success of the socialist theft depends on Orwellian doublespeak
to equate dependence on government with freedom. Freedom from
individual adult responsibility awards total social control to the government. It is why *freedom is slavery* in Orwell's socialistic society, why Dr.
Lyle Rossiter identifies the regressive liberal agenda as antithetical to
freedom, and why the collapse of the American family is a passage from
bonding to bondage in America.

CHAPTER 26

Who Launched the Cultural Revolution and Hostile Takeover of America?

The will to power is nothing new; megalomania simply expanded its frontiers as the world became a smaller place through science and technology. For centuries, the Great Wall of China provided protection against foreign invasion. Airplanes rendered the Wall irrelevant as a defense, and now the Great Wall of China is a popular tourist attraction.

The United States of America has been in the crosshairs of Great Britain since the United States won its War of Independence in 1776. Are you surprised? British history is one of continuous conquest and colonialism. Its unapologetic objective—world domination under British rule.

In the *Last Will and Testament of Cecil J. Rhodes*[106] (1853–1902), the British imperialist and mining magnate who founded DeBeers diamond mines, famously left his fortune for:

> The furtherance of the British Empire, for the bringing of the whole uncivilised world under British rule, for the recovery of the United States, for the making the Anglo-Saxon race but one Empire. What a dream! But yet it is probable. It is possible. (p. 59)

Rhodes believed that world peace would be attained through British hegemony. A very interesting article, "How the British Invented Globalism,"[107] written by Richard Poe, April 29, 2021, examines the familiar term *globalism*. Poe writes:

> Most patriots agree that we are fighting something called "globalism." But what is it? First and foremost, it is a British invention. Modern globalism was born in Victorian England, and later promoted by Britain's Fabian socialists. It is now the dominant belief system of today's world.

Poe argues that Alfred Tennyson's 1842 poem, "Locksley Hall,"[108] envisioned the globalist age of "universal law," a "Parliament of man," and a "Federation of the world."

Tennyson's vision is antithetical to the sovereign state dreamed by our forefathers, a government of the people, by the people, and for the people. Globalism, regardless of its origin, is a return to the binary feudal system of rulers and ruled. It is diametrically opposed to the freedoms and upward mobility dreamed by our Founding Fathers.

Poe describes Winston Churchill as the father of modern globalism and shows how Churchill's vision of global governance was parallel to Cecil Rhodes' view:

> Churchill called for a "world organization" backed by a "special relationship" between English-speaking countries. On February 16, 1944, Churchill warned that, "unless Britain and the United States are joined in a special relationship . . . within the ambit of a world organization—another destructive war will come to pass." Accordingly, the United Nations was founded on October 24, 1945.

Tennyson, Rhodes, and Churchill represent the British version of Gramsci's cultural hegemony. The establishment of the United Nations brought the United States into the field. This brings us to a discussion of the faces of globalism.

Orwell warned of the British globalists who represent the Western face of globalism seeking world domination, but today the British have competition. The Russians seek world domination, the Islamists seek world domination, and the Communist Chinese seek world domination.

What the competing faces of globalism share is their common cause to destroy the sovereignty of the United States of America. None can ascend to world hegemony without collapsing America first.

The globalist axis is an alliance of convenience that will continue until America falls; then the axis members will battle each other for dominance. There is no room for partners in globalist hegemony. It is a winner-take-all tournament, and we are still in the qualifying rounds.

War makes strange bedfellows, and the war on America is no exception. America's enemies within are by far our strangest and most deadly adversary. David Rockefeller, an unapologetic globalist and eugenicist, was America's connection to the British globalists and the infamous Alfred Kinsey, whose purpose was to destroy the morality and family structure of America.

Dr. Judith Reisman's forty-year battle to expose the monstrous crimes of Alfred Kinsey and the Kinsey Institute exposed a horrifying reality: Kinsey and the Institute were being protected by the U.S. government, which refused to prosecute them. It was a staggering realization for her. Why was this happening? What was the purpose of protecting Kinsey and the Institute? Who could be that immoral to promote the assault on innocent children? Why would anyone want to promote Kinsey's perverse ideas? Who benefited from burying the evidence about Kinsey?

These questions launched the next phase of Dr. Reisman's inquiry. Her exhaustive research connected the breakdown of sexual mores and Judeo-Christian morality to the Rockefeller Foundation and the CIA. The breakdown of the moral fiber of America and the accompanying breakdown in the American family was planned—the sexual revolution did not happen by chance. Dr. Reisman documented the catastrophic social effects and identified the two institutions responsible for protecting Kinsey and the Kinsey Institute.

Dr. Reisman presented her stunning findings in a comprehensive white paper published on August 10, 2020. The executive summary and thesis provide an overview exposing the crimes, protections, and methods for the madness. The entire paper is available on The Reisman Institute[109] website, and includes documentation of how MKUltra, the CIA's mind-control program, used non-consenting mental patients for its horrific experiments.

MKULTRA, KINSEY & ROCKEFELLER: Instruments of the New World Order[110]

The Executive Summary:

> In 1932 communist W. Z. Foster predicted the destruction of America's "education, morality, ethics, science, art, patriotism, religion" was necessary to establish a "New World Order."[i] [footnotes listed at end of chapter] America's social, economic, and sexual stability rested on Judeo-Christian beliefs and laws—abstinence before and faithfulness during consensual heterosexual marriage. Her

national health and wealth testified to the success of this *normal biopsychological sexual model.* From 1941, when America entered WWII, the Rockefeller Foundation (RF) began funding the work of Dr. Alfred Kinsey, who would have been known to RF as a sadomasochistic bi/homosexual. RF backing ensured Kinsey's 1948 book, S*exual Behavior in the Human Male,* instant popularity; "the Kinsey scale" codified "fluid sexuality" for the future, ensuring his enduring international fame.

RF connected Kinsey with a wider network of RF-funded scientists. From c.1946 Kinsey partnered with RF's *Columbia-Greystone Brain Project* at New York's "Snake Pit," *Rockland Mental Hospital.* The results of Kinsey's studies of sexual responses of lobotomized patients are sanitized in Kinsey's 1953 book, *Sexual Behavior in the Human Female.* This paper provides new evidence that the ~2,034 infants and children sexually violated for Kinsey's globe-changing "scientific proof" of infant/child orgasm were sourced from these and similar entities. 82% of Kinsey's child sex experiments are a match with the "Enhanced Interrogation Techniques" used on terrorism suspects at Guantanamo Bay.

Since Kinsey's definition of "orgasm" involves symptomatology indistinguishable from epileptic fit, terror/distress and/or electric shock treatment, the physiological responses he declared as child "orgasm" were true trauma responses. This is a newly uncovered Kinsey fraud represented as "science" by his RF funders. Very far from the organic "shock" of a scientific break-through advertised, this paper argues that Kinsey's sex work served as part of a broader psyops,[2] as rationale for thorough social change. As recently as 2020, RF claimed credit for "funding a sexual revolution" via the "Kinsey Reports."

From 1954 Congressional efforts to investigate Kinsey's sex work and the causal connection between pornography and ever-rising levels of child sexual abuse have been successfully blocked. Those acting in Rockefeller interests have prevented Kinsey's exposure while promoting his conclusions. From 1953, Hefner, "Kinsey's pamphleteer," marketed RF/Kinsey's lies to young college men via *Playboy.* The sexual restraint of previous generations—responsible for building America—were reframed as a web of hypocritical lies; premarital, extramarital, meaningless, love-free sex glamorized; and a generation, with Hefner its guru, embraced cynicism about human relationships, nihilism and rejection of all received wisdom.

The 1955 RF-funded Model Penal Code (MPC), drafted by RF's approved team, citing Kinsey, would overturn prior sex laws, including obscenity laws by 1957, and trivialized sexual abuse. In 1964, the Sexuality Information and Education Council of the United States (SIECUS), funded by *Playboy* and based at the Kinsey Institute, taught schools to disparage chastity, heterosexuality and monogamy. Soon, with "obscenity exemptions" allowed for "education" K–12 instructed in exotic sexual behaviors. Ever greater upticks in child rape, pornography and deadly STDs have, predictably, followed.

In 2014, the Kinsey Institute (KI) won United Nations consultative status for "educational" materials which aimed at overriding the most basic instinct for self-preservation in children of all ages, effectively preparing them to cooperate with RF's social change agenda. Since 2019 the KI's App., the "Kinsey Reporter", solicited "citizen scientists" (of any age) to record/report all sex acts/crimes *anonymously. Congressional investigation of a criminal nexus of RF, KI, Big Pharma, Big Porn, Big Abort and "sexual health" providers and educators, past and present, is critically needed to halt the damage these entities inflicted on three successive generations in their obsession for a New World Order.* (p. 2)

The Thesis:

For over seven decades, powerful entities prevented official investigation of Dr. Alfred Kinsey and promoted his conclusions as "truth". The result is that public policy, education, and law have been guided by the lies of a psychopathic[ii] [footnotes listed at end of chapter] pedosadist.[iii] [footnotes listed at end of chapter] Instead of protecting children and scaffolding the family, government policy has facilitated the agenda of allied interest groups which benefit personally, financially, and/or politically from sexual exploitation of the vulnerable and the destruction of the nuclear family. Notable among these beneficiaries are the very elites who, wishing to establish a New World Order, initiated and funded Kinsey's work, sold his lies to the public, and obstructed investigation of Kinsey and the Institute that bears his name and continues his work to this day. Official investigation of Kinsey—and the cultural transformation he set in motion—is long overdue. (p. 6)

Dr. Reisman's comprehensive examination and documentation of Alfred Kinsey's fraud is essential to understanding the malevolence and deliberateness of the Sexual Revolution as an intrinsic part of the globalist Culture War on America.

Dr. Judith Reisman, a brilliant, courageous, intrepid warrior for the safety of our nation's children and the family's families that protect them, died suddenly on April 9, 2021.

Footnotes from the Executive Summary and Thesis:

[i] William Z.Foster. (1932/2016). Toward Soviet America. Hauraki Publishing. Kindle Edition. P. 313.

ii The use of such a term "psychopath" is not simply hyperbole. It is used in the clinical sense of the word. Academic researchers, such as Robert Hare, Ph.D, (1) and James Fallon, Ph. D. (2), and forensic clinicians who have spent years working with incarcerated psychopaths in long-term solitary and in general population, such as Jon K. Uhler, LPC (3), each concur that the clinical definition of a psychopath can be boiled down to someone lacking conscience, empathy, and remorse:

(1) http://www.psychology-criminalbehavior-law.com/2015/01/hare-psychopath/ (2)https://www.crimetraveller.org/2015/07/inside-mind-of-psychopath-psychopathic-killer/
(3) https://www.quora.com/Why-do-certain-psychologists-mix-up-cluster-B-traits-and-deem-the-combination-a- sociopath/answer/Jon-K-Uhler
Given that Kinsey elected to sexually abuse children, allow other deviant adults to sexually abuse them under the guise of scientific experiments, and the fact that he would do so to so many children, and never experience any signs of remorse or contrition would clearly categorize him well within the realm of psychopathy. In fact, given that he would then take such "results" from such diabolically abusive "treatment" of children which would no doubt have profound life-altering and life-long consequences on those children, and use that in such a brazen manner so as to appear as having done legitimate research (as opposed to having

perpetrated and sanctioned the perpetration of children), for the purpose of creating a belief about the supposed sexuality of children, in order to craft public opinion, public policy, judicial decisions, and impact state and federal legislation reveals a profoundly psychopathic agenda-driven mind, intent upon shifting the culture toward a greater acceptance of child sexuality and the narrative of mutual love and sexual expression between persons, regardless of age. After all, were now told that, "Love is Love", "Love knows no boundaries", and "Love knows no age". https://www.growingbolder.com/love-has-no-age-3020496/

iii While "pedophile" and "pederast" has been used to describe those who desire to, or who do, sexually violate, exploit children, the term means "child-lover" ("philia" the Greek for love or more recently, "friendly feeling toward," https://www.merriam- webster.com/dictio-nary/-philia). From his 11+ years of clinical forensic work with hundreds of incarcerated male child offenders, Jon Uhler notes that 100% of offenders with child victims possessed child-rape porn, 98% with child-rape porn distribution. One who uses children sexually is clinically psychopathic (arousal derived from pain and suffering in the victim). Hence, we have chosen to be clinically accurate using the term "pedosadist," versus the misleading "pedophile" or "pederast."

CHAPTER 27

The Weapons of the Ruling Class: Weaponized Education, Weaponized Media, and Weaponized Entertainment

Investigative journalist Daniel Estulin has written two extraordinary books documenting the covert 100-year globalist war on America that is manipulating the public into accepting globalist one-world governance. The first, *The True Story of the Bilderberg Group* (2005, updated 2009), identifies the institutional infrastructure of organizations, research facilities, think tanks, and media partners working collaboratively in common cause. The second, *Tavistock Institute: Social Engineering the Masses* (2015), exposes the psycho-social methodologies using Lewin's change model to *unfreeze* family bonding and Judeo-Christian norms, *change* society into socialist dependence and scientism, then *refreeze* our nation into one-world government bondage and compliance. *Tavistock Institute* will be discussed in Chapter 30.

An extraordinary book review by Stephen Lendman, "'The True Story of the Bilderberg Group' and What They May Be Planning Now,"[111] originally published on *Global Research* in June 2009 and reposted in May 2019, is a comprehensive and timely summary of the globalist scheme to fundamentally transform America.

> Daniel Estulin has investigated and researched the Bilderberg Group's far-reaching influence on business and finance, global politics, war and peace, and control of the world's resources and its money.

> His book, *The True Story of the Bilderberg Group*, was published in 2005 and is now updated in a new 2009 edition. He states that in 1954, "the most powerful men in the world met for the first time" in Oosterbeek, Netherlands, "debated the future of the world," and decided to meet annually in secret. They

called themselves the Bilderberg Group with a membership representing a who's who of world power elites, mostly from America, Canada, and Western Europe with familiar names like David Rockefeller, Henry Kissinger, Bill Clinton, Gordon Brown, Angela Merkel, Alan Greenspan, Ben Bernanke, Larry Summers, Tim Geithner, Lloyd Blankfein, George Soros, Donald Rumsfeld, Rupert Murdoch, other heads of state, influential senators, congressmen and parliamentarians, Pentagon and NATO brass, members of European royalty, selected media figures, and invited other—some quietly by some accounts like Barack Obama and many of his top officials.

Always well represented are top figures from the Council on Foreign Relations (CFR), International Monetary Fund (IMF), World Bank, Trilateral Commission, European Union (EU), and powerful central bankers from the Federal Reserve, the European Central Bank's (ECB) Jean-Claude Trichet, and Bank of England's (BoE) Mervyn King.

For over half a century, no agenda or discussion topics became public nor is any press coverage allowed. The few invited fourth estate attendees and their bosses are sworn to secrecy. Nonetheless, Estulin undertook "an investigative journey" that became his life's work. He states, "Slowly, one by one, I have penetrated the layers of secrecy surrounding the Bilderberg Group, but I could not have done this without help of 'conscientious objectors' from inside, as well as outside, the Group's membership." As a result, he keeps their names confidential.

Whatever its early mission, the Group is now "a shadow world government . . . threatening to take away our right to direct our own destinies (by creating) a disturbing reality" very much harming the public's welfare. In short, Bilderbergers want to supplant individual nation-state sovereignty with an all-powerful global government, corporate controlled, and check-mated by militarized enforcement.

> "Imagine a private club where presidents, prime ministers, international bankers and generals rub shoulders, where gracious royal chaperones ensure everyone gets along, and where the people running the wars, markets,

and Europe (and America) say what they never dare say in public."

Early in its history, Bilderbergers decided "to create an 'Aristocracy of purpose' between Europe and the United States (to reach consensus to rule the world on matters of) policy, economics, and (overall) strategy." NATO was essential for their plans—to ensure "perpetual war (and) nuclear blackmail" to be used as necessary. Then proceed to loot the planet, achieve fabulous wealth and power, and crush all challengers to keep it.

Along with military dominance, controlling the world's money is crucial for with it comes absolute control as the powerful 19th century Rothschild family understood. As the patriarch Amschel Rothschild once said: "Give me control of a nation's money and I care not who makes its laws."

Bilderbergers comprise the world's most exclusive club. No one buys their way in. Only the Group's Steering Committee decides whom to invite, and in all cases, participants are adherents to One World Order governance run by top power elites. . . .

Bilderberg Objectives

The Group's grand design is for "a One World Government (World Company) with a single, global marketplace, policed by one world army, and financially regulated by one 'World (Central) Bank' using one global currency." Their "wish list" includes:

— "one international identity (observing) one set of universal values";

— centralized control of world populations by "mind control"; in other words, controlling world public opinion;

— a New World Order with no middle class, only "rulers and servants (serfs)," and, of course, no democracy;

— "a zero-growth society" without prosperity or progress, only greater wealth and power for the rulers;

— manufactured crises and perpetual wars;

— absolute control of education to program the public mind and train those chosen for various roles;

— "centralized control of all foreign and domestic policies"; one size fits all globally;

— using the UN as a de facto world government imposing a UN tax on "world citizens";

— expanding NAFTA and WTO globally;

— making NATO a world military;

— imposing a universal legal system; and

— a global "welfare state where obedient slaves will be rewarded and non-conformists targeted for extermination."

Secret Bilderberg Partners

In the US, the Council on Foreign Relations (CFR) is dominant. One of its 1921 founders, Edward Mandell House, was Woodrow Wilson's chief advisor and rumored at the time to be the nation's real power from 1913–1921. On his watch, the Federal Reserve Act passed in December 1913 giving money creation power to bankers, and the 16th Amendment was ratified in February creating the federal income tax to provide a revenue stream to pay for government debt service.

From its beginnings, CFR was committed to "a one-world government based on a centralized global financing system. . . ." Today, CFR has thousands of influential members (including important ones in the corporate media) but keeps a low public profile, especially regarding its real agenda. . . .

The Trilateral Commission (discussed below) is a similar group that "brings together global power brokers." Founded by David Rockefeller, he's also a leading Bilderberger and CFR Chairman Emeritus, organizations he continues to finance and support.

Their past and current members reflect their power:

— nearly all presidential candidates of both parties;

— leading senators and congressmen;

— key members of the fourth estate and their bosses; and

— top officials of the FBI, CIA, NSA, defense establishment, and other leading government agencies, including state, commerce, the judiciary and treasury.

For its part, "CFR has served as a virtual employment agency for the federal government under both Democrats and Republicans." Whoever occupies the White House, "CFR's power and agenda" have been unchanged since its 1921 founding.

It advocates a global superstate with America and other nations sacrificing their sovereignty to a central power. CFR founder Paul Warburg was a member of Roosevelt's "brain trust." In 1950, his son, James, told the Senate Foreign Relations Committee: "We shall have world government whether or not you like it—by conquest or consent."

Later at the 1992 Bilderberg Group meeting, Henry Kissinger said:

> "Today, Americans would be outraged if UN troops entered Los Angeles to restore order; tomorrow, they will be grateful. This is especially true if they were told there was an outside threat from beyond, whether real or promulgated, that threatened our very existence. It is then that all people of the world will plead with world leaders to deliver them from this evil. . . individual rights will be willingly relinquished for the guarantee of their well-being granted to them by their world government."

CFR planned a New World Order before 1942, and the "UN began with a group of CFR members called the Informal Agenda Group." They drafted the original UN proposal, presented it to Franklin Roosevelt who announced it publicly the next day. At its 1945 founding, CFR members comprised over 40 of the US delegates.

According to Professor G. William Domhoff, author of *Who Rules America*:

"The Council on Foreign Relations, while not financed by government, works so closely with it that it is difficult to distinguish

Council action stimulated by government from autonomous actions. (Its) most important sources of income are leading corporations and major foundations." The Rockefeller, Carnegie, and Ford Foundations to name three, and they're directed by key corporate officials.

Dominant Media Partners

Former CBS News president Richard Salant (1961–1964 and 1966–1979) explained the major media's role: "Our job is to give people not what they want, but what we decide they ought to have."

CBS and other media giants control everything we see, hear and read—through television, radio, newspapers, magazines, books, films, and large portions of the Internet. Their top officials and some journalists attend Bilderberg meeting—on condition they report nothing.

The Rockefeller family wields enormous power, even though its reigning patriarch, David, will be 94 on June 12 and surely near the end of his dominance. However, for years "the Rockefellers (led by David) gained great influence over the media. (With it) the family gained sway over public opinion. With the pulse of public opinion, they gained deep influence in politics. And with this politics of subtle corruption, they are taking control of the nation" and now aim for total world domination.

The Bilderberger-Rockefeller scheme is to make their views "so appealing (by camouflaging them) that they become public policy (and can) pressure world leaders into submitting to the 'needs of the Masters of the Universe.'" The "free world press" is their instrument to disseminate "agreed-upon propaganda. . . ."

CFR Cabinet Control

"The National Security Act of 1947 established the office of Secretary of Defense." Since then, 14 DOD secretaries have been CFR members.

Since 1940, every Secretary of State, except James Byrnes, has been a CFR member and/or Trilateral Commission (TC) one.

For the past 80 years, "Virtually every key US National Security and Foreign Policy Advisor has been a CFR member.

Nearly all top generals and admirals have been CFR members.

Many presidential candidates were/are CFR members, including Herbert Hoover, Adlai Stevenson, Dwight Eisenhower, John Kennedy, Richard Nixon, Gerald Ford, Jimmy Carter (also a charter TC member), George HW Bush, Bill Clinton, John Kerry, and John McCain.

Numerous CIA directors were/are CFR members, including Richard Helms, James Schlesinger, William Casey, William Webster, Robert Gates, James Woolsey, John Deutsch, George Tenet, Porter Goss, Michael Hayden, and Leon Panetta.

Many Treasury Secretaries were/are CFR members, including Douglas Dillon, George Schultz, William Simon, James Baker, Nicholas Brady, Lloyd Bentsen, Robert Rubin, Henry Paulson, and Tim Geithner.

When presidents nominate Supreme Court candidates, the CFR's "Special Group, Secret Team" or advisors vet them for acceptability. Presidents, in fact, are told who to appoint, including designees to the High Court and most lower ones.

Programming the Public Mind

According to sociologist Hadley Cantril in his 1967 book, *The Human Dimension—Experiences in Policy Research*:

Government "Psycho-political operations are propaganda campaigns designed to create perpetual tension and to manipulate different groups of people to accept the particular climate of opinion the CFR seeks to achieve in the world."

Canadian writer Ken Adachi (1929–1989) added:

> *"What most Americans believe to be 'Public Opinion' is in reality carefully crafted and scripted propaganda designed to elicit a desired behavioral response from the public.*
>
> *And noted Australian academic and activist Alex Carey*

(1922–1988) explained the three most important 20th century developments, "The growth of democracy, the growth of corporate power, and the growth of corporate propaganda as a means of protecting corporate power against democracy."

Web of Control

Numerous think tanks, foundations, the major media, and other key organizations are staffed with CFR members. Most of its life-members also belong to the TC and Bilderberg Group, operate secretly, and wield enormous power over US and world affairs.

The Rockefeller-Founded Trilateral Commission (TC)

On page 405 of his Memoirs, David Rockefeller wrote:

"Some even believe we are part of a secret cabal working against the best interests of the United States characterizing my family and me as 'internationalists' and conspiring with others around the world to build a more integrated global political and economic structure—one world, if you will. If that's the charge, I stand guilty, and I am proud of it."

In alliance with Bilderbergers, the TC also "plays a vital role in the New World Order's scheme to use wealth, concentrated in the hands of the few, to exert world control." TC members share common views and all relate to total unchallengeable global dominance. . . .

CFR's leadership must make "an end run around national sovereignty, eroding it piece by piece," until the very notion disappears from public discourse.

Bilderberg/CFR/Trilateralist success depends on finding "a way to get us to surrender our liberties in the name of some common threat or crisis. The foundations, educational institutions, and research think tanks supported by (these organizations) oblige by financing so-called 'studies' which are then used to justify their every excess. The excuses vary, but the target is always individual liberty. Our liberty" and much more.

Bilderbergers, Trilateralists and CFR members want "an all-encompassing monopoly" over government, money, industry, and property that's "self-perpetuating and eternal. . . ."

After the [2009 Bilderberg] meeting, Estulin got a 73-page report on what was discussed. He noted that "One of Bilderberg's primary concerns . . . is the danger that their zeal to reshape the world by engineering chaos (toward) their long-term agenda could cause the situation to spiral out of control and eventually lead to a scenario where Bilderberg and the global elite in general are overwhelmed by events and end up losing their control over the planet."

Estulin also noted some considerable disagreement between "hardliners" wanting a "dramatic decline and a severe, short-term depression (versus others) who think that things have gone too far" so that "the fallout from the global economic cataclysm" can't be known, may be greater than anticipated, and may harm Bilderberger interests. Also, "some European bankers (expressed great alarm over their own fate and called the current) high wire act 'unsustainable.'"

There was a combination of agreement and fear that the situation remains dire and the worst of the crisis lies ahead, mainly because of America's extreme debt level that must be resolved to produce a healthy, sustainable recovery.

Topics also included:

— establishing a Global Treasury Department and Global Central Bank, possibly partnered with or as part of the IMF;

— a global currency;

— destruction of the dollar through what longtime market analyst Bob Chapman calls "a stealth default on (US) debt by continuing to issue massive amounts of money and credit and in the process devaluing the dollar," a process he calls "fraud";

— a global legal system;

— exploiting the Swine Flu scare to create a WHO global department of health; and

— the overall goal of a global government and the end of national sovereignty.

In the past, Estulin's sources proved accurate. Earlier, he predicted the housing crash and 2007–2008 financial market decline, preceded by the kind of financial crisis triggered by the Lehman Brothers collapse. Watch for further updates from him as new information leaks out on what the world's power elites have planned going forward.

Stephen Lendman is a Research Associate of the Centre of Research for Globalization. He lives in Chicago and can be reached at lendmanstephen@sbcglobal.net.

Also visit his blog site at sjlendman.blogspot.com and listen to The Global Research News Hour on RepublicBroadcasting.org Monday—Friday at 10AM US Central time for cutting-edge discussions with distinguished guests on world and national issues. All programs are archived for easy listening.

© Copyright Stephen Lendman, Global Research, 2009

The URL address of this article is: www.globalresearch.ca/index.php?context=va&aid=13808

The Bilderberg Plan for 2009: Remaking the Global Political Economy by Andrew G. Marshall

New World Order (The Movie)

The Bilderberg Group on Dandelion Salad

CHAPTER 28

The Great Reset Planned for the United States of America

The Great Reset is the name given to the 50th annual World Economic Forum (WEF) meeting in Davos, Switzerland, in June 2020. The WEF is a private, *not-for-profit*, international non-governmental organization (NGO) founded in 1971 by executive chairman Klaus Schwab. Headquartered in Geneva, Switzerland, the WEF describes itself as committed to "improving the state of the world." Mentored by Henry Kissinger, Klaus Schwab is an unapologetic globalist who believes improving the world requires planetary governance by the globalist elite.

The Great Reset is also the latest name for United Nations Agenda 21, United Nations Agenda 2030, the Fourth Industrial Revolution, and the New World Order. It is the creation of the Davos globalist network including the WEF, the Council on Foreign Relations (CFR), and the CFR media networks.[112]

No matter what it is called, the Great Reset is the same old elitist dream of rulers and ruled. It is a return to feudalism on a planetary scale that deceitfully presents bondage as freedom. The Great Reset profits the ruling class exclusively, which is why the WEF standing as a *not-for-profit* entity is so misleading. The WEF itself may not profit as an organization, but its membership certainly does.

Sustainable is a reference to the globalist solution to the Malthusian dilemma of increasing population and decreasing natural resources, and to the fiction of *man-made* global warming. The earth has been going through natural cycles of heating and cooling for millennia. Man is responsible for pollution, which must be addressed, but the notion that man's behavior heats or cools the earth is preposterous.

Absurdity does not get in the way of determined globalists, and no lie is too big to tell. In fact, the bigger the lie, the better. The fiction of global warming began as the 20th century lie used to redistribute wealth from industrialized to non-industrial nations. It is socialism on a planetary scale.

In 1991, the Club of Rome, part of the WEF network promoting global governance by a technocratic elite, published a book titled _The First Global Revolution_.[113] It offered diabolical depopulation policies and visions of one-world planetary governance—ruled by themselves, of course. The Club of Rome decided that their policies would be supported only if the public could identify and unite to fight a common enemy. They settled on mankind itself and dreamed up man-made global warming:

> In searching for a new enemy to unite us, we came up with the idea that pollution, the threat of global warming, water shortages, famine and the like, would fit the bill. In their totality and in their interactions these phenomena do constitute a common threat which demands the solidarity of all peoples. But in designating them as the enemy, we fall into the trap about which we have already warned, namely mistaking symptoms for causes. All these dangers are caused by human intervention and it is only through changed attitudes and behaviour that they can be overcome. The real enemy, then, is humanity itself. (p. 115)

The idea was to unite mankind against itself as both the _cause_ and the _cure_ for catastrophic disasters. In true dialectical fashion, the globalists presented a false assumption, that natural disasters are _man-made_. Then manipulated the public toward their predetermined _solution_, with messaging from the non-stop media echo chamber, the entertainment media, and educational indoctrination.

Man-made global warming ran into trouble when the earth's natural temperature fluctuations resulted in a cooling trend. That is when global warming became _climate change_. Still, the doomsday projections, relentless fear mongering, and blame did not redistribute enough wealth to achieve globalist planetary governance.

Klaus Schwab published _The Fourth Industrial Revolution_[114] in January 2017. The book describes the artificial intelligence of today as the 21st-century fourth industrial revolution. It follows the steam engine, which launched the first industrial revolution in the 18th century, electricity in the 19th century, and computers in the 20th century.

In a January 10, 2016, interview[115] on Swiss channel RTS, Schwab explained that human beings will soon receive a chip in their body in order to merge with the digital world. When asked about implanted chips, Schwab responded matter-of-factly:

> Certainly, within the next ten years. And at first, we will implant them in our clothes. And then we could imagine that we will implant them in our brains, or in our skin. And in the end maybe there will be a direct communication between our brain and the digital world. What we see is a kind of fusion of the physical, digital, and biological world…It is a servant that with artificial intelligence learns, and that is not only your assistant for manual work, but that can really be an intellectual partner of you.

The Fourth Industrial Revolution (4IR), in blurring the boundaries between physical, digital, and biological worlds, challenges what it means to be human. It fuses man and machine through artificial intelligence (AI), robotics, the Internet of Things (IoT), 3-D printing, genetic engineering, and quantum computing. It relies on technological surveillance rather than the rule of law to maintain order in society. These technological advances depend on fifth-generation (5G) mobile network technology for speed and connectivity.

Schwab claims the seismic changes of the Fourth Industrial Revolution are so sweeping that they redefine everything, including how we relate to one another, the way we work, the way we do business, how governments function, and even what it means to be human. The tools of the 4IR are so powerful that they enable new forms of surveillance and social control, including intrusion into our minds, reading our thoughts and influencing our behavior. Schwab argues that we must embrace the changes and build an ethical, inclusive, sustainable, and prosperous future.

That sounds an awful lot like the United Nations jibber-jabber hawking planetary one-world government—and so it is. As with every force in nature, the elements of the Fourth Industrial Revolution can be used for either construction or destruction. Klaus Schwab's elitist vision for planetary governance is lipstick painted on the same destructive aristocratic pig rejected by our Founding Fathers.

Hillary Clinton was expected to win the 2016 election and make Schwab's globalist dreams come true. Instead, Donald J. Trump won the presidential election and he remains the existential enemy of globalism—a proud American patriot, defender of the U.S. Constitution, and protector of national sovereignty.

President Trump's America-first policies strengthened the United States in every sector and posed a serious obstacle to the globalist campaign for planetary governance. The economy was booming, and President Trump was certain to be reelected in 2020.

The globalists had a time-sensitive political problem. Their man-made global warming narrative had failed to frighten the public into childlike compliance and surrender to UN planetary governance. The COVID-19 *plandemic* provided the escalation of fear required to launch the fourth industrial revolution. In October 2019, the Johns Hopkins "Center for Health Security" held "Event 201," a pandemic response exercise sponsored by the Bill & Melinda Gates Foundation and the World Economic Forum.

The coronavirus SARS-CoV-2 was released from Wuhan, China, in late 2019. In March 2020, the China-centric World Health Organization declared the disease it caused, COVID-19, a pandemic. In 2020, Klaus Schwab said that COVID-19 is a "rare but narrow window of opportunity to rethink, reinvent, reset our world."

The COVID-19 "pandemic" is the big lie of the 21st century, used to destroy the American economy and Trump's presidency, and launch the Great Reset—it is political medicine disguised as public health. The WEF propaganda video, *The Great Reset*,[116] was posted on June 3, 2020, with this announcement:

> There is an urgent need for global stakeholders to cooperate simultaneously managing the direct consequences of the COVID-19 crisis. To improve the state of the world, the World Economic Forum is starting the Great Reset. The World Economic Forum is the international organization for Public-Private Cooperation. The Forum engages the foremost political, business, cultural, and other leaders of society to shape global, regional and industry agendas.

The Great Reset is actually a system of globalized, one-world government overseen by the United Nations. It is beyond the deceitful socialist promises of global sustainability, social justice, and economic equality. It is a total restructuring of the global economy and the complete transformation of humanity into a transhumanist nightmare akin to the world depicted in Aldous Huxley's 1932 novel, *Brave New World*.

International banking consultant Marilyn MacGruder Barnewall explains the importance of 5G in achieving Reset objectives:

> It is impossible to implement a world government without a world economic system. It is impossible to have a world economic system without a world currency. It is impossible to control a world currency without it being cryptocurrency—this prevents a President in some small nation somewhere in the world from changing the value of the currency because, if it is computer based, it can only be changed from one central location controlled by the world government. The only way to do that is a computer system that can handle billions of transactions daily and quickly—from credit and debit cards to major international lending and payment to . . . you name it if it involves currency—please note I did not say money. The only way to provide a computer system that handles the demands required of a world economic system is to implement 5G.

The WEF effort is a self-serving attempt to rebuild the world society and economy in a binary "sustainable" way following the COVID-19 debacle. "Build back better" is the slogan of the Great Reset—it is globalist doublespeak for *you will own nothing, and you will be happy.*

South African author and public speaker Douglas Kruger discusses the slogan in a 12-minute video titled <u>You will OWN NOTHING, and you will be HAPPY</u>.[117]

Kruger identifies the stakeholders—the globalist elite in banking, finance, and business, who are conspiring with governments in a public-private effort to rebuild the covid-collapsed economies using the socialist promise of the "greater good" that eliminates private property.

The globalist elite are selling feudalism by calling it freedom. The Great Reset turns the multi-national corporations working with government into overlords, and the world population into their economically enslaved serfs.

Collectivist ownership is a communist lie, because if the government controls the manufacture and distribution of goods and services, ownership is a moot point: the government controls your life. China is a one-party communist state that operates on a social credit score. This means the government controls your life. If you do or say anything that the government disapproves of, your social credit score drops and the government can "ghost" you—lock you out of your life.

The United States of America was founded on freedom and property rights. Kruger quotes George Washington: *Freedom and property rights are inseparable. You cannot have one without the other.*

Kruger warns us that the overlords of the Great Reset will confiscate all your private property, including your home, your heirlooms, anything and everything you have ever earned and accumulated. Your speech and private thoughts will be controlled by the government. Each succeeding generation will have property values reset to zero, and will be completely dependent upon the government and their social credit scores. The United States of America becomes a permanent welfare state.

Self-sufficiency has always been the U.S. ideal, with the goal of lifting people out of welfare dependence. The Great Reset establishes a permanent global welfare state. It is a return to the feudal order of rulers and ruled, and the most colossal humanitarian hoax in world history.

CHAPTER 29

The Permanent Global Welfare State

The permanent global welfare state was not the ideological creation of Klaus Schwab. It was envisioned eighty years ago by American philosopher and political theorist James Burnham (1905–1987).

Burnham began his career as an avowed communist and eventually became an ardent anticommunist. He formally rejected Marxism as impractical in 1940, and the next year published his own vision of the future in *The Managerial Revolution: What Is Happening in the World.*[118] Burnham forecast Schwab's Great Reset and its particular answer to the Malthusian dilemma of increasing population and decreasing natural resources.

Burnham taught in the philosophy department at New York University from 1929 to 1953. He took a leave of absence during World War II to work for the Office of Strategic Services (OSS), a precursor to the Central Intelligence Agency (CIA).

Burnham is best remembered for his book's 1941 prediction that sovereign nations would be replaced by super-states determined by their advanced industry:

> The world political system will coalesce into three primary super-states, each based upon one of these three areas of advanced industry, and the nuclei of these three super-states are . . . Japan, Germany and the United States. (pp. 175–176)

In fact, only two super-powers emerged—the United States and the Soviet Union. Burnham remained a vocal critic of containment strategies to undermine Soviet power, advocated instead a more aggressive response to communism.

What Burnham did predict correctly was the emergence of a managerial revolution based in scientism, what is being promoted by

Klaus Schwab as the Great Reset. Burnham may have been an ardent anticommunist, but he possessed the supremacist mindset that imagined the managerial revolution. He simply painted lipstick on the same binary socio-political feudal pig and replaced one tyranny with another. This is how it works.

Obfuscating language is the key to social control. Ayn Rand knew that private property is the key to freedom. When the government (or managerial class) controls the property you "own," you don't really own it.

So, for example, if you have a million dollars in the bank, but the government managers say you cannot access it—either they close the bank or in a cashless society simply deny access digitally—you do not own the money in "your" bank account. You may be a millionaire on paper, but you are not a millionaire in objective reality. It is a question of the meaning of the word ownership.

Americans understand the word *ownership* in the colloquial sense: the individual controls what he owns. In the obfuscators' world, ownership is yet another humanitarian hoax—a cashless society for our convenience and for own good, of course.

Burnham understood that obfuscating language is essential for the transition from capitalism to the managerial state:

> Of course, some of the words of the capitalist ideologies are taken over: such words as "freedom" are found in many ideologies since they are popular and, as we have seen, can be interpreted in any manner whatever.
>
> These concepts, and others like them, help break down what remains of capitalism and clear the road for the managers and managerial society. They prepare the psychic atmosphere for the demolition of capitalist property rights, the acceptance of state economy and the rule of a new kind of state, the rejection of the "natural rights" of capitalism (that is, the rights of the capitalists in the private market place), and the approval of managerial war. When enough people begin thinking through these instead of the capitalist categories, the consolidation of the managerial structure of society is assured. (*The Managerial Revolution*, p. 191)

Canadian researcher and political analyst Cynthia Chung is co-founder of the <u>Rising Tide Foundation</u>[119] (Montreal, Canada) and contributing writer to <u>Strategic Culture Foundation</u>.[120] Chung has written an excellent two-part analysis of James Burnham and his theoretical future: <u>"The Great Reset: How a 'Managerial Revolution' Was Plotted 80 Years Ago by a Trotsky-turned-CIA Neocon"</u>[121] and <u>"How the Great Reset Was First Thought Up by the Original Proselytizer of Totalitarianism and the Father of Neo-Conservatism."</u>[122]

The analysis is clear and concise. In part 1 Chung details Burnham's personal path to managerial revolution, from Trotsky and dialectical materialism to Bertrand Russell and globalist elitism:

> *"We cannot understand the revolution by restricting our analysis to the war [WWII]; we must understand the war as a phase in the development of the revolution."*

—James Burnham, "The Managerial Revolution"

In Burnham's "<u>The Managerial Revolution</u>,"[123] he makes the case that if socialism were possible, it would have occurred as an outcome of the Bolshevik Revolution, but what happened instead was neither a reversion back to a capitalist system nor a transition to a socialist system, but rather a formation of a new organizational structure made up of an elite managerial class, the type of society he believed was in the process of replacing capitalism on a world scale.

He goes on to make the case that, as seen with the transition from a feudal to a capitalist state being inevitable, so too will the transition from a capitalist to managerial state occur. And that ownership rights of production capabilities will no longer be owned by individuals but rather the state or institutions, he writes:

> *"Effective class domination and privilege does, it is true, require control over the instruments of production; but this need not be exercised through individual private property rights. It can be done through what might be called corporate rights, possessed not by individuals as such but by institutions: as was the case conspicuously with many societies in which a priestly class was dominant."* [p. 39]

Burnham proceeds to write:

> "*If, in a managerial society, no individuals are to hold comparable property rights, how can any group of individuals constitute a ruling class?*
>
> *The answer is comparatively simple and, as already noted, not without historical analogues. The managers will exercise their control over the instruments of production and gain preference in the distribution of the products, not directly, through property rights vested in them as individuals, but indirectly, through their control of the state which in turn will own and control the instruments of production. The state—that is, the institutions which comprise the state—will, if we wish to put it that way, be the 'property' of the managers. And that will be quite enough to place them in the position of the ruling class.*" [p. 69]

Burnham concedes that the ideologies required to facilitate this transition were not yet fully worked out [in 1941] but goes on to say that they can be approximated:

> "*from several different but similar directions, by, for example: Leninism-Stalinism; fascism-nazism; and, at a more primitive level, by New Dealism and such less influential [at the time] American ideologies as 'technocracy'. This, then, is the skeleton of the theory, expressed in the language of the struggle for power.*" [p. 70]

This is, to be sure, a rather confusing paragraph but becomes clearer when we understand it from the specific viewpoint of Burnham. As Burnham sees it, all these different avenues are methods in which to achieve his vision of a managerial society because each form stresses the importance of the state as the central coordinating power, and that such a state will be governed by his "managers". Burnham considers the different moral implications in each scenario irrelevant; as he makes clear early on in his book, he has chosen to detach himself from such questions.

Burnham goes to explain that the support of the masses is necessary for the success of any revolution; this is why the masses must be led to believe that they will benefit from such a revolution, when in fact it is only to replace one ruling class with another and nothing changes for the underdog. He explains that this is the case with the dream of a socialist state, that the universal equality promised by socialism is just a fairy tale told to the people so that they fight for the establishment of a new ruling class, then they are told that achieving a socialist state will take many decades, and that essentially, a managerial system must be put in place in the meantime.

In part 2 Chung makes a stunning connection between the *intellectuals* described by Burnham and then by Aldous Huxley, as useful idiots for the managerial state, whose purpose is to persuade people to love their servitude:

In Burnham's "The Managerial Revolution,"[124] he writes:

> "*Most of these intellectuals are not in the least aware that the net social effect of the ideologies which they elaborate contributes to the power and privilege of the managers and to the building of a new structure of class rule in society. As in the past, the intellectuals believe that they are speaking in the name of truth and for the interests of all humanity…Indeed, the intellectual, without usually being aware of it, elaborate the new ideologies from the point of view of the position of the managers.*" [p. 70]

What this means is that the intellectuals themselves do not understand who in fact will benefit in the end by the philosophies and theories they support and defend, they are mere instruments for the propagation of a new ruling class and hold no true power. Aldous Huxley's, who also promoted a managerial ruling class in his "Brave New World," [1962] speech to naïve Berkeley students, titled "The Ultimate Revolution"[125] comes to mind…

As Huxley put it:

> "*There will be, in the next generation or so, a pharmacological method of making people love their servitude,*

> *and producing dictatorship without tears, so to speak, producing a kind of painless concentration camp for entire societies, so that people will in fact have their liberties taken away from them, but will rather enjoy it."*

Burnham's vision and Huxley's prediction are fast becoming the new reality for America. Its new ruling class is neither Democrat nor Republican; it comprises an immoral globalist elite who are building Burnham's managerial state by collapsing American capitalism.

Following Burnham's playbook, the managerial class is a self-defined ruling class:

> We have defined "ruling class" as consisting of the group of persons which has (as a matter of *fact*, not necessarily of law or words or theory), as against the rest of the population, a special degree of control over access to the instruments of production and preferential treatment in the distribution of the products of those instruments. (p. 154)

> In managerial society, however, politics and economics are directly interfused; the state does not recognize its capitalist limits; the economic arena is also the arena of the state. Consequently, there is no sharp separation between political officials and "captains of industry." The captain of industry is, by virtue of his function, at the same time a state official. The "supreme planning commission" is indistinguishably a political and an economic institution. (pp. 156–157)

A stunning article by Justin Haskins on The Federalist website on October 22, 2021, "How Global Capital's Social Credit Systems Force Corporate America to Lurch Left,"[126] explains how investment firms Vanguard, BlackRock, and State Street are rulers in the managerial state.

> BlackRock, the world's largest investment management corporation, now controls nearly $10 trillion in assets. (Just one year ago, it controlled less than $8 trillion.) And that's just one of many large investment firms. The ten largest management firms have more than $41 trillion in assets under management, nearly double the annual gross domestic product for the United States (about $21 trillion).

Investment firms don't use the fortunes they manage to build swimming pools of money; they buy assets, especially stock and real estate, in order to provide a good return for their investors and to increase their stranglehold on Wall Street. Investment firms like BlackRock now control so much stock, in fact, that they can effectively force virtually any large corporation in the United States to do—well, pretty much anything they want.

BlackRock, State Street, and others are using their stock [holdings] to force companies to adopt policies and social causes promoted by elites, many of which align with left-wing goals.

The most important tool for accomplishing this strategy is environmental, social, and governance (ESG) standards, a new framework for evaluating businesses. Under an ESG model, which has already been widely adopted by corporate America, companies are rewarded or punished based on how they score on dozens of metrics developed by bankers, investors, activists, and, in some cases, government officials.

For example, one influential ESG model developed by the International Business Council of the World Economic Forum—one of the leaders of the international "Great Reset" movement—evaluates businesses based on their commitment to the Paris Climate Accords, water use, "ecological sensitivity," and, among many other things, the "Percentage of employees per employee category, by age group, gender and other indicators of diversity (e.g. ethnicity)."

It is important to understand that investment firms are not brokerage houses. Brokerage firms buy and sell stocks on behalf of the investor—they are the middleman between buyer and seller. Investment firms make investments on behalf of investors who have invested funds in the investment company itself. It is a different business model. So, BlackRock owns the shares of the companies it buys, and the investor owns shares of BlackRock.

The ESG standards comport with UN Agenda 2030, the global initiative to impose one-world government, and explain why so many corporations echo the same propagandized narrative embraced by the Biden administration. The radical leftist policies, including critical race theory and opposition to voter identification policies, are leading the nation into Burnham's managerial state.

The Great Reset fully intends to *build back better* without the nuclear family. Instead, its own state managers will regulate family function. As in Communist China, state managers will dictate how many children are allowed; who goes to college; who works in the mines; who gets an apartment; who can travel; what citizens are allowed to eat; and so on and so on. It will all be determined by their ESG scores.

The managerial state is literally what its name defines. Citizens are totally managed from cradle to grave by a totalitarian surveillance state with absolute control. The collapse of the American family is the essential element of collapsing Humanity 1.0 and what it means to be a human being. Human identity, human interaction, and the human social structure that has been organized through family bonds and loyalty must be destroyed for social acceptance of man as machine.

So, the essential philosophical question is "Who will control the artificial intelligence in the machine?" Someone plans to remote-control the humanoids. The answer is, of course, the globalist elite managers themselves.

The globalist elite managers with their technocrat collaborators have taken megalomania where no man has ever gone before. They are unapologetic transhumanist supremacists who expect to live forever and control the world. They reject both Judeo-Christian life after death and Buddhist concepts of reincarnation and never-ending life forms. Transhumanists believe in eternal life on earth through the blending of man and machine. They are introducing a new life form through artificial intelligence, Humanity 2.0.

The current efforts to blur boundaries between male and female are designed to blur the established biological definitions of male and female, and then of humanity itself. What is a man? What is a woman? What is a human? Words matter. The definition of what it means to be a human being is what is contested in the movement toward Humanity 2.0 and the collectivist utilitarian ethics that animate it.

The Great Reset is a replacement ideology being forced upon citizens of the United States by the globalist elite on both sides of the corrupt American political aisle. The vehicle is political medicine and the fraudulent COVID-19 narrative. Its highest priority is the acceptance of "vaccine" mandates by the American people. With economic and political pressure from above, and medical pressure from below, the Great Reset will squeeze Americans into believing snow is black.

CHAPTER 30

Political Medicine Threatens American National Security

L
ike American education, American medicine, including the National Institutes of Health (NIH), the Centers for Disease Control and Prevention (CDC), medical research, and medical education, has experienced a seismic shift away from established Judeo-Christian norms protective of individualism toward secular bioethics and collectivist theories focusing on efficacy and the common good.

Greek physician Hippocrates of Kos (460–370 BC), considered to be the Father of Medicine, established high moral standards for treating patients that focused on protection of the individual and the physician's primary duty to the patient. Hippocrates' code of ethics became known as the Hippocratic Oath,[127] a pledge of moral conduct made by physicians of the time to the Greek gods. The oath was translated into English in the 1700s, and Western medical schools began regularly incorporating the ancient oath into graduation ceremonies.

In 1948 the Hippocratic Oath was updated to include the Declaration of Geneva, adopted by the General Assembly of the World Medical Association in response to the atrocities committed by Nazi doctors. The Declaration of Geneva[128] physician's oath pledged not to use medical knowledge to violate human rights or civil liberties, and to practice medicine without discrimination or bias.

The 1964 Hippocratic Oath,[129] rewritten by Dr. Louis Lasagna, Academic Dean at Tufts University School of Medicine, provided a secular version in response to surgical procedures, like abortion, that presented moral and religious conflicts for physicians. Most medical schools no longer require the Hippocratic Oath; instead, they allow incoming students to select or create their own oaths. Here is the oath taken by medical students of the New York Medical College[130] class of 2024 at their white coat orientation ceremony:

As a member of the New York Medical College Class of 2024, beginning this journey during these unforeseen circumstances, I stand here today, before my loved ones and fellow members of the medical community, to accept my white coat and the responsibilities with which it comes.

I take this oath with the goal of becoming the best physician I can be.

I pledge to remain humble, open-minded and to honor the legacy of the physicians who have come before me by paying it forward in the same scholarly tradition.

I recognize my duty to adapt to the dynamic landscape of medicine and to the tremendous growth in biotechnology.

I pledge to help each individual entrusted to my care to the best of my ability, in line with the founding principles of New York Medical College.

I recognize that my treatment of patients should not only reflect scientific knowledge, but also the art of empathetic care.

I pledge to be an effector of positive change in society and an advocate for the collective health of humankind.

I recognize that my newly afforded position bestows upon me unique responsibilities, which I will use to make our field of medicine a safe space by promoting equity, inclusion, and belonging.

I pledge to care for myself and my peers so that together we can provide the best service to our patients and community.

I recognize that medical school is a challenging and arduous endeavor and I must ensure my well-being in order to provide consistent care as a physician in training.

I recognize that our collective success means the best outcome for all and I will utilize inter-professional collaboration to enhance the patient experience.

With humility, honor, and gratitude, we, the students of New York Medical College Class of 2024, accept these white coats as we embark on our journey to become both skilled physicians and genuine healers.

You will notice the similarity in language between medical *change agents* who advocate for the collective health of humankind; educational *change agents* who advocate for the collective education of humankind exposed by Dr. Charlotte Iserbyt; and sexual *change agents* who advocate for the collective "sexual rights" of humankind's children exposed by Dr. Judith Reisman. The change agents marching through these institutions are implementing the seismic shift from individualism to collectivism necessary to collapse America into socialism. It is a process of controlled demolition, escalated during the Carter and Obama administrations, that negatively affects the family.

The President's Commission for the Study of Ethical Problems in Medicine and Biomedical and Behavioral Research was created by Congress at the request of President Carter in 1978, the year before he established the Department of Education.

Bioethicist Dianne Irving, MA, PhD, presented her clarifying essay "What is "Bioethics?"[131] at the Tenth Annual Conference: Life and Learning X in June 2000 at Georgetown University. Excerpts below document the seismic shift in medical ethics away from focus on the individual over the last four decades.

Dr. Irving explains how, since 1979, the utilitarian principle of *the greater good* became the ethical standard in a new field named *bioethics*, "created by Congressional fiat and immediately applied to Federal government's regulations to determine the 'ethics' of the use of human beings as research subjects." (p. 2)

Principlism, a system of ethics based on defined moral principles, was introduced to address the ethical problems of using human subjects in medical research.

I. Introduction

Contrary to "popular opinion", bioethics, as predominantly practiced today—especially as embedded in formal governmental regulations, state laws and a myriad of other documents, committees, guidelines, guidebooks, etc., around the world—is not the same thing as "ethics per se". .... As we will see, bioethics understood as "principlism" is an academic theory of ethics which was formally articulated in 1979 by the Congressionally-mandated 11-member National Commission in their Belmont Report. That Report, as mandated, identified three bioethical principles: respect for persons [autonomy], justice and beneficence. (p. 1)

IV. From World War II to the National Commission

The contemporary history of medical ethics began after World War II, especially over controversies involving medical research. Medical ethics found itself increasingly confounded as medical science advanced and medical interventions became increasingly technical. As Jonsen notes, the important bonds of the physician/patient relationship began to suffer, and it was no longer clear what was "benefit" and what was "harm." Is it "harm" to experiment on a dying person to generate better ways of curing disease for the "benefit" of other patients, even if it wouldn't "benefit" that individual patient? How should the growing intimacy of medical practice and medical research with government, commerce, and the new technologies be handled? If some patients cannot pay for medical care, who should? Who should live, and who should die? How should the limited resources of health care be justly distributed? How should the benefits and burdens of research be justly distributed? How far could individual physicians, medical investigators and the government go in advancing scientific knowledge and providing for our national security? And, of course, who should decide the answers to these difficult questions?

These were, after all, issues that philosophy, theology and the law had previously pondered, rather than medicine. These disciplines were about to find their new home in the new field of secular bioethics, but with a difference. There would be a major shift from considerations of standard medical care and practice to those of cutting-edge medical scientific research, thus eventually blurring the distinction between the respective subject matters, methods and goals of these two very different fields of endeavor, and between the roles of physician and researcher. Further, the traditional roots of "medical ethics" in the

Hippocratic Oath, religion and theology would be drastically cut as attempts to secularize "ethics" were rapidly articulated—especially for use in our "pluralistic, multicultural, democratic" societies. . . .

Of note too was the attitude of elitism exuded on all sides in the face of such complex dilemmas. Dubos explained: "We are not assembled here to solve problems. Our purpose is to air problems . . . to state our problems as clearly and thoughtfully as we can, so that they can be better analyzed by the scientific community and so that the community at large—lay people—can struggle under our guidance to form its own opinions. . . ." As Sir Charles Snow concluded, the way to deal with such problems is by foresight and intelligence and, above all, by scientists telling the truth. But "it is not enough for scientists to make statements of the greatest possible truth; [scientists] must have the courage to carry those statements through because they alone know enough to be able to impress their authority upon a world which is anxious to hear." And as Jonsen notes, "The public was only rarely invited to partake in resolving these great problems . . . for the most part, the public is seen as an audience, waiting for scientists to bring solutions to the problems they have created. . . ."

Scientists took sides for and against programs of eugenics and thought control. J.B.S. Haldane described a vision of his own "utopia," imagining the biological possibilities in the next ten thousand years. His "utopia" included broad control of physiological and psychological processes, achieved largely by pharmacological and genetic techniques, including cloning and deliberate provocation of mutations, to suit the human product for special purposes in the world of the future.

VII. The National Commission and Bioethics: A Short Analysis

B. Problems with the principles: [summary]

While the Commissioners of the *Belmont Report* gave a nod to the traditional Hippocratic understanding of Beneficence as "doing good for the patient," their definition is essentially and predominantly utilitarian, with particular emphasis placed in that *Report* on the "good" for society at large—or roughly, "the greatest good for the greatest number of people." Utilitarianism has always had a serious problem with defining in practice what "good" is, but it is generally reduced to some sort of lack of pain, or pleasure. It is clear, however, that their formula leaves minorities and the vulnerable out in the cold. There are no moral absolutes here—only "rules" or risk/benefit ratios, which are by definition relative. As utilitarian, the general norm or standard against which one determines if an individual action is right or wrong is "utility"; i.e., if that action is useful to achieving *good consequences*, those being defined as "the greatest good for the greatest number." The principle of Justice, too, is ultimately defined along utilitarian lines. Even the principle of Autonomy eventually ends up serving "the greatest good"—as I will indicate in a moment. At any rate, after all is said and done, bioethics is reduced to some form of utilitarianism or relativism, where "consequences" are the only morally relevant condition and the "good" of the individual person is clearly *not* top priority. (p. 3)

XI. Conclusion

This [bioethics as "principlism"] has resulted not only in the politicization of "ethics," but in the politicization of medicine and science as well—including and especially the science of human embryology. Scientific facts are now to be determined to be factually true or false by "democratic" representatives with absolutely no expertise in those fields, using a "democratic" process of "consensus" in place of the scientific method proper to the lab. Science itself has become "relative," depending on a public or political "consensus" for its verification. The consequences for health care and public policy alone will be profound.

But more disturbing is the possibility that in a deep sense we have really come full circle. It was not just the "arrogance" of the early physicians and scientists that resulted in the systemic abuse of so many human subjects in research, but often the arrogance of physicians and scientists of an essentially eugenic mindset. Much as we have tried to "distance" ourselves from the eugenic atrocities of the Nazi era and similar more recent events, our official "silence" on eugenics in the academy and elsewhere has served only to blind us to its creeping acceptance in principle in the corridors of academe and government. Has "a Eugenic Age" indeed finally arrived, or is it still just the stuff of sci-fi novels? One only has to hear the many voices of many of the current leaders of the bioethics community around the world to ascertain an accurate answer. But that assumes that we know who these bioethics leaders are, and that we listen to what they are saying. (p. 7)

One named bioethics leader is Dr. Ezekiel Emanuel, senior fellow at the radical left, Soros-funded Center for American Progress, founded by radical leftist John Podesta and run by Patrick Gaspard, past president of George Soros' Open Society Foundation.

On November 9, 2020, President-elect Joe Biden named Ezekiel Emanuel to be one of the sixteen members of his COVID-19 Advisory Board.

Dr. Emanuel is currently Vice Provost for Global Initiatives at the University of Pennsylvania. He holds a joint appointment at the University of Pennsylvania School of Medicine which announced his departure as chair of the Department of Medical Ethics and Health Policy in May 2021: "With a donation from Bill Gates, Dr. Emanuel created and co-directs the Healthcare Transformation Institute [at the University of Pennsylvania], which focuses on developing and evaluating interventions, mainly in the area of physician payment and behavior change."

Dr. Emanuel is an unapologetic globalist and eugenicist who has stated publicly that no one over 75 should receive health care. The Federalist Papers[132] website published an article in 2014 with Dr. Emanuel supporting his conviction with a graph showing that at age 75 and over, the senior's "last contribution" to society likely occurred more than a decade earlier. This completely collectivist utilitarian view, antithetical to Judeo-Christian norms that value individual human life, is being espoused by a member of President Biden's COVID-19 Advisory Board.

In a July 27, 2020, National Review article, "Ezekiel Emanuel Wants to Shut Down the Country Again,"[133] Wesley Smith describes Emanuel's totalitarian attitude:

If Ezekiel Emanuel thinks it is wise policy, the country's preem-
inent bioethicist generally wants to mandate it. For example,
he repeatedly called for <u>mandatory national shutdowns</u>. He has
urged that <u>all children be forced to have a flu shot</u> every year.
He also advocated that different levels of <u>government impose
vaccine mandates</u>. He also believes that doctors should be <u>re-
quired to perform abortions</u> when asked, or find an abortionist
for the patient if they have a conscientious objection. "Mandate"
should be Emanuel's middle name.

Bioethics under Ezekiel "Mandate" Emanuel's utilitarian tutelage is
medical tyranny and unconscionably manipulative. In a July 14, 2021,
article on the website STAT that Emanuel co-wrote with Matthew Guido
and Patricia Hong, he actually tried to shame health care workers into
getting jabbed. (More about STAT below.) The article, "<u>Vaxxed or axed:
To protect patients, every health care worker must be vaccinated</u>,"[134] is
an outrage, the antithesis of American values. According to Emanuel:

> Mandating vaccination isn't just the right thing to do, it's also
> the ethical thing to do. All health care workers pledge that their
> highest duty is to promote the best interests of their patients.
> In the words of the <u>Hippocratic Oath</u>, physicians pledge that,
> "Into whatever homes I go, I will enter them for the benefit of
> the sick. . . ." (There were no hospitals at the time of Hippo-
> crates, only home care.) <u>Nurses pledge</u> to "devote myself to the
> welfare of those committed to my care." And on it goes for all
> health care workers, from phlebotomists to <u>pharmacists</u>: They
> all pledge to use their skills to "assure optimal outcomes for my
> patients."
>
> A vaccine mandate simply puts into effect health care workers'
> promise to patients and the community. . . . It's one thing for a
> retail worker not to get vaccinated. It's unethical and appalling
> for a health care worker.

Let's talk about STAT, sometimes called STAT News, a health-oriented
website launched in 2015 by globalist John W. Henry, owner of the
leftist *Boston Globe* that endorsed Hillary Clinton in 2016 and Joe
Biden in 2020. STAT is not an independent medical journal that presents both sides of the COVID-19 controversy. STAT simply parrots the
political medicine provided by the CDC as *settled science*. In medicine,

the word STAT refers to a diagnostic or therapeutic procedure that needs to be performed immediately.

Ezekiel Emanuel is the quintessential tyrant of political medicine who spews his radical leftist agenda as if it was legitimate science. He ignores the thousands of doctors and scientists worldwide who discredit his CDC claims with legitimate scientific studies. In contrast, Ezekiel Emanuel uses the Hegelian dialectic to support his political agenda disguised as public health.

The political medicine disseminated by the CDC and advanced by Ezekiel Emanuel claims that to protect patients, health care workers must be "vaccinated." It is an entirely false assumption that the entire mandate is based upon! Even the CDC has finally admitted that the experimental mRNA treatments are NOT legally vaccines because they do not provide immunity or prevent transmission. So, how exactly are experimental jabs protecting patients from their health care workers?

Saying something does not make it true, unless of course you are living in the magical subjective reality of political medicine. Propaganda thrives in its world of feelings and subjective reality. Ezekiel Emanuel uses his position as a "bioethicist" to promote the globalist political medicine of the CDC. His mandates rob citizens of their individual freedom by making an experimental jab a condition of employment, entertainment, shopping, travel, and basically living one's life in a free society of ordered liberty.

Ezekiel Emanuel's tyrannical mandates usurp parental rights by denying parents their constitutional rights and freedom to make health choices for their children. Political medicine is a deceitful vehicle for total social control. Families no longer have the authority to make family health decisions—the state has awarded itself that authority through "vaccine" mandates. When families are denied their familial rights, they cease to exist as a meaningful entity in society.

Tyrannical mandates rob individual citizens of their constitutional rights by denying them the freedom to make health choices for themselves. When individuals are denied their individual rights, they cease to exist as a meaningful entity in society.

Political medicine is the colossal humanitarian hoax that awards the state total social control in the name of public health. Dr. Ezekiel Emanuel, a 21st-century *bioethicist*, and Dr. Anthony Fauci (see Chapter 31) are two prime-time hucksters.

Dr. Emanuel's February 2021 white paper, "The Future of Value-Based Payment: A Road Map to 2030,"[135] is a prelude to socialized medicine that awards the state total control of the health care sector. Ezekiel "Mandate" Emanuel lives up to his epithet with his proposed government takeover of health care.

What Ezekiel Emanuel describes in glowing terms as moving U.S. health care system "from volume to value" is the government takeover of private health care. In Emanuel's "value-based" system the government determines the value of services rendered. Doctors become pawns in the "bioethics" of utilitarian collectivism, and the government controls the distribution of health services and the payment for those services. Welcome to socialized medicine—for your own good, of course.

Ezekiel Emanuel co-wrote an article with then-wife, Linda, published in JAMA 1992.[136] The article presents and compares four models of the physician-patient relationship: *informative*, *interpretive*, *deliberative*, and *paternalistic*. All four models have a differentiating role for patient autonomy and are compared on that basis. Patient autonomy is described as:

> Informative: Choice of, and control over, medical care
>
> Interpretive: Self-understanding relevant to medical care
>
> Deliberative: Moral self-development relevant to medical care
>
> Paternalistic: Assenting to objective values

What interested me most was his fifth model, the *instrumental* model, which excludes patient autonomy as irrelevant:

> The four models are not exhaustive. At a minimum there might be added a fifth: the *instrumental* model. In this model, the patient's values are irrelevant; the physician aims for some goal independent of the patient, such as the good of society or furtherance of scientific knowledge. The Tuskegee syphilis experiment[i–iii] [footnotes listed at end of chapter] and the Willowbrook hepatitis study[iv-v] [footnotes listed at end of chapter] are examples of this model. As the moral condemnation of these cases reveals, this model is not an ideal but an aberration. Thus, we have not elaborated herein.

The instrumental model, rejected in 1992, is the accepted 2021 socialist utilitarian model that Ezekiel Emanuel is unapologetically advancing in America today.

Ezekiel Emanuel's utilitarian bioethics supports the collective. Collectivism is antithetical to individualism and to the family. In collectivism, parents are loyal to the state, not to each other and not to their children. George Orwell's lesson in *Animal Farm* is twofold: children removed from their parents and raised by the state are loyal to their masters, and the elite always take care of themselves. In Orwell's words, "some animals are more equal than others."

Russia's Nikita Khrushchev predicted Ezekiel Emanuel's eventual success with the collectivist *instrumental* model in a message to the UN on September 29, 1959:

> Your children's children will live under communism, You Americans are so gullible. No, you won't accept communism outright; but we will keep feeding you small doses of socialism until you will finally wake up and find you already have communism. We will not have to fight you; we will so weaken your economy, until you will fall like overripe fruit into our hands. The democracy will cease to exist when you take away from those who are willing to work and give to those who would not.

Footnotes from the JAMA 1992 article:

Four Models of the Physician-Patient Relationship Ezekiel J. Emanuel, MD, PhD, Linda L. Emanuel, MD, PhD, JAMA, April 22/29, 1992. Vol 267, No 16

[i] Jones JH. Bad Blood. New York, NY: Free Press, 1981

[ii] Final Report of the Tuskegee Syphilis Study Ad Hoc Advisory Panel. Washington, DC: Public Health   Service; 1973.

[iii] Brandt AM. Racism and research: the case of the Tuskegee Syphilis Study. Hastings Cent Rep. 1978;8:21–29.

[iv] Krugman S, Giles JP. Viral hepatitis: new light on an old disease. JAMA. 1970;212:1019–1029.

[v] Ingelfinger FJ. Ethics of experiments on children. New England Journal Med. 1973;288:791–792.

CHAPTER 31

Personnel Is Policy

Personnel is policy. The Biden/Obama/Harris regime is staffed with radical leftists whose anti-American collectivist views continue to become policies that dismantle traditional American norms and destroy American families. The most dangerous of all the political medicine players continues to be the lethally corrupt Dr. Anthony Fauci. He is the mouthpiece for the globalist elite, promoter of *the greater good*, director of the National Institute of Allergy and Infectious Diseases (NIAID) since 1984, and chief medical advisor to President Biden and former President Trump.

The website Washington News Daily reported on October 4, 2021, "Dr. Anthony Fauci declares Americans should 'give up' individual freedom 'for the greater good of society.'"[137]

> "I think what people have to appreciate, that indeed you do have personal liberties for yourself and you should be in control of that," Fauci began. "But you are a member of society, and as a member of society, reaping all of the benefits of being a member of society, you have a responsibility to society."

> "I think each of us, particularly in the context of a pandemic that's killing millions of people, you have got to look at it and say, 'There comes a time when you do have to give up what you consider your individual right of making your own decision for the greater good of society,'" he explained.

> "There is no doubt that that's the case," Fauci added.

Anthony Fauci is the quintessential example of how the politicized and ethically compromised medical establishment has partnered with Big Pharma and embraced the pharmacological germ/vaccine theory of disease that supports *scientism*. Scientism is rooted in the collectivist *bioethics* of the *instrumental* model where the patient's values are irrelevant and the physician aims for some goal independent of the patient, such as the good of society or furtherance of scientific knowledge.

Scientism is an exaggerated trust in the power of scientific knowledge and techniques applied to all areas of investigation (as in philosophy, the social sciences, and the humanities). It is a worldview that science is the best and only objective means by which society should determine both its values, and what distinguishes justified belief from mere opinion.

For many members of society, scientism has replaced traditional religion as the moral and ethical authority, and it supports the seismic changes in American medical ethics. *"Trust the science"* is now a colloquial expression.

The limitation of scientism is that not all questions can be answered with science. The failure of scientism is that it relies solely on the integrity of scientists—not science itself. Scientism is a dangerous humanitarian hoax that supports political medicine in the name of public health, and political consensus in the name of science.

Using the utilitarian *instrumental* model of bioethics described by Ezekiel Emanuel in 1992, scientism created political medicine, a gross perversion of honest science in medicine. Political medicine has an agenda that defies the research honesty demanded prior to the '60s shift. When political *ends justify the means*, the results are falsification of data, manipulated statistics, exaggerated claims, and failure to do requisite safety studies.

The orchestrated 2020 COVID-19 "pandemic" is scientism's masterpiece. Based in the Hegelian dialectic that denies objective reality and blurs boundaries between truth and lies, the *bioethics* of scientism presents its political agenda as science, and its politicians as scientists.

In December 2016, just after the presidential election, President Donald Trump contacted Robert F. Kennedy Jr. to discuss vaccine safety. In a <u>12-minute video interview</u>,[138] Robert F. Kennedy Jr. describes the meeting, with the president telling him he thought vaccines were making people sick. The president had three women friends whose young, healthy children were perfectly healthy until being vaccinated at their wellness visits at about two years of age.

President Trump asked Kennedy to chair a vaccine safety commission. Kennedy recommended opening the existing medical databases to study the issue, and was appointed to lead an investigation into vaccine safety. A week later, pharmaceutical giant Pfizer made a $1 million contribution to Trump's inaugural celebration. Afterward, the White House enthusiasm for the Kennedy commission cooled.

The vaccine safety meetings continued with Anthony Fauci. Kennedy insisted all they had to do was open the Vaccine Safety Datalink and review the existing records for the top nine HMOs; independent scientists could study the data. But that never happened. Anthony Fauci made sure nobody got the information.

Vaccine safety requires honest scientific inquiry. It is not a political construct; it is a public health issue addressed with the safety of the individual as its highest priority. Political medicine is driven by consensus of the stakeholders. Pharmaceutical companies are driven by profit and their globalist agenda. Vaccine safety is not Big Pharma's highest priority, since they were indemnified from vaccine harm in 1986. This inherent conflict of interest would be disqualifying in traditional medical ethics, but in utilitarian bioethics the stakeholders determine the *greater good.*

Trump appointed Pfizer's lobbyist, Scott Gottlieb, to run the Food and Drug Administration (FDA) and Eli Lilly's lobbyist, Alex Azar, to run Health and Human Services (HHS). They immediately shut down Kennedy's vaccine safety investigation.

Personnel is policy, and hiring Big Pharma to run our public health institutions was the lethal error of Trump's presidency. Trusting the untrustworthy destroyed Trump's presidency, the American economy, and world health.

The entire manufactured hysteria surrounding COVID-19 is political medicine, not medical science. It is a psychological operation (PSYOP) using fear to manipulate behavior. Thought precedes behavior, and fear is an extremely powerful motivating force.

The COVID-19 jabs are not legally vaccines. They neither provide immunity nor prevent transmission. They are the sinister vehicle for totalitarian social control deceitfully labeled "vaccines" to dupe the public into believing that they provide protection.

The CDC actually changed the definition of vaccine to disguise its deception. The Federalist Papers[139] reports that from May 16, 2018, to September 1, 2021, the CDC[140] listed the definitions for vaccine and vaccination as:

> **Vaccine:** A product that stimulates a person's immune system to produce immunity to a specific disease, protecting the person from that disease. Vaccines are usually administered through needle injections, but can also be administered by mouth or sprayed into the nose.

> **Vaccination:** The act of introducing a vaccine into the body to produce immunity to a specific disease.

Notice that the definitions for vaccine and vaccination state that they "produce immunity."

As of September 1, 2021, the CDC had switched[141] the definitions:

> **Vaccine:** A preparation that is used to stimulate the body's immune response against diseases. Vaccines are usually administered through needle injections, but some can be administered by mouth or sprayed into the nose.

> **Vaccination:** The act of introducing a vaccine into the body to produce protection from a specific disease.

Now, according to the CDC, vaccines will "stimulate the body's immune response" rather than "produce immunity," and vaccinations produce "protection" rather than "immunity."

Using dialectical deceit, the CDC redefined the terms to deceive the public.

Even worse, from its inception, the entire coronavirus "pandemic" narrative has operated on George Soros' principle of reflexivity, which refers to economic markets' reflexive response to news—fake or factual. This is how it works:

Soros is an unapologetic globalist and heavy contributor to liberal mainstream media outlets. According to Media Research Center[142] (MRC), Soros has direct ties to thirty mainstream news outlets including the *New York Times, Washington Post*, The Associated Press, National Public Radio, CNN, and ABC. These outlets have many high-level employees who serve on the boards of Soros-funded media operations. Columbia Journalism Review (CJR), which describes itself as "a watchdog and a friend of the press in all its forms," lists seven different investigative reporting projects funded by Soros' Open Society Institute including ProPublica, Center for Public Integrity, Center for Investigative Reporting, The Lens, and The Columbia School of Journalism which operates CJR.

So, media outlets disseminating fake news deliberately manipulate public opinion and, therefore, public behavior. If Soros wants to drive stock prices down, his television lackeys ominously predict a serious downturn and the public predictably responds with panic selling. The false prediction of a downturn results in an actual downturn (reflexivity[143]) and Soros goes on a buying spree. When stock prices return to their appropriate levels, Soros sells the stock and makes millions more to finance the ambitions of his radical leftist Open Society Foundation.

The globalists running the COVID-19 operation are using the same principles of reflexivity to sell "vaccines" for social control—not immunizations for public health.

The initial COVID-19 projections were wildly exaggerated intentionally to cause massive public fear → reflexive public hysteria → reflexive economic shutdown → worldwide economic collapse → Bill & Melinda Gates Foundation commits more than $1.9 billion to support the global response to COVID-19 including efforts at detection, treatment, and vaccine development → Gates is hailed as a savior by the colluding media for providing COVID-19 deliverance as he makes billions selling dangerous UNNECESARY mRNA "vaccines" equipped to track and thereby control every citizen of the world.

This is globalist Armageddon—the last-ditch all-out globalist power grab using the coronavirus economic bioweapon developed with illegal U.S. NIAID gain-of-function funds in China's Wuhan Institute of Virology, against the world population to achieve absolute global control by exploiting the reflexivity of fear. It is a monstrous humanitarian hoax peddling Gates' "vaccines" as deliverance from the plague when, in fact, it is the "vaccines" that will enslave the world's population.

The propaganda campaign promoting Covid-19 "vaccines" is reinforced by politicized education that supports scientism, and its fraudulent claims established by consensus.

The military-industrial complex that Eisenhower warned us about in 1961 is now a multiplex. Academia is an integral part of the effort to collapse America into socialism. A closed, politicized educational system graduates indoctrinated *experts*, who continue to parrot the collectivist curriculum content they were propagandized with. Anthony Fauci is in charge of NIAID research grants, so it is difficult for anyone to speak out against him or get funding for opposing theories.

Senator Rand Paul, a physician and vocal critic of Anthony Fauci, exposed how Fauci lied to Congress when he repeatedly denied that his agency's grant funding went to gain-of-function research on novel coronavirus research at the Wuhan Institute of Virology.

Anthony Fauci is director of the U.S. National Institute of Allergy and Infectious Diseases (NIAID). The NIAID is part of the National Institutes of Health (NIH), which is an Operating Division within the Department of Health and Human Services (HHS). This <u>organizational structure</u>[144] helps explains how Fauci is able to mislead, obfuscate, and deny his culpability in the gain-of-function research funded by American taxpayers. Dr. Christine Grady, Anthony Fauci's wife, is Chief of the Department of Bioethics at the NIH and also serves as Head of the Section on Human Subjects Research.

Nine hundred pages of recently released documents acquired through the Freedom of Information Act (FOIA) prove that the NIH funded gain-of-function research on coronaviruses via EcoHealth Alliance, a U.S. based non-governmental organization, and its subrecipient the Wuhan Institute of Virology.

Americans have entrusted their public health to the NIH and its subsidiaries. It is essential for Americans to know that the information they are receiving from Anthony Fauci is as false and misleading as the information Fauci gave to then-president Trump.

The Book of Humanitarian Hoaxes: Killing America with 'Kindness',[145] released the summer before the 2020 election, included this iconic photograph and meme of President Trump:

> *In reality they're not after me, they're after you. I'm just in the way.*

Donald J. Trump ✓
@realDonaldTrump

IN REALITY
THEY'RE NOT AFTER ME
THEY'RE AFTER YOU

I'M JUST IN THE WAY

10:49 PM · Dec 18, 2019 · Twitter for iPhone

Because of the stolen 2020 election, President Trump is no longer in the way. Joe Biden is now in the White House, and Americans are under direct attack by the radical leftist administration and its assaults on our individual freedom, including medical freedom. Dr. Ezekiel Emanuel's attempts to mandate "vaccines" for all Americans is a case in point.

Knowing that medical education is funded largely by Big Pharma and the Rockefeller Foundation is essential in understanding the public health vector in the globalist race for a one-world government. Anthony Fauci is America's spokesman for political medicine and its globalist objectives.

The military/industrial/medical/academia complex supports the pharmaceutical/medical model. It is a closed, politicized model that claims *settled science* by consensus. The public is offered political medicine disguised as public health, and then *bioethicist* Ezekiel Emanuel proclaims it is the "moral responsibility" of health care workers to get the jab. It is a closed system of medical propaganda designed for totalitarian control.

Public education, with its insidious indoctrinating curricula from K–12 through university, graduates anti-American, pro-collectivism students in preparation for world citizenship. Similarly, medical schools are graduating impassioned "experts" in the pharmaceutical/vaccine model they have been indoctrinated with.

Social policies and public health policies are no longer determined by the scientific method and pure science; they are the products of politicized medicine and doublespeak consensus. The objective of the current military/industrial/academia/pharmaceutical model is total social control, served up on a vaccine platter "for your own good," of course.

Robert F. Kennedy Jr. has just released his 2021 blockbuster *The Real Anthony Fauci: Bill Gates, Big Pharma, and the Global War on Democracy and Public Health*. Kennedy's introduction states:

> I wrote this book so that Americans—both Democrat and Republican—can understand Dr. Fauci's pernicious role in allowing pharmaceutical companies to dominate our government and subvert our democracy, and to chronicle the key role Dr. Fauci has played in the current coup d'état against democracy.

Politicized medicine and politicized education are lethal weapons being used against Americans by the enemy within, to collapse America. The perpetrators are being protected by the politicized FBI, CIA, and Justice Department.

The enemies of American freedom have created a closed information system that indoctrinates unsuspecting Americans with collectivist propaganda. It is a system that relies on *disinformed* consent to succeed. The enemy within is the most deadly because it hides in plain sight.

CHAPTER 32

Psychiatry: Covert Weapon of the Ruling Class

Psychiatry, like every other force in nature, can be used for either construction or destruction. The asymmetric information war being waged against America includes an overarching psychological component that targets Americans and is designed to unfreeze → change → refreeze society into socialism using Kurt Lewin's change model[146] (see Chapter 8).

Daniel Estulin's second book, *Tavistock Institute: Social Engineering the Masses*,[147] exposes the sinister use of psychiatry to melt American minds and brainwash Americans against themselves.

Tavistock Institute's singular goal is to break down the psychological strength of the individual so that he or she is incapable of opposing globalism's New World Order. Techniques that break down family unity, and family values of religion, honor, patriotism, and sexual behavior, are all weaponized to destabilize the individual (unfreeze) and encourage behaviors antithetical to established norms (change). The reeducated individual, unable to form permanent, stable, lasting relationships, is socially engineered into a submissive citizen of the New World Order (refreeze).

Estulin's introduction states:

> Tavistock in Sussex, England, "is the world's center for mass brainwashing and social engineering activities." From a crude beginning at Wellington House, grew a sophisticated organization that was to shape the destiny of the entire planet, and in the process, change the paradigm of modern society. . . .

> During WWII, "Tavistock was the headquarters of the British Army's Psychological Warfare Bureau, which, through the arrangements of the Special Operations Executive also dictated policy to the United States Armed Forces in the matters of psycholog-

ical warfare."

Tavistock Institute began as an outgrowth of Tavistock Clinic, where British army psychiatrists worked to rehabilitate soldiers after World War II. Kurt Lewin's early work provided extraordinary insights into the human mind and social conditioning possibilities that were used at Tavistock Clinic, and later at Tavistock Institute.

In 1947, Britain's Tavistock Institute of Human Relations (TIHR) was established through a grant from the American Rockefeller Foundation. Tavistock Clinic's early rehabilitative military work provided the foundation for the multifaceted social engineering through psychological manipulation that has attacked the United States and the nuclear American family since the end of World War II. Daniel Estulin explains:

> What's under assault are not only our individual human rights, but rather the very institution of the "nation state" republic from the oligarchy's "massive social engineering program conducted through Tavistock Institute of Human Relations and other much larger, integrated network of centers of applied social psychology and social engineering that emerged in the aftermath of WWII." These groups regard us and the principles of nation states as their axiomatic philosophical enemy. . . . Each new measure viewed on its own may seem an aberration, but a whole host of changes as part of an ongoing continuum constitutes a shift—towards total enslavement. (pp. 2, 4)

America fought World War II to defeat the expansionism and megalomania of Hitler, Mussolini, and Hirohito. The end of the war did not, however, end the will to power or desire for world dominance. President Eisenhower was not interested in global domination, and chose instead the reconstruction of Europe under the Marshall Plan. His objective was to create allies and trading partners, and preserve the Westphalian world order of sovereign, cooperating, independent nations.

A political split ensued that divided America. Eisenhower's side chose the Marshall Plan and national sovereignty; the Rockefeller side chose globalism and the establishment of one-world planetary governance. Eisenhower ended his presidential term with an ominous warning at his farewell address[148] on January 17, 1961:

> Until the latest of our world conflicts, the United States had

no armaments industry. American makers of plowshares could, with time and as required, make swords as well. But now we can no longer risk emergency improvisation of national defense; we have been compelled to create a permanent armaments industry of vast proportions. Added to this, three and a half million men and women are directly engaged in the defense establishment. We annually spend on military security more than the net income of all United States corporations.

This conjunction of an immense military establishment and a large arms industry is new in the American experience. The total influence—economic, political, even spiritual—is felt in every city, every state house, every office of the Federal government. We recognize the imperative need for this development. Yet we must not fail to comprehend its grave implications. Our toil, resources and livelihood are all involved; so is the very structure of our society.

In the councils of government, we must guard against the acquisition of unwarranted influence, whether sought or unsought, by the military-industrial complex. The potential for the disastrous rise of misplaced power exists and will persist.

We must never let the weight of this combination endanger our liberties or democratic processes. We should take nothing for granted; only an alert and knowledgeable citizenry can compel the proper meshing of huge industrial and military machinery of defense with our peaceful methods and goals, so that security and liberty may prosper together.

Akin to, and largely responsible for, the sweeping changes in our industrial-military posture has been the technological revolution during recent decades.

In this revolution, research has become central; it also becomes more formalized, complex, and costly. A steadily increasing share is conducted for, by, or at the direction of, the Federal government.

Today, the solitary inventor, tinkering in his shop, has been overshadowed by task forces of scientists in laboratories and testing fields. In the same fashion, the free university, historically the fountainhead of free ideas and scientific discovery, has experienced a revolution in the conduct of research. Partly because of the huge costs involved, a government contract becomes virtually a substitute for intellectual curiosity. For every old blackboard there are now hundreds of new electronic computers.

The prospect of domination of the nation's scholars by Federal employment, project allocations, and the power of money is ever present and is gravely to be regarded.

Yet, in holding scientific research and discovery in respect, as we should, we must also be alert to the equal and opposite danger that public policy could itself become the captive of a scientific-technological elite.

It is the task of statesmanship to mold, to balance, and to integrate these and other forces, new and old, within the principles of our democratic system—ever aiming toward the supreme goals of our free society.

Eisenhower's warning in 1961 was at the beginning of the third industrial revolution—the digital revolution. He spoke to the nation before home computers were introduced in 1970, and before the World Wide Web became publicly accessible in 1991. Eisenhower could only hint at the possibilities of a fourth industrial revolution that would blur the boundaries between the physical, digital, and biological worlds—still science fiction in 1961.

Yet Eisenhower understood that any partnership between government and private industry could threaten American freedom and sovereignty by tilting the balance of power toward a scientific-technological elite.

The singular goal of Tavistock Institute was to foster globalism by conditioning the American public to reject Americanism and embrace globalism through psychological manipulation. The opposing factions for the future of America were defined and the enemy within activated.

Globalism is the existential enemy of a sovereign United States of America as a constitutional republic. The strategy and tactical plan devised 70 years ago was for the United States to be destroyed from within. The three pillars of American greatness—family, faith, and freedom—were all targeted by the enemies of American freedom and American sovereignty.

Alliances were forged and the globalist narrative echoed throughout the world. Corporations and educational, economic, and medical institutions partnered with the lethally corrupt United Nations to propagandize generations into believing that globalism's reimagined humanity and binary New World Order of rulers and ruled is deliverance from evil.

Tavistock's operating principle is simple:

* First, the more familiar something is, the more accepted it is.

* Second, whoever controls the educational curriculum controls the future.

* Third, truth is what the media say it is, so the fake news media determine truth, not the facts—objective reality is replaced with subjective reality.

Those who ran Tavistock Institute realized that television was the single greatest vehicle for mass indoctrination and social engineering ever created. News and entertainment programming offered by globalist companies, using mass media technologies, presented propagandized content to indoctrinate the masses. Contrast and compare how the family was presented in the 1950s with how the family is presented today.

Yuri Bezmenov, a former KGB propagandist, worked as a "journalist" inside the Western countries he was tasked with subverting. Bezmenov defected to Canada in 1970 and began giving lectures and interviews to warn Western nations about ongoing Soviet tactics being used to subvert their countries.

In his 1984 interview[149] with G. Edward Griffin, Bezmenov explained that the main focus of the KGB is not espionage. The emphasis is on ideological subversion, active measures, or psychological warfare. During the interview Bezmenov defined[150] the four stages of ideological subversion involved in a communist takeover of a Western country as:

> I. DEMORALIZATION (15–20 years)
> Indoctrination with Marxism-Leninism.
> Takes 15–20 years to educate one generation without any counter-balance.

II. DESTABILIZATION (2–5 years)
Destabilize economy, foreign relations, and military.

III. CRISIS (6 weeks)
Violent change of power.

IV. NORMALIZATION (indefinitely)
Creation and acceptance of the new normal. Lasts indefinitely.

Bezmenov explained that the Marxist goal is to change perceptions of reality to such an extent that no one is able to come to sensible conclusions to defend himself, his family, or his country. It is brainwashing, to the extent that facts no longer matter. Tavistock's goal is the same. Both are variations on Bertrand Russell's psychological warfare articulated in *The Impact of Science on Society*, when he advocates weaponizing education such that children will eventually believe that snow is black.

Psychiatry is the covert weapon of the ruling class. In 1956 Dutch psychiatrist Dr. Joost Meerloo published *The Rape of the Mind*.[151] This extraordinary book explores how a free human mind can be transformed into an automatically responding machine. He wrote the book for the general public after World War II *to bring order to the chaos of our particular epoch*. (p. 15)

Meerloo describes brainwashing, thought control, and menticide as the methods by which man's integrity can be violated. He brings awareness as a warning of the dangers which threaten a free society. Dr. Meerloo coined the word *menticide*, which literally means to kill the mind:

> Menticide is an old crime against the human mind and spirit but systematized anew. It is an organized system of psychological intervention and judicial perversion through which a [ruling class] can imprint [their] own opportunistic thoughts upon the minds of those [they] plan to use and destroy. (p. 28)

Dr. Meerloo escaped the Nazis and became Chief of the Psychological Department of the Netherlands Forces in England. He interviewed victims of Nazi terror and torture, and learned how the Nazis extracted false confessions in order to use the prisoners for propaganda purposes.

Meerloo describes how totalitarians use menticide:

> deliberately, openly, unashamedly, as part of their official policy,

as a means of consolidating and maintaining their power, though, of course, they give a different explanation to the whole procedure—it's all confession of real and treacherous crimes. (p. 35)

False confessions are the result of brainwashing so that facts no longer matter. What was once a weapon used by foreign enemies against prisoners of war is now being used domestically. The enemy within is using anti-American propaganda and brainwashing techniques to melt American minds.

Schools and universities across America are indoctrinating students with anti-American critical race theory (CRT) that posits America is a systemically racist evil empire. The goal of its false premise is false confessions used for propaganda purposes to demand social justice in the form of collectivism.

The war against Christianity is not merely the elimination of Christmas in schools—it is the globalist elite's deliberate attempt to destroy American Judeo-Christian morality and replace it with leftism's moral relativism, historical revisionism, political correctness, and critical race theory.

The Tavistock-generated identity politics of leftist victimhood has duped two generations of Americans into believing that one-world government will provide "social justice" for their perceived victimhood. The reality is that one-world government has no middle class, no upward mobility, no national sovereignty, and no individual freedoms. One-world government is a binary socio-political system consisting of a small ruling class and an enslaved population that serves them.

What defines intersectionality and identity politics? The twin foundational psychodynamics of identity politics are victimhood and regression. The branding of Americans animates identity politics. Black Americans, white Americans, gay Americans, straight Americans, rich Americans, poor Americans, etc., etc., are all divisive labels used by the Biden regime to separate Americans into a house divided.

Globalist media and business corporations echo the same false premises for the same purpose of exacting false confessions from a confused public. The value of false confessions for propaganda is essential to understanding the current media and educational indoctrination of critical race theory and how it affects the nuclear and national American families.

A political bifurcation has been created between parents and their children, brothers and sisters, extended family members, friends and neighbors, and co-workers. The purpose of the war on the nuclear family is to destroy its moral authority and shift family loyalty to the state. The nuclear family in America is being shattered, the new religion of leftism is replacing traditional Judeo-Christian norms, and globalism is replacing Americanism as the international ethos.

Perhaps the most divisive issue facing our nation is the COVID-19 debacle. American psychiatrist Dr. Peter R. Breggin has spent his career fighting abuses in the medical and psychiatric fields, especially the abuses of electroshock therapies, psychosurgery, and psychotropic drugs. He has a 29-page resume and has testified against drug companies hundreds of times. Dr. Breggin and his wife have written an authoritative, scholarly, extensively researched and documented book, *COVID-19 AND THE GLOBAL PREDATORS: WE ARE THE PREY.*[152]

The 600-page colossus is a stunning summary of the entire globalist effort to enslave the world. The truth of it brought me to tears. The preface, "The Pandemic Is the Opening Salvo," introduces the Breggins' purpose for writing the book:

> Our book, *COVID-19 and the Global Predators,* began with an inquiry into the source of the obviously irrational, contradictory, and harmful public health policies implemented in the name of COVID-19. Eventually, it grew so broad and deep in scope that it now requires an introductory summation of some of our major discoveries and conclusions. (p. iii)

The Breggins chronicle the stunning coordination and reach of what they named the Global Predator Network:

> We uncovered a loose but coordinated array of billionaires, tech companies, public health schools and authorities, major worldwide corporations, and their allies had been planning for at least four years to make a financial killing on what they defined and repeatedly predicted as the inevitable and soon-to-arrive pandemic. Four years ahead of time, the globalists began making massive marketing expenditures to prepare the world

> for accepting dangerously rushed vaccination programs in the future. The propaganda splurge was stunning, and before 2017 was over, they were already predicting and preparing the world specifically for a SARS-CoV pandemic through which to impose their vaccines on humanity at the first opportunity. (p. vii)

The collaborating globalists include America's top tech corporations:

> Microsoft, Apple, Alphabet (Google and YouTube), Facebook, Twitter. Almost every single billionaire remains deep in the predatory morass: Jeff Bezos, Bill Gates, Warren Buffet (a partner with Gates until he recently resigned), Mark Zuckerberg, the Waltons, Steve Balmer, Larry Page, and Michael Bloomberg. All are deeply invested in China. . . .

> Meanwhile the coalition continues to include surrogates for the top predators. Two of the most powerful are Anthony Fauci (very close to Bill Gates) and Tedros of WHO (also very close to Bill Gates and even closer to the Chinese Communists). (p. viii)

The master plan for fulfilling their predatory goals was presented in July 2017 in a 21-page PowerPoint presentation[153] made by the Coalition for Epidemic Preparedness Innovations (CEPI) to the World Health Organization (WHO).

CEPI was founded in January 2017 by the health fund Wellcome Trust, the Bill & Melinda Gates Foundation, Klaus Schwab's World Economic Forum, and a consortium that included pharmaceutical giant GlaxoSmithKline (GSK) and governments of Norway, Japan, and Germany. The fund was created as a solution to the problems encountered in developing and distributing vaccines, and empowers its founders to run the next pandemic.

Dr. Breggin writes:

> In the CEPI master plan, which WHO adopted, Bill Gates manages the vaccine production and profits from the coming pandemic while WHO manages the medical and scientific community. WHO's major role became managing the pandemic in the interest of the Chinese Communist Party and Bill Gates, two of the largest donors to the WHO. (p. xi)

Global predators are driven by power and money; internationalism suits them. As the Breggins note, "Their ethics are relativist, situational, and tailored to meet their greater goals." This comports with Dr. Ezekiel Emanuel's situational bioethics and reflects the familiar operating principle of tyrannical regimes: *The ends justify the means.*

The Breggins discuss how the entire political establishment has become entwined with the "highest circles of worldwide industry and finance and the Chinese government." They emphatically state that any denial of the Communist Chinese Party goals of reshaping the world into a Communist empire with itself as supreme ruler is self-deluding and suicidal.

Corrupt American politicians on both sides of the aisle are deeply invested in communist China, a situation which presents a financial conflict of interest that threatens American national security. It would be madness to pursue policies that enrich and empower an enemy of the state, but global predators have no loyalty to any particular state— they are internationalists, desiring unlimited power and wealth in an unrestricted global marketplace.

Klaus Schwab has become the spokesperson for the Global Predator Network. His 2020 book, *COVID-19 and the Great Reset,* describes the insidious predation. Breggins writes:

> The Great Reset aims to further empower people of great wealth and influence to use docile top-down governments to exploit the world. In the process, it plans to distort human nature and contemporary societies to create more conformist people. The newly engineered human, this product of transhumanism, will happily live under their guidance, despite crushing deprivations of personal freedom and quality of life. Population control will help enable the remaining people to have enough food and limited amenities, while preserving planet Earth by reducing the number of human consumers and polluters. . . .
>
> He [Schwab] acknowledged the greatest threat to globalist ambitions [is] the patriotic democratic republics, especially the United States with its love of individualism and freedom. He admitted that the nemesis of globalism was President Donald Trump. (p. viii)

The Breggins share my personal assessment that the lethal error of Trump's presidency was that he trusted the untrustworthy:

> After heroically standing up to the global predators on polit-
> ical and economic issues, President Trump played into their
> hands by refusing to fight their totalitarian assault in the guise
> of treating COVID-19. . . . All of President Trump's accomplish-
> ments were erased or set back by his submission to the totali-
> tarian COVID-19 strategies of the global predators. (pp. xiv–xv)

The Breggins' book is an encyclopedic documentation of the Global
Predator Network—its goals, tactics, successes, failures, challenges, and
most importantly, its abusive strategy of terrorizing us to tame us. Using
their covert weapon, the predatory globalists are achieving the Marxist
goal of changing public perceptions of reality.

COVID-19 totalitarianism is using the same brainwashing techniques
used against prisoners of war to destabilize them and break their hold
on objective reality; it is menticide. Maintaining an atmosphere of
fear, creating the sense of emergency, isolating people from family and
friends, masking, inconsistent messaging, and never-ending threats—all
are psychological manipulations to change our perceptions of reality
to such an extent that no one is able to come to sensible conclusions
to defend himself, his family, or his country. It is what Yuri Bezmenov
described as brainwashing to the extent that facts no longer matter.

The war between objective and subjective reality has bifurcated our
country, collapsing the nuclear and national American families as
family members battle over what is real. *A house divided against itself
cannot stand.*

Abraham Lincoln's famous "House Divided Speech"[154] delivered in
1858 was about slavery. Today we are facing an equivalent battle between defending freedom in our constitutional republic or surrendering to the slavery of predatory globalism.

CHAPTER 33

Transhumanism and Technocracy

The evolution to transhumanism is an attack on the American family. Transhumanism eliminates the nuclear family and transfers family functions, family authority, and family loyalty to whoever or whatever controls the transhuman. In the case of the Great Reset, family functions, authority, and loyalty are transferred to the predatory globalist managerial state.

Whether an idea is used for construction or destruction depends upon the user. The Global Predator Network is collapsing the American family by using its influence for deconstruction. The difference between theory and practice is determined by the practitioner. Education depends upon the educator, science depends upon the scientist, and public policy depends upon the politician. The Hegelian dialectic blurs the boundary between practice and practitioner to promote indoctrination as education, scientism as science, and transhumanism as human progress.

Transhumanism is the fusion of human and machine. There are, of course, constructive and marvelous blendings of humans and machines: prosthetics allow amputees to walk, cochlear implants allow children to hear, and pacemakers record heart rhythms for remote medical monitoring.

Implants are part of the Internet of Things (IoT), physical objects that are embedded with sensors, processing ability, software, and other technologies that collect, connect, and exchange data with other devices and systems over the Internet or other communications networks. Implants are an example of the technological advances relying on 5G network technology for connectivity (discussed Chapter 28).

IoT is promoted as one of the most important technologies of the 21st century because it enhances connectivity and communications between people, processes, and things. IoT allows people and machines to "talk" with each other. Conversational artificial intelligence (AI) has provided natural language processing to IoT devices and created digital personal assistants like Alexa and Siri.

AI advancements in image recognition use artificial neural networks to solve artificial intelligence problems: the machine learns. Artificial neural networks mimic neural brain activity and use complex mathematical algorithms for information processing. Machine analyses of highly complex eye scans and image recognition are being used for self-driving cars and to augment interpretation of three-dimensional medical images for cancer screening.

Machines and applications acquire new skills using data processed by complex algorithms. The new skills enable the machines to learn and make decisions. The ability to make decisions raises the stature of machines and applications to a new level. Machines can "think."

The blurring of the boundaries between human and machine raises fundamental questions about *who* controls the machine. If cars are driven remotely, who controls the car? The car? The programmer? If human beings are implanted with programmable devices, who controls the human beings? Will humans be remotely driven like cars?

Let's consider the societal and security implications of programmable devices, applications, and AI learning algorithms for use in human genetic modification. CRISPR, the controversial genetic engineering technique, can be applied constructively in medicine to replace a mutant disease-causing gene with its correct sequence and cure the disease. But CRISPR, like any other technology, can be also be used for destruction. Who will control CRISPR systems and the bioethics that will determine how they are used?

The Internet of Things has been expanded to the Internet of Bodies. On June 23, 2020, a stunning article appeared on the Nature Portfolio Bioengineering Community blog, "Internet of Bodies (IoB): Using CRISPR to electrically connect with and control the genome."[155] Scientist Naren Bhokisham writes:

> Just like Internet of Things (IoT), IoB refers to access and control of the human body via the internet. Here, we detail how CRISPR can be used to electrically connect with the genome and as a proof of concept display control over transcriptional

informational networks inside E. coli and Salmonella.

Technology has played a transformative role in our lives and its impact on human health is never felt more than in the current times of the Covid-19 global pandemic. . . .

To aid in our pursuit, we exploited the CRISPR technology that provides the means to target any specific target in the genome. Specifically, we used the dCas9 based transcriptional activator to electrically activate and repress select genes of interests. . . .

Overall, we expect that electrical control of transcriptional networks in cells would find many biotechnology applications such as engineered probiotic bacteria that could be programmed to respond to electric stimuli in the gut. In the longer term, similar to how DNA based vaccines are being electroporated into the human body to fight Covid-19, we may expect that electrogenetic promoter circuits will be inserted into human cells to open a new modality of bioelectronic signaling.

Electroporated? Electroporation is a technique in which cells are subjected to an electrical impulse that leads to the temporary formation of pores in the cell membrane. The pores provide openings that allow foreign materials such as new DNA, vaccines, or drugs to pass into the cell.

Bhokisham's scientific study, "A redox-based electrogenetic CRISPR system to connect with and control biological information networks,"[156] was published May 15, 2020, in Nature Communications. The abstract explains how the goal of communication is the efficient transmission of information, not just in electronics but also in biology. Electronics uses electromagnetics to communicate, biology utilizes biomolecular communication. Establishing the electromagnetic to biomolecular communication channel in biological systems would be transformative for science and society. Bhokisham's team successfully interfaced the two, and established a revolutionary methodology they named electrogenetic CRISPR (eCRISPR) that enables direct communication between biological and electronic systems:

> In conclusion, we propose an electrogenetic methodology in which direct connection between electronic signals and bacterial cells can mediate expression of target genes. Emergence of eCRISPR provides the capability to electronically target specific

genes in the genome of organisms and importantly, the integration of CRISPR with electronics provides the capability to electrically turn ON and OFF several genes simultaneously. In this way, electronically programmed information is transmitted to and within biology using a medium of redox as a communication channel.

What this means is that science has found the way to deliver CRISPR therapies into the human body with user-specified control. Who will control the use and users of eCRISPR technology and the new modality of bioelectronic signaling in medicine? *Bioethicist* Ezekiel "Mandate" Emanuel? Christine Grady at NIH? Fauci at NIAID? Political medicine does not concern itself with public health, and its "vaccines" are experimental mRNA treatments. Political medicine seeks to impose transhumanism.

Transhumanism is the defining feature of the Fourth Industrial Revolution, a seismic economic and power shift that moves humankind into a new dimension—Humanity 2.0, the worldwide transmutation called the Great Reset.

Klaus Schwab's article "The Fourth Industrial Revolution: What It Means and How to Respond"[157] describes the shift in glowing terms. Originally posted December 12, 2015, in *Foreign Affairs*, a publication of the Council on Foreign Relations (CFR), it was reposted January 14, 2016, on the World Economic Forum (WEF) website:

> We stand on the brink of a technological revolution that will fundamentally alter the way we live, work, and relate to one another. In its scale, scope, and complexity, the transformation will be unlike anything humankind has experienced before. We do not yet know just how it will unfold, but one thing is clear: the response to it must be integrated and comprehensive, involving all stakeholders of the global polity, from the public and private sectors to academia and civil society.

> The First Industrial Revolution used water and steam power to mechanize production. The Second used electric power to create mass production. The Third used electronics and information technology to automate production. Now a Fourth Industrial Revolution is building on the Third, the digital

> revolution that has been occurring since the middle of the last century. It is characterized by a fusion of technologies that is blurring the lines between the physical, digital, and biological spheres . . . these changes herald the transformation of entire systems of production, management, and governance. . . .

> The possibilities of billions of people connected by mobile devices, with unprecedented processing power, storage capacity, and access to knowledge, are unlimited. And these possibilities will be multiplied by emerging technology breakthroughs in fields such as artificial intelligence, robotics, the Internet of Things [IoT], autonomous vehicles, 3-D printing, nanotechnology, biotechnology, materials science, energy storage, and quantum computing.

Schwab's enthusiastic sales pitch provides familiarity, continuity, and the recurrent promise of social justice and income equality:

> Like the revolutions that preceded it, the Fourth Industrial Revolution has the potential to raise global income levels and improve the quality of life for populations around the world . . . technological innovation will also lead to a supply-side miracle, with long-term gains in efficiency and productivity.

He soothes the reader's concerns by voicing and dismissing them:

> The revolution could yield greater inequality, particularly in its potential to disrupt labor markets. As automation substitutes for labor across the entire economy, the net displacement of workers by machines might exacerbate the gap between returns to capital and returns to labor. On the other hand, it is also possible that the displacement of workers by technology will, in aggregate, result in a net increase in safe and rewarding jobs.

Schwab forecasts safe, rewarding jobs, plus increased engagement for citizens of the world as the fusion of technologies continues to transmute mankind. He presents the fundamental shift in the definition of humanity that dehumanizes and robotizes mankind as empowering and uplifting in the new world collective:

> As the physical, digital, and biological worlds continue to converge, new technologies and platforms will increasingly enable

citizens to engage with governments, voice their opinions, coordinate their efforts, and even circumvent the supervision of public authorities. Simultaneously, governments will gain new technological powers to increase their control over populations, based on pervasive surveillance systems and the ability to control digital infrastructure. . . .

The Fourth Industrial Revolution, finally, will change not only what we do but also who we are. It will affect our identity and all the issues associated with it: our sense of privacy, our notions of ownership, our consumption patterns, the time we devote to work and leisure, and how we develop our careers, cultivate our skills, meet people, and nurture relationships. It is already changing our health and leading to a "quantified" self, and sooner than we think it may lead to human augmentation. . . .

In its most pessimistic, dehumanized form, the Fourth Industrial Revolution may indeed have the potential to "robotize" humanity and thus to deprive us of our heart and soul. But as a complement to the best parts of human nature—creativity, empathy, stewardship—it can also lift humanity into a new collective and moral consciousness based on a shared sense of destiny. It is incumbent on us all to make sure the latter prevails.

The Great Reset is the colossal humanitarian hoax of transhumanism and predatory globalist planetary governance. It is the consummate Hegelian dialectic used to obliterate the family, absorb sovereign nations into one-world government, and drive humanity from freedom into slavery. The entire narrative is fraudulently promoted as *for our own good.*

Patrick Wood, editor-in-chief of Technocracy News, explains the connection between technocracy and transhumanism in his July 11, 2021, article, "The Evil Twins of Transhumanism and Technocracy":[158]

Technocracy is to the transformation of society as Transhumanism is to the transformation of the human condition of people who would live in that society.

Wood documents the birth of technocracy:

Formalized in 1932 by scientists and engineers at Columbia

University, the movement defined itself in a 1938 edition of its magazine, *The Technocrat*:

> Technocracy is the science of social engineering, the scientific operation of the entire social mechanism to produce and distribute goods and services to the entire population.... For the first time in human history, it will be done as a scientific, technical, engineering problem.

> There will be no place for Politics, Politicians, Finance or Financiers, Rackets or Racketeers.... Technocracy will distribute by means of a certificate of distribution available to every citizen from birth to death.

Today, Technocracy is embodied in the World Economic Forum's **Great Reset** and the various United Nations' manifestations of Sustainable Development: Agenda 21, 2030 Agenda, New Urban Agenda, etc.

Wood explains how transhumanism is the means to Technocracy's ends:

> The means to the end is ultimately genetic engineering that takes over and speeds up evolution theory to create Humanity 2.0. Since the advent of CRISPR gene-editing technology, transhumans have saturated universities and private corporations to modify all categories of living things, including humans.

> What is preached as the preservation of biodiversity by the United Nations is really the takeover of genetic material, which was noted as early as 1994, just two years after the debut of Sustainable Development and Agenda 21 at the UN Conference on Economic Development (UNCED) in Rio de Janiero, Brazil....

> It is little wonder today that the pharmaceutical industry is producing gene therapy shots using genetically modified RNA to transform the body's immune system. They have been working hard since 1992 to advance the technology needed to hijack the human genome and begin the transformative pathway to Humanity 2.0.

> However, it is Technocracy that has used its "science of social engineering" techniques to manipulate twenty-two percent of the world's population into willingly accepting the transhumans'

gene-altering injections.

The consummate, predatory social engineering technique is the fraudulent coronavirus fearmongering narrative that has terrified and regressed the world's population into childish compliance. This is how it works.

The globalist narrative presents the false assumptions of scientism: Man-made climate change is killing the physical planet, and the COVID-19 pandemic is killing human life on the planet.

Then the globalists offer to "save" the planet and humanity with their experimental gene-altering messenger RNA (mRNA) treatments deceitfully labeled "vaccines." The catastrophic economic consequences launch the Great Reset and the nightmare of planetary governance in the feudal system of transhuman masters and slaves.

The Great Reset is a computer analogy that infers the *new normal* of transhumanism and technocracy. It is a slogan that redefines what it means to be human. In the reimagined serfdom of Humanity 2.0, the rulers are able to control their super-slaves' thoughts, moods, and behavior.

There is no mother, father, sister, or brother in the New World Order. The entire concept of family has been erased.

The New World Order of the Great Reset is often compared to Aldous Huxley's 1932 dystopian novel, *Brave New World.*[159] The novel opens in the World State city of London in the year 2540. World citizens are engineered in artificial wombs, educated with indoctrination programs, placed in predetermined classes based on intelligence and labor, and constantly soothed with the happy-drug Soma—Humanity 2.0. The totally engineered World State society is contrasted by the Savage Reservation in New Mexico, where natural-born people live with aging, disease, different languages, religions, cultures, and emotional outbursts—Humanity 1.0.

The world we are now facing is predatory and dystopian, but most definitely *not* brave. It is a cowering return to the feudal structure of rulers and ruled, where humanity will be reduced to a transhuman existence of mechanized totalitarianism. Americans are being duped into accepting a totalitarian surveillance state like that of communist China, where citizens' access to anything and everything is based on their social credit score that is part of the digital infrastructure.

Compliance with government mandated "moral" behavior establishes a social credit score that determines the distribution of all goods and services. Individual citizens, companies, and government organizations are monitored, scored, and ranked for compliance to the moral tenets defined by the leadership.

The Culture War on America with its inexorable march through American institutions is part of the overarching effort to collapse America in preparation for globalist domination in a planetary managerial surveillance state. The stealth attack on the nuclear American family uses medical tyranny and educational indoctrination to disrupt family cohesion and foment divisiveness. Children are the future of every society on the planet. Education is a business—its products are the students it graduates. There is nothing *progressive* about illiteracy and indoctrinated students engineered to become compliant global citizens in a binary feudal technocracy of rulers and ruled. It is the return to a jungle of predators and prey.

CHAPTER 34

Connecting the Dots . . . the Grayson File

The nuclear American family has been targeted for decades by the globalist enemies of freedom seeking planetary governance. Their will to power and megalomania is well documented and well planned. The long-term globalist strategy for the Great Reset separates children from their parents; denies family loyalty; replaces family bonding with bondage to the state; redefines the "rights" of children; and enslaves them in the transhumanist Fourth Industrial Revolution using globalized educational indoctrination.

The supremacist attitude of the globalist elite is difficult for most Americans to fathom. In case there are readers still clinging to the belief that the war on America documented in this book is hyperbole or wild conspiracy theory, please consider the Grayson File.

The Grayson File is the smoking gun that implicates the United States of America in an international technology initiative to globalize education through the United Nations Educational Scientific and Cultural Organization (UNESCO).

Investigative reporter John Klyzcek documents his discovery of the file and its contents in a shocking June 1, 2021, expose of the secret plan, "From UNESCO Study 11 to UNESCO 2050: Project BEST and the Forty-Year Plan to Reimagine Education for the Fourth Industrial Revolution,"[160]

Klyczek read the file and realized, "For over forty years, coalitions of academics, governments, corporations, and world governance bodies have colluded to build a global ed-tech [educational technology] schooling system meant to shackle children to the transhumanist Fourth Industrial Revolution."

It turns out *progressive* education is Orwellian doublespeak for progress toward the reimagined education required for the Fourth Industrial Revolution.

Excerpts from the Grayson File below will help the reader grasp the depth and breadth of the scheme to reeducate American students unbeknownst to their parents.

To read the complete "Grayson File," including UNESCO Study 11, along with the entirety of Project BEST and other related documents from the U.S. Department of Education, the reader can subscribe to John Jake Klyczek's database at his website: schoolworldorder.info.[161]

Excerpts from Klyczek's investigative report:

> I recently visited former Senior Policy Advisor to the US Office of Educational Research and Improvement, Charlotte Thomson Iserbyt, who gave me access to her archive of files that she collected from the US Department of Education. After digging through a collection of files collated by Lawrence P. Grayson, who was the Advisor for Mathematics, Science and Technology at America's National Institute of Education (NIE), I discovered that the Department of Ed's Project BEST (Basic Education Skills through Technology), which Iserbyt leaked in 1981, was actually the USA's domestic version of an international technology initiative spearheaded by the United Nations Educational Scientific and Cultural Organization (UNESCO).
>
> While stationed at the NIE, Grayson was also the US Department of Ed's liaison with UNESCO's educational technology programs, including "Study 11: New Technologies in Education", which he procured for Iserbyt in a bundle of interrelated memorandums and journals. Labeled as the "Grayson File," this folder compiled the following documents:
>
> • UNESCO Study 11 whitepapers that issue ed-tech directives to a region of 14 nation states grouping together communist, socialist, and capitalist countries;
>
> • US Department of Ed memorandums which stipulate American collaboration with Study 11 and other UNESCO technology programs;
>
> • Law journals that call for restructuring legal systems in order to globalize the computerized "information technology"

(IT) revolution necessary to streamline international ed-tech markets;

- Academic journals containing ed-tech promotionals from Project BEST contractors and UNESCO Study 11 representatives published alongside commercial advertisements and order forms for Project BEST courseware and other e-learning products being sold by the very same companies, including Microsoft, Apple, and IBM, that are endorsed in the UNESCO Study 11 whitepapers.

This compilation of "Grayson File" documents shows that UNESCO's Study 11 was carried out through international public-private partnerships between communist, socialist, and capitalist countries coordinating efforts between multinational telecommunications and computer corporations. Working in concert with academic institutions and national government agencies, Study 11 affiliates lobbied to restructure laws in order to globalize school systems through proto-internet technologies manufactured by Big Tech companies, such as <u>Microsoft</u>, <u>IBM</u>, and <u>Apple</u>, which are now steering the <u>Fourth Industrial Revolution</u> into a new political system of <u>communitarian technocracy</u> driven by a new economic system of "stakeholder capitalism" through "community-based" <u>public-private partnerships</u> that are managed by <u>Big Data</u>.

While this techno-fascist Fourth Industrial Revolution is being accelerated under the duress of coronavirus panic, global <u>COVID lockdowns</u> are sealing the deals for UNESCO Study 11 and <u>Project BEST</u> as schools around the entire world are forced to rely on the technocratic IT infrastructure that has been set up by Study 11 and Project BEST through their public-private partnerships with Microsoft, Apple, and IBM. These partnerships are now converting brick-and-mortar schoolhouses into virtual classrooms that digitally data-mine students through computer hardware devices, such as <u>Apple iPads and Macbooks</u>, which transmit video teleconferencing through software programs, including <u>Microsoft Teams</u>, supplemented by adaptive-learning courseware and other artificial-intelligence applications like <u>IBM's Watson Education</u>.

Now that the IT infrastructure set up by Study 11 and Project BEST is firmly in place, globalist oligarchs at the World Economic Forum (WEF) are calling for a "Great Reset" to purportedly save the planet from COVID-19 by rushing into the Fourth Industrial Revolution with the help of WEF members, including Microsoft, Apple, and IBM, which are exploiting lockdowns in order to "reset" the global economy and "Reimagine Education" through ed-tech that is programmed to data-mine students' "learning analytics" through "Social Credit" systems of "surveillance capitalism." In the final equation, these "geospatial intelligence" systems will be hooked up to transhumanist neurotechnologies plugged into the "internet-of-things." In the meantime, a UNESCO 2050 project is building on the IT infrastructure of Study 11 through the new UNESCO "Futures of Education" study, which advocates for a communitarian assimilation of AI ed-tech in order to "Reframe Humanism" to accelerate society's evolution into the "more-than-human world" at the crux of the Fourth Industrial Revolution.

UNESCO "Study 11: New Technologies in Education" from Corporatism to Communism

This UNESCO Joint Study of communist, socialist, and capitalist National Commissions was regionalized to cooperatively investigate the "current and planned applications of new technologies to education," including ed-tech applications of "computers, videotex/teletext, interactive video (including videodisc), communications satellites, multichannel cable/fibre optics, teleconferencing (audio/video/computer), as well as new developments in video, audio, and audiographs." More specifically, this UNESCO Study 11 investigated the comprehensive impacts of such evolving technologies on "learning theory, the quality of education, access to education, the role of the teacher, organization of education, financing of education, issues related to privacy and freedom, the interfaces between school and working life, school and home, education and state, education and society in general, and others."

By regionalizing a single bloc of communist, socialist, and capitalist states under an advisory panel of cognitive scientists and technocrats, UNESCO Study 11 aimed not just to "upgrade" schools with hi-tech computers, but to dialectically integrate communist and socialist systems of educational statecraft with capitalist ed-tech markets. This communo-fascist synthesis would radically alter student privacy and educational freedom through global transformations of school governance and finance managed by computerized IT. . . .

In sum, UNESCO Study 11 commissioned a coalition of communist, socialist, and capitalist nations to cooperate in their efforts to proliferate computerized ed-tech, such as "videotex/teletext" and "teleconferencing" software that is now a booming industry across the globe under the worldwide COVID lockdown being pushed by the WEF's Great Reset. This global "reset" is calling for a new world economic system of communitarian "stakeholder capitalism" through techno-fascist public-private partnerships that enforce government lockdowns while mandating virtual "distance learning" through commercial e-learning technologies that are manufactured by WEF members, including Microsoft, Apple, and IBM. Their objective is to digitally data-mine students' psychometrics for the purposes of Social Credit surveillance in the bourgeoning Fourth Industrial Revolution. . . .

How UNESCO and Project BEST Set the Stage for Globalist Virtual Charter School Corporations

Roughly forty years later, the globalist virtual charter school industry resulting from BEST sub-projects, such as the internet e-learning pilots of NWREL's RICE-SPIN network and Spady's High Success Schools, has provided the online-learning infrastructure to "Reset" and "Reimagine" education for the Fourth Industrial Revolution. Expanding on these virtual charter school markets, the techno-oligarchs of the Fourth Industrial Reset are executing an ed-tech takeover that is exploiting government lockdowns to force all schools into computerized "distance learning" facilitated by Big Tech corporations, including WEF members like Microsoft, Apple, and IBM, in order to data-mine students' "learning analytics" through AI surveillance algorithms. . . .

UNESCO's Transhumanist "Futures of Education" 2050

Now, in the midst of the COVID lockdown reset, UNESCO is convening an International Commission to oversee the "Futures of Education: Learning to Become" project, which is "a global initiative to reimagine how knowledge and learning can shape the future of humanity and the planet" through "digital, biotechnology and neuroscience developments" that will drive the Fourth Industrial Revolution. This UNESCO 2050 initiative takes Study 11 to the next level as it charts a "more-than-human," or transhuman, future in which Homo *sapiens* will "evolve" with a global IT economy integrated with biotech and neurotech systems of Big Data managed by an international "commons" of "stakeholder" corporations. Looking to this 2050 future envisioned by UNESCO, global "stakeholder" companies, through communitarian public-private partnerships, are on a trajectory to blanket the planet with posthuman AI ed-tech in order to "Reframe Humanism" by data-mining students' biopsychosocial algorithms for the purposes of "unleash[ing] an engineering of human beings previously inconceivable," according to UNESCO. . . .

Of course, this transhumanist agenda can be traced all the way back to the eugenic roots of UNESCO's first Director General, Julian Huxley [Aldous Huxley's brother], who was the President of the British Eugenics Society before calling for a global eugenics program in his 1946 UNESCO: Its Purpose and Its Philosophy. Later, in a 1957 book titled New Bottles for New Wine, Huxley coined the term "transhumanism" as the next phase in eugenic evolution. According to Huxley, the eugenic goals of biologically engineering human evolution should be refined through transhumanist technologies, which combine the eugenic methods of genetic engineering with neurotech that merges humans and machines into a new organism.

It is worth noting here that Malthusian eugenics has also been a cornerstone of the World Economic Forum's global governance agenda going as far back as 1978 when the third annual meeting of the WEF showcased a population control speech on "The Limits of Growth" by Aurelio Peccei, who co-founded the

Club of Rome with Alexander King, the Director-General for Scientific Affairs of the OECD's Committee for Science Policy. A little over a decade later, King authored The First Global Revolution: A Report by the Council of the Club of Rome, which reiterated the Malthusian-eugenic population control policies of The Limits to Growth: A Report for the Club of Rome's Project on the Predicament of Mankind. In this 1991 book, The First Global Revolution, King declared that, in order to save the planet from over-population, societies must rally in opposition to "a common enemy against whom we can unite." In quintessential Malthusian-eugenic fashion, King resolved that "[t]he real enemy then is humanity itself."

"Reimagining" Project BEST and UNESCO Study 11 for a Transhumanist Fourth Industrial Revolution

Following its trans-eugenic mission statement, UNESCO carried out Study 11 to promote the global distribution of ed-tech products from multinational technology corporations, such as Microsoft, Apple, and IBM, in partnership with the United States and other national governments for the purposes of building the computerized IT infrastructure of the "information age." All of this was done in order to pave the way for a <u>Fourth Industrial Revolution</u> driven by AI systems of "<u>geospatial intelligence</u>" through a <u>blockchain "internet-of-things"</u> hooked up to transhumanist biotechnologies linked to the "<u>internet-of-bodies</u>."

As the ed-tech building blocks of the Fourth Industrial Revolution were being laid out by the US Department of Education in partnership with UNESCO and the OECD, Assistant Secretary Senese <u>reported</u> that "the OECD also decided to study strategies for countering resistance to the introduction and use of the new technologies in schools." Now, in 2021, resistance to the techno-fascist ed-tech takeover is being suppressed by the COVID lockdown propaganda of the billionaires at the World Economic Forum as they hype their "<u>Great Reset</u>" with pathos fallacies stirred up to scare and shame working-class people into capitulating to the WEF, which is partnering with Microsoft, Apple, and IBM, as it rams forward with its technocratic visions of a Fourth Industrial Revolution.

In tandem with the Great Reset, Google and the Bill & Melinda Gates Foundation, which are both <u>WEF members</u>, are "<u>Reimagining Education</u>" by setting up <u>Big Data networks</u> that link "learning analytics" from Learnsphere databases to the Cortex database on a Gates-funded InnovateEdu platform that partners with Google's BigQuery, which contracts with ChainLink "middleware" in order to monetize, or tokenize, Social Credit data, such as student-learning algorithms, through "smart contracts" on blockchain, hashgraph, and other "distributed ledger technologies" (DLTs). By building this Social Credit surveillance infrastructure through Big Data school systems hooked up to a <u>DLT</u> <u>internet-of-things</u>, Big Tech is laying the groundwork for the <u>internet-of-bodies</u>, which will plug students into <u>transhumanist biotechnologies</u> for the purposes of trans-eugenically re-engineering, or reimagining, the human species.

It should be noted here that <u>Microsoft</u>, <u>Apple</u>, and <u>IBM</u> are all developing <u>digital</u> COVID <u>vaccine passports and immunity passports</u> stored on iPhones and other mobile devices through <u>blockchain</u> DLT apps which can be <u>expanded to track and trace</u> other biopsychosocial data, such as biometric and psychometric data extracted from <u>transhumanist wearables and implantables</u>. At the same time, the <u>World Economic Forum </u>is <u>sponsoring</u> the <u>CommonPass</u> immunity passport, while the <u>United Nations</u> is endorsing the <u>COVI-PASS</u>™ <u>Digital Health Passport</u>, which is also built upon a blockchain platform that can be expanded to <u>interface</u> with transhumanist biotech and neurotech that aggregate the total spectrum of an individual's biopsychosocial data into a DLT Social Credit system.

To be sure, this was always UNESCO's endgame. Even back in 1978, Lawrence P. Grayson, who was the International Coordinator for UNESCO Study 11, wrote an article in the Educational Communication and Technology Journal, which predicted "the potential of computers to read thought patterns in the human mind" through "a special helmet" that utilizes a "biocybernetic" system that can "identify and monitor the electroencephalographic signals (EEG) in the brain that are associated with language." Today, thanks to Study 11, and with the help of Tech Baron corporations such as <u>IBM</u> and <u>Microsoft</u>, which are con-

nected to eugenics enterprises, UNESCO is now on the preci-
pice of finally realizing its 75-year mission to trans-eugenically
re-engineer a new human species in the "reimagined" image of
computerized techno-fascism.

CHAPTER 35

Prove That You Love Me

The globalist war on America goes where no man has gone before. Beyond the realm of national sovereignty, beyond the realm of individual autonomy, the globalist war on America is a war on humanity that demands unconditional surrender to globalist transhumanist technocrat managerial rule.

To understand the profound malevolence of this toxic megalomania, it is helpful to examine the microcosm and macrocosm of the nuclear and national American families.

Groups large and small require an organizing principle to define the structural elements of power and control. Our Founding Fathers rejected the centralized power and control of the British monarchy. The U.S. Constitution is an unprecedented document in world history. It defines a decentralized government, the limits of its powers and controls, and the unalienable rights and privileges of its citizens.

The constitutional separation of powers provides checks and balances to control federal government overreach. The responsibilities, authorities, and powers of the executive, legislative, and judicial branches are kept separate. Powers not granted to the federal government belong to the states and to the people.

Our national American family is bound by our constitutional laws, and the individual freedoms it guarantees. The U.S. Constitution is the organizing principle and common denominator that binds us one to the other. It is the social contract between individual citizens to live by its tenets, and the political contract between government and individual citizens for both to abide by its tenets. Generation after generation pledging allegiance to the flag of the United States of America is a commitment to the American ideals of freedom, liberty, and the generational responsibilities required to preserve them.

THE COLLAPSING AMERICAN FAMILY   233

The traditional nuclear American family begins with the parents, whose love and protection modulate their power and control. As the children grow up and become more responsible, the power and control shift away from the parents toward the young adults who have acquired the skills and maturity required to preserve American freedom and liberty.

The nuclear American family is the generational fulcrum on which American national sovereignty and social order pivots.

> The family unit is the first government; an incubator for a growing child's values and affections. Trust is the mortar that holds these precious units together to form a storm-resistant society—Jonathan Mooers

Family is the organizing principle of American society and American values. This makes its disorganization, according to Alinsky's *Rules for Radicals* (see Chapter 15), required to collapse society. Disrupting family bonds is the motivation for targeting the American nuclear and national families in the Culture War that convulses America today.

Contemporary America is experiencing a stunning and expanding level of family rupture. The nuclear and national families are splintering along political lines. Decades of educational indoctrination have undermined family unity by challenging parental authority and traditional American values.

Parents and grandparents are being bludgeoned with the racist narratives of critical race theory expounded by their indoctrinated children and grandchildren. It is a *take it or leave it* proposition—leftist intolerance is absolute. Either the parents/grandparents surrender to the orthodoxy of leftism, or adult children choose estrangement.

There is no respectful agreeing to disagree, there is no challenge to leftist disinformation allowed, there is only surrender or rupture. The surrender must be unconditional or the adult children weaponize the grandchildren and withhold them if the grandparents refuse to comply. It is a lose-lose proposition for grandparents. The grandparents either lose their integrity or lose their families.

The consequence of losing their families is excruciating heartbreak. The consequence of losing their integrity is the loss of the republic. This is not hyperbole. Family estrangement transfers family loyalty and parental authority to the grasping socialist state.

The unconditional surrender that adult children demand is parallel to the unconditional love they also demand. It is an infantile view of the world appropriate to infants and young children that is incompatible with the demands of ordered liberty in a constitutional republic.

The leftist offer of social justice and income equality in the socialist state fails to mention that freedom is the price for free stuff. Indoctrinated adult children who demand their parents' surrender to leftism are demanding that their parents participate in the collapse of America. The indoctrinated adult children are too mesmerized by the glitter of free stuff to realize the bargain requires relinquishing their freedom and individual rights to the state.

Leftist adult children are trading free stuff for eternal childhood where they will remain forever children, forever powerless and controlled. The structural elements of power and control in the socialist state are the opposite of the structural elements of power and control in a constitutional republic.

Socialism requires collectivist dependency in a centralized government that retains all the power and control. A constitutional republic requires adult independence in a decentralized government that awards the power and control to the individual. The difference is a matter of *agency*.

Agency is the condition of being in action—the ability to effect change. An individual is said to have agency if that individual has the power to act. The difference between freedom and enslavement is agency. In a constitutional republic, citizens have agency because they can direct their own lives. Agency is the core of American life, American freedom, and the American dream.

The globalist war on America seeks to collapse America into socialism, and then into planetary governance where the citizens of the world no longer have agency. The deceitful worldwide COVID-19 fear campaign is the vehicle for escalating governmental restrictions that increasingly deprive citizens of agency, and often end in family rupture.

In an extraordinary November 19, 2020, article, "Do or Die,"[162] Judd Garrett explains the psychodynamics of the sinister manipulation, and how politicians use love to control us. Garrett writes:

> In the movie *The Green Mile*, when the bad guy "Wild Bill"
> Wharton breaks into a house to rape and kill the two young
> girls, he keeps the girls silent by telling them, "<u>You love your
> sister? You make any noise, . . . I'm gonna kill her instead of
> you</u>." As the protagonist of the movie John Coffey observed, "<u>He
> killed them with their love</u>." The killer used their love against
> them. Neither girl wanted to be responsible for her sister's
> death, so both girls remained silent, and complied. And their
> silence allowed him to kill them both. That is the way evil works.
> Evil uses good people's love against them, to control them, and
> to even kill them.
>
> Since the start of the pandemic, when people have told us that
> we must wear masks, they would say, "<u>you are not doing it to
> protect yourself, you are *only* doing it to protect other people</u>."
> I never understood the logic of that. Does the corona-virus only
> penetrate the blue side of the mask, and not the white side?
> Couldn't we just flip our masks over? If the mask protects other
> people, it only follows that it would also protect the wearer. But
> we are told wearing the mask *only* protects the other person
> because the people who want to control us are using our love
> against us. They are using our love of our families or our
> fellow man to force us to comply with their wishes. They know
> if people were told that the mask protected the wearer, many
> people would say, 'I'm not wearing it, I'll take my chances of
> getting sick.' And there would be no guilt because other people
> would be protected by their own masks.

So it is in families today. Adult children are told they are protecting
their parents and grandparents, parents are told they are protecting
their children and their parents. Love for each other is being used
against them to end family gatherings, weddings, funerals, Christmas
gatherings, business parties. Family love and loyalty are being manipulated to isolate and splinter families.

I will repeat: Family love and loyalty are being used to splinter families.

Consider the parents who reject the fearmongering of political medicine, who understand its destructive political purpose. These parents

are diametrically opposed to the views of their indoctrinated adult children. Parents are offered the choice of conforming to their adult children's philosophical demands or suffering family rupture. It is the childish demand: *Prove that you love me.*

The choice is a lose-lose dilemma for the parents. The parents love their children but are being pressured to surrender their integrity to have a relationship with them. Emotional extortion is not love, and demanding political conformity is not tolerance.

Today's indoctrinated adult children are so fragile they are unwilling to agree to disagree. Some even require safe spaces and distance to protect themselves and their young children from the toxic ideas of conservative parents/grandparents. The generation gap today is defined by politics.

America's indoctrinated adult children have become ideological warriors. What they have not yet understood is that they are participating in their own destruction. The objective of political medicine is social control, submission, and centralized planetary governance. Parents must ask themselves, is it more loving to surrender to your adult children's demand to wear masks, social distance, and be jabbed? Or is it more loving to reject their demands for conformity and stand for freedom? What is a lose-lose dilemma for parents is a win-win situation for the cunning social engineers.

It is time for courageous parents of adult children to do what courageous parents of young children have begun to do: *Just say NO!* COVID-19 lockdowns and school closures resulted in remote learning and homeschooling across the country. Parents became painfully aware of the egregious anti-American, racist, dumbed-down content of public education. Angry parents started attending school board meetings and complaining about woke ideology, critical race theory, pornographic sex education, and educational overstep regarding COVID-19 policies.

In response, on September 29, 2021, the National School Boards Association (NSBA), sent an incendiary letter[163] to Joe Biden asking for federal assistance to

> investigate, intercept, and prevent the current threats and acts of violence against public school officials through existing statutes, executive authority, interagency and intergovernmental

task forces, and other extraordinary measures to ensure the safety of our children and educators, to protect interstate commerce, and to preserve public school infrastructure and campuses. . . .

Specifically, NSBA asks that the U.S. Department of Justice, Federal Bureau of Investigation, U.S. Department of Homeland Security, and the U.S. Secret Service and its **National Threat Assessment Center** focus their expertise and resources on the level of risk to public schoolchildren, educators, board members, facilities, and campuses. NSBA also requests that the U.S. Postal Inspection Service intervene against threatening letters and cyberbullying attacks that have been transmitted to students, school board members, district administrators, and other educators. . . .

Read NSBA's <u>complete letter</u> to President Biden.

In classic leftist political theater hyperbole, the NSBA letter claims that "America's public schools and its education leaders are under an immediate threat." As stated earlier, leftism is an orthodoxy that does not tolerate opposing points of view.

In response, the Biden regime has relabeled free speech as *hate speech*, and Attorney General Merrick Garland has proposed labeling angry parents protecting their children at school board meetings *domestic terrorists*.

The pillars of Americanism are family, faith, and freedom. The Biden regime rejects all three pillars in favor of leftism and the global predator network. The slogan of the Great Reset is extremely important to understand: *You will own nothing, and you will be happy.*

Individual freedom has two central components—freedom of speech and private property. Political predators are attempting to eliminate free speech by criminalizing dissent. They are attempting to eliminate private property by destroying the economy of the middle class through politically driven covid restrictions.

Political medicine is not about public health—it is the vehicle for totalitarian control and imposition of the Great Reset. Our indoctrinated adult children do not recognize the malevolence and pathology of those who seek absolute control. "Vaccines," masks, and social distancing will not protect them, their parents, or their grandparents any more than the sisters could protect each other from Wild Bill in *The Green Mile.*

Prove that you love me persuades many parents to accept their adult children's catastrophic demands for conformity. The global predators and political social engineers just sit back and watch American families either capitulate or implode. The precious individual freedoms our ancestors fought and died for are being surrendered in the name of love.

> Men fight for liberty and win it with hard knocks. Their children, brought up easy, let it slip away again, poor fools. And their grandchildren are once more slaves—D. H. Lawrence

Final Thoughts

Freedom Is an Adult Enterprise

In 1995, when I wrote the manuscript for *Dear America: Who's Driving the Bus?* [164] my concern was the increasingly regressive behavior I witnessed in adults that was clearly detrimental to individuals and to society as a whole. My goal was to help people understand their behavior so they could change it. At that time, it did not occur to me that the societal pressures toward regression were deliberate, sinister, and a coordinated plan to collapse America from within. I published the book in 2011. It begins:

> Dear America,
>
> I am writing to express my deepest concern for the state of our union. As I reflect upon the grandeur and possibilities of our great nation, I am overcome by a feeling of profound sadness and foreboding. I sense the dividing of our country, and I know that this schism is not fomented by an enemy abroad; it is an internal battle fought within the individual citizen and an external battle fought one citizen against another. America is embroiled in a second civil war that it is unaware of and that threatens our way of life, The civil war in this country is being fought over the same issue that all great wars are fought over: *power.* But in this war, the adversaries are ourselves. Civil War II is not a race war, an economic war, or a war between states. It is a psychological battle between states of mind that will determine who has the power in our society, who is in control. (p. 13)
>
> Psychological growth is the universal challenge of childhood. Every society in the world needs its children to grow into physical and psychological adulthood in order to continue the cycle of life. Theoretically, if a society were to remain a nation of children it would necessarily collapse and extinguish itself. (p. 14)

In the preface to my second book, *The Book of Humanitarian Hoaxes:*

Killing America with 'Kindness', I explain how our extraordinary individual freedoms and ordered liberty require a citizenry of emotional adults. That was when I realized that a nation of children is easily controlled, and that the enemies of the United States were deliberately infantilizing Americans to collapse America from within.

The Collapsing American Family: From Bonding to Bondage demonstrates how the infantilization of America using the COVID-19 fear campaign, scientism, educational indoctrination, and the associated media propaganda has successfully resulted in families rupturing over what is truth and reality. If families are extinguished, what then?

Los Angeles psychiatrist, Dr. Mark McDonald, offers his answer in a January 21, 2022, interview with Dr. Joseph Mercola. Discussing his new book, *United States of Fear: How America Fell Victim to Mass Delusional Psychosis*, Dr. McDonald explains that this is a psychological war. Without fear, they cannot rob us of our freedoms:

> My concern is that the underlying motivation of this psychological campaign has been for a long time, and it is still today, an attack on the core structures, foundations, institutions of our country. . . . Certainly, in all the anglophone countries, there has been an attack for many, many years on the core archetypes of the male and the female, the masculine and the feminine. The goal is to take away the interest, the capacity, the comfort, both internally and also on a societal level, of men and women coming together. If men and women stop coming together, if they stop desiring one another, if they stop speaking to one another, if they stop dating, getting married, having children, then we no longer have families. We have single parents.
>
> If we don't have families, we don't have civic organizations. We don't have churches. We don't have communities. All we have are single parents running around with their own children, relying on, most likely, government, to help keep them financially and physically safe. So, the role of the father, the role of the mother is simply eliminated.
>
> The state then steps in and the state supplants the role of the father and begins to take over. . . . So, I really do believe that the attacks on masculinity, and on femininity, are specifically de-

signed to end the family unit and to cause all men and women to turn towards government for their security rather than to one another, as has traditionally been the case.

Once the family structure has been eliminated and the government steps in, what then?

The answer is the metaverse—the next iteration of the internet where reality and unreality converge. To enter the fake utopia of the metaverse the individual simply dons a headset and then feels himself to be anyone, anywhere he chooses to be. The metaverse blurs the lines between physical, digital, and biological identities. In the artificial reality of the metaverse anything and everything is possible. The enhanced AI computer algorithms of the metaverse upgrade the virtual reality of gaming to immersion in virtual environments. The escape into the virtual worlds of the metaverse is an escape into the unreality of drugs without the drugs. User addiction is the goal, because in the metaverse you will literally own nothing and be happy.

The telecommunications infrastructure for the metaverse is already here. Enabling the metaverse requires increased wireless speeds. The 5G networks launched in 2019 will expand to 6G to accommodate the connectivity demands.

In an extraordinary October 29, 2021, Technocracy News article, Patrick Wood discusses the metaverse and asks the question, "Meta: The Final Disconnect from Reality?"[165]

Wood begins:

> Mark Zuckerberg hasn't lost his mind, but he wants you to lose yours… to the metaverse.

An enchanted and smiling Mark Zuckerberg, the creator of Facebook, is shown presenting artificial reality as a game. The problem, of course, is when humanitarian huckster Zuckerberg puts on the required headgear, he is not playing; he is selling unreality—the *feeling* of being somewhere when you are not *really* there. The psychopaths who are socially and genetically re-engineering humanity are not playing games. They know that familiarity breeds acceptance. Gaming is the marketing strategy Zuckerberg is using to familiarize his billion Facebook users with the artificial reality of the metaverse, along with Facebook's new name, Meta.

The games, rooted in *feelings*, are designed to persuade an infantilized public to accept a future where fact and fiction converge into a virtual existence—a magical world of childhood fantasy where no boundaries exist between fact and fiction. The metaverse is the dreamworld where Johnny can fly because he *feels* like a bird.

The globalist megalomaniacs driving the movement to the managerial state are interested only in absolute power. They are seducing a regressed, captivated public with fun, games, and feelings because no one ever seduced a child with spinach.

In the metaverse, everything is a matter of perception. This means that once you put the headgear on, if you perceive yourself as a king in a castle you *are* a king in a castle. In the metaverse, Johnny *is* a bird that can fly.

Being out of touch with objective reality is the traditional definition of insanity. The difference between sanity and insanity is knowing what is real and what is not real. The malevolence of the metaverse is that its goal is to blur the boundaries between reality and unreality so that the public is no longer willing or able to distinguish between the two. The public is literally being driven insane as it plays the game.

Patrick Wood warns:

> For those who embrace it, the metaverse will completely rewire the human brain. It will get into your brain. It will dominate your brain. It will provide an endless source of dopamine hits as you are visually, mentally and emotionally stimulated.
>
> It will dominate the workforce, the social world, the classroom and education and entertainment.
>
> The metaverse will not necessarily tell you what to think, but it will entirely change the way you think. It will rearrange your logic circuits in a way that you cannot distinguish between what is real and what is not. Your metaverse will become as real to you as the nose on your face.

The metaverse is the ideological subversion that Yuri Bezmenov warned of, where facts no longer matter. It is the quintessential manifestation

of Bertrand Russell's sinister educational goal to convince students that
snow is black, plus the tyranny of political medicine.

> Diet, injections, and injunctions will combine, from a very early
> age to produce the sort of character and the sort of beliefs that
> the authorities consider desirable, and any serious criticism of
> the 'powers that be' will become psychologically impossible.
> (*The Impact of Science on Society*, 1953, p. 45)

The artificial reality of the metaverse is the objective reality of a schizophrenic. In the metaverse, insanity is perceived as sane.

The psychopaths driving the movement for planetary governance are
in the process of persuading the public that objective reality does not
exist. They intend to replace objective reality with artificial reality—the
metaverse—where people living in the Great Reset will own nothing
(including themselves) and be happy. The perpetrators, however, will
remain in objective reality where they are empowered to control you,
your mind, and every aspect of your enslaved life.

Using Lewin's three-stage theory of change, the masters of the
metaverse will exploit science and technology to create their own
21st-century iteration of Orwell's dystopian society. The future in the
globalist managerial state is forecast in *1984*:

> The real power, the power we have to fight for night and day,
> is not power over things, but over men. . . . Power is in tearing
> human minds to pieces and putting them together again in
> new shapes of your own choosing. . . . Already we are breaking
> down the habits of thought which have survived from before
> the Revolution. We have cut the links between child and parent,
> and between man and man, and between man and woman. No
> one dares trust a wife or a child or a friend any longer. But in
> the future there will be no wives and no friends. Children will
> be taken from their mothers at birth, as one takes eggs from
> a hen. The sex instinct will be eradicated. Procreation will be
> an annual formality like the renewal of a ration card. We shall
> abolish the orgasm. Our neurologists are at work upon it now.
> There will be no loyalty, except loyalty toward the Party. There
> will be no love, except the love of Big Brother. There will be no
> laughter, except the laugh of triumph over a defeated enemy.

There will be no art, no literature, no science. When we are omnipotent we shall have no more need of science. . . . But always—do not forget this, Winston—always there will be the intoxication of power, constantly increasing and constantly growing subtler. . . . If you want a picture of the future, imagine a boot stamping on a human face—forever.[166]

Transhumanism is the ultimate quest of the megalomaniac. Transhumanism represents not just absolute power but absolute power in an infinite lifetime. Transhumanism is the battle against the finiteness of actual time in objective reality. We all live on this earth until we die. Some accept life on earth as the beginning and end of existence. Some believe in an afterlife. Others believe in reincarnation. Transhumanism seeks eternal life on earth. Why is this a problem?

Let's return to Karl Marx and his belief in the superiority of communism and its historical inevitability. Marx insisted that capitalism would fall to socialism, and then socialism to communism, which would necessarily evolve into a worldwide communist utopia. The millions who died on communism's path to utopia were considered simply collateral damage. Karl Marx and the communist leaders who followed, whether Russian, Chinese, or Western, share the supremacist/aristocratic attitude discussed at length in this book.

The aristocratic attitude is without conscience because supremacists do not consider other people's lives equivalent to their own. *The end justifies the means* is a supremacist's anthem. The civilized mind has great difficulty processing how the terms *end* and *means* are interpreted by a supremacist. Words matter. Let's be clear: transhumanism, the goal of the Great Reset, is the *end* and the COVID-19 *planned pandemic* is the *means* for global predators seeking world domination and immortality. Their slogan *build back better* is the path from family bonding to feudal bondage.

Transhumanists believe in the evolutionary certainty of the singularity. The singularity is the moment in time when artificial intelligence and other technologies are so advanced that humanity undergoes a seismic and irreversible change: human and machine become one. Transhumanists are literally promoting a new evolutionary life form. It is their 21st-century answer to humanity's existential dilemma—the knowledge that humans eventually die.

No other animals have awareness of their inevitable death. They are not confounded by this knowledge or challenged to manage the anxiety it creates. In the premodern era religion was the source of truth and reality. Religion offered moral structure and escape from the anxiety of our existential dilemma and aloneness.

Our Founding Fathers rejected the supremacist attitude of aristocratic minds. The constitutional republic they established required a philosophical and psychological commitment to the belief that other people's lives are as important as our own. It is the operating principle of a nation of the people, by the people, and for the people. Our founding morality was rooted in the Ten Commandments and brotherly love. It is the ethos of our nuclear and national American families.

Humans seek escape from their aloneness in multiple ways. Some accept the existential dilemma that death is the inevitable end of life on earth. They choose constructive solutions and commit themselves to family, faith, and freedom in this life on earth. Others attempt to defeat death.

In the modern era, science (scientism) has challenged America's Judeo-Christian tradition as the source of truth and reality. Scientism offers no solace, comfort, or moral structure. Its ethics are utilitarian and deny the value of the individual in favor of the collective. It is prelude to the scientific dictatorship Carl Sagan warned of. In his 1996 interview, Sagan bemoaned the lack of science knowledge in the general public. Without a basic understanding of science, the public is vulnerable to the deceit and lies of scientism's corrupt scientists.

In the postmodern era of the metaverse, truth and reality are defined by the individual and his personal life's experience. There is no objective reality for the postmodernist—he lives in a world of total relativism, consensus, and Hegelian contradictions. This is very convenient for the transhumanist and for the advancement of scientism.

The metaverse is the envisioned future of the internet and will become the next major computing platform. An article by Stefan Hall and Cathy Li posted on the World Economic Forum website October 29, 2021, "What is the metaverse? And why should we care?"[167] explores the metaverse.

Facebook recently changed its name to "Meta" to align the company with its ambitions to build the "metaverse."

Microsoft and Nvidia are also working on their own versions of the metaverse. . . .

If the concept can be actualized it will be as transformative to society and industry as the mobile phone.

The internet today is often the main entry point for millions of us to access information and services, communicate and socialize with each other, sell goods, and entertain ourselves. The metaverse is predicted to replicate this value proposition—with the main difference being that distinction between being offline and online will be much harder to delineate.

This could manifest itself in several ways, but many experts believe that "extended reality" (XR)—the combination of augmented, virtual and mixed reality—will play an important role. Central to the concept of the metaverse is the idea that virtual, 3D environments that are accessible and interactive in real time will become the transformative medium for social and business engagement. If they are to become practical, these environments will be dependent on widespread adoption of extended reality.

Until now, XR technologies have mostly been limited to a subset of video games and niche enterprise applications. However, as games increasingly become platforms for social experiences, the likelihood increases that their characteristics—discoverable and continuous virtual worlds, mediums for open and creative expression, and conduits for pop culture—can and will be applied to other contexts.

The success of the metaverse is dependent upon acceptance of extended reality and the expansion of wireless speeds into 6G network technology. The metaverse is the Orwellian dreamworld provided by the global predatory network to make the Great Reset palatable to a dehumanized, roboticized, enslaved public.

On May 27, 1996, in his last interview with Charlie Rose, world-renowned American astronomer, planetary scientist, and astrophysicist Carl Sagan[168] warned of the consequences of a technologically advanced civilization where the population is vastly ignorant of both science and technology. He warned of a scientific dictatorship able to manipulate, abuse, and exploit the ignorance of the population with devastating results.

Carl Sagan observed:

> One of the saddest lessons of history is this: If we've been bamboozled long enough, we tend to reject any evidence of the bamboozle. We're no longer interested in finding out the truth. The bamboozle has captured us. It is simply too painful to acknowledge, even to ourselves, that we've been taken. Once you give a charlatan power over you, you almost never get it back.

COVID-19, the Great Reset, transhumanism, and the metaverse are the great bamboozle of the 21st century. Freedom in a constitutional republic is an adult enterprise. We must acknowledge the bamboozle and reject it in all its forms. If we fail, tomorrow's children will be enslaved by today's Global Predator Network and the regression into *extended* reality it demands.

Freedom requires its citizens to live in the adult world of objective reality where they cannot be bamboozled. Rational adulthood is the defense against insanity and enslavement, because freedom is an adult enterprise.

Space is no longer the final frontier—reality is.

ENDNOTES

URLs that have disappeared from the Internet are retrievable on the Internet Archive Wayback Machine; https://archive.org/web/web.php

How to use Wayback Machine;
https://www.youtube.com/watch?v=HDpPz5om3Wc

CHAPTER 2: *America and the Family Business Rule*

1. American dream; https://en.wikipedia.org/wiki/American_Dream

CHAPTER 3: *Selling Socialism to America*

2. Marxism, the Frankfurt School, and the Leftist Takeover of the College Campus; https://www.americanthinker.com/articles/2019/03/marxism_the_frankfurt_school_and_the_leftist_takeover_of_the_college_campus.html

3. I Won't Grow Up; https://www.lyrics.com/lyric/1201351

CHAPTER 4: *The Relationship Charade: Walking on Eggshells is not Reconciliation*

4. *Dear America*; Linda Goudsmit, *Dear America: Who's Driving the Bus?*, Contrapoint Publishing (2011), p. 14

CHAPTER 5: *The Educational Battlefield: the deliberate dumbing down of america*

5. The Hand That Rocks the Cradle Rules the World; http://holyjoe.org/poetry/wallace.htm

6,7,8,9,10,11 *the deliberate dumbing down of america*; http://deliberatedumbingdown.com/ddd/wp-content/uploads/2018/04/DDDoA.pdf

CHAPTER 6: *John Dewey: The Father of Weaponized Education in America*

12. The Dewey Deception; http://www.improve-education.org/id42.html

13. John Dewey is a Fraud; https://www.americanthinker.com/articles/2012/10/john_dewey_is_a_fraud.html

14. Education Establishment; http://www.crossroad.to/Excerpts/chronologies/nea.html

15. *Saving K-12: What Happened to Our Public Schools? How Do We Fix Them*, Bruce Deitrick Price, Anaphora Literary Press, pp. 22, 23

16. coda; http://www.improve-education.org/id42.html

CHAPTER 7: *The Hegelian Dialectic*

17. *the deliberate dumbing down of america*; http://deliberatedumbingdown.com/ddd/wp-content/uploads/2018/04/DDDoA.pdf

CHAPTER 8: *The Mathematics of the Culture War on America*

18. Hegelian Dialectic; http://noisyroom.net/blog/2014/01/23/hegelian-dialectics-for-dummies/

19. Lewin's equation, B = F (pe); https://en.wikipedia.org/wiki/Kurt_Lewin

20. Force-field analysis; https://en.wikipedia.org/wiki/Force-field_analysis

21. genidentity; http://philsci-archive.pitt.edu/9388/1/Padovani_Lewin-Reichenbach-BerlinGroup.pdf

22. rubber-sheet geometry; https://psychology.wikia.org/wiki/Topology

23. topological psychology; https://www.psychologydiscussion.net/learning/learning-theory/lewins-field-theory-of-learning-education/2525

CHAPTER 9: *Sexual Predators Threaten the American Family*

24. Exposing Sick Roots of 'Sex Ed' - Kinsey, CIA & Child Abuse; https://thenewamerican.com/alex-newman-exposing-sick-roots-of-sex-ed-kinsey-cia-child-abuse/

25. American Law Institute; https://ali.org/about-ali/how-institute-works/

26. Playboy; http://www.drjudithreisman.com/reisman_won_playboy_libel_suit.html

27. NCJRS Abstract; https://www.ojp.gov/ncjrs/virtual-library/abstracts/role-pornography-and-media-violence-family-violence-sexual-abuse-2

28. The Reisman Institute; https://www.thereismaninstitute.org

CHAPTER 10: *The Scheme and the Schemers Determined to Reeducate America*

29. Why the Deep State is Sexualizing Kids; https://thenewamerican. com/why-the-deep-state-is-sexualizing-kids/?mc_cid=56990a1778&mc_ eid=0f1b890ecc

30. Problematic Women: Planned Parenthood Ideology 'Killing the Family,' Ex-Volunteer Says; https://www.dailysignal.com/2020/08/20/problematic-women-planned-parenthood-ideology-killing-the-family-ex-volunteer-says/

31. It Takes a Family; https://ittakesafamily.org

CHAPTER 11: *Pushback against Reeducating America*

32. Transgenderism: A Mental Illness Is Not a Civil Right; Transgenderism: A Mental Illness Is Not a Civil Right

33. The Pedophile Project: Your 7-year-old Is Next on The Sexual Revolution's Hit Parade; https://thefederalist.com/2019/02/21/pedophile-project-7-year-old-next-sexual-revolutions-hit-parade/

34. Overton Window; https://www.mackinac.org/overtonwindow

35. Availability Cascade; https://papers.ssrn.com/sol3/papers.cfm?abstract_ id=138144

36. Queens, New York; https://www.amny.com/news/queens-library-drag-story-hour-1.18422964/

37. drag queen story times; https://losangeles.cbslocal.com/2017/10/16/draq-queen-library-lgtbq-kids/

38. Lactatia; https://www.youtube.com/watch?v=ajeFAhW0hlM

39. to get other children; https://www.dailymail.co.uk/femail/article-5228857/A-10-year-old-drag-queen-founded-drag-club-kids.html

40. TED Talk; https://www.youtube.com/watch?v=egiBgmvv8wA

41. December 2018 article; https://link.springer.com/article/10.1007/s12119-

018-9519-1#citeas

42. mass delusion; https://thefederalist.com/2015/06/08/how-to-escape-the-age-of-mass-delusion/

43. Stop CSE; https://www.comprehensivesexualityeducation.org/about/

44. The War on Children: Exposing the Comprehensive Sexuality Education Agenda; https://www.comprehensivesexualityeducation.org/film/

CHAPTER 12: *Political Predators Threaten America with Extinction*

45. Saul Alinsky; https://steelonsteel.com/saul-alinsky-rules-for-radicals/

46. *Rules for Radicals*; Saul Alinsky, Vintage Books (1989), pp.116, 130, 133

47. Why BLM Yawns at Police-Shooting Statistics; https://cms.frontpagemag.com/fpm/2020/07/why-blm-yawns-police-shooting-statistics-john-perazzo

48. U.S. Subsidizes Soros Radical Leftist Agenda Worldwide; https://www.judicialwatch.org/corruption-chronicles/u-s-subsidizes-soros-radical-leftist-agenda-worldwide-judicial-watch-special-report-shows/

49. investigative report; https://www.judicialwatch.org/documents/soros-judicial-watch-special-report-open-society-foundations-2018/

50. New York Times; https://www.nytimes.com/2021/09/25/us/politics/capitol-riot-fbi-informant.html

51. Report: FBI Handler Had Tap on Jan.6, Plant in Crowd Working for Him; https://www.westernjournal.com/report-fbi-handler-tap-jan-6-plant-crowd-working/?utm_source=Email&utm_medium=WJBreaking&utm_campaign=breaking&utm_content=western-journal&ats_es=840b120646ee0053956a3a0c91294c8d

52. Attorneys: Jan.6 Detainee Held in Confinement 23 Hours a Day, Conditions Violate 'Every Single Basic Human Right'; https://www.westernjournal.com/attorneys-jan-6-detainee-held-confinement-23-hours-day-conditions-violate-every-single-basic-human-right/?ff_source=Email&ff_medium=WJBreaking&ff_campaign=breaking&ff_content=western-journal

53. Capitol incursion; https://www.westernjournal.com/confirmed-

disguised-leftists-infiltrated-trump-crowd-jan-6-said-told-fbi-infiltrate-maga/?ff_source=Email&ff_medium=WJBreaking&ff_campaign=breaking&ff_content=western-journal

54. pursued; https://www.westernjournal.com/red-alert-online-sleuths-hunting-trump-supporters-entered-capitol-jan-6/?ff_source=Email&ff_medium=WJBreaking&ff_campaign=breaking&ff_content=western-journal

55. 2020 riots; https://www.westernjournal.com/blms-mostly-peaceful-riots-cost-1000x-damage-jan-6-capitol-unrest/?ff_source=Email&ff_medium=WJBreaking&ff_campaign=breaking&ff_content=western-journal

56. *Gateway Pundit*; https://www.thegatewaypundit.com/2021/09/heartbreaking-letter-jan-6-prisoner-solitary-confinement-dc-gitmo-violates-international-codes-torture/

57. specifically The Nelson Mandela Rules; https://www.un.org/en/events/mandeladay/mandela_rules.shtml

CHAPTER 13: *The Collapsing American Family: Macrocosm and Microcosm*

58. Classic Communist Divide-And-Conquer Tactic; https://thefederalist.com/2020/09/29/critical-race-theory-is-a-classic-communist-divide-and-conquer-tactic/

CHAPTER 14: *Leftist Socialism: The Toothfish of Modern Politics*

59. Toothfish; https://www.upworthy.com/5-fish-got-different-names-and-now-theyre-so-expensive-it-hurts

60. Social democracy; https://en.wikipedia.org/wiki/Social_democracy

61. Social Democrats, USA; USA; https://en.wikipedia.org/wiki/Socialist_Party_of_America

62. Toothfish as Chilean Sea Bass; https://priceonomics.com/the-invention-of-the-chilean-sea-bass/

63. *The Naked Communist*; http://www.ecjones.org/1963_Communist_Goals. pdf, Congressional Record, Vol. 109 88th Congress, 1st Session Appendix Pages A1-A2842 Jan. 9-May 7, 1963 Reel 12

CHAPTER 15: *Obama's Grand Plan: Fundamental Transformation*

64. *Rules for Radicals*; https://archive.org/details/RulesForRadicals/page/ n129/mode/2up

65. Race to the Top; https://truthinamericaneducation.com/race-to-the-top/

66. Common Core Standards Mission Statement: http://www.uwosh.edu/ coehs/cmagproject/common_core/documents/CC_Standards_Myths.pdf

67. Global Education First Initiative; http://www.unesco.org/new/en/gefi/ about/

68. The 3 Priorities; http://www.unesco.org/new/en/gefi/priorities/

69. Connect All Schools; https://us.iearn.org/programs/connect-all-schools

70. WND; https://www.wnd.com/2013/01/muslim-brotherhood-group-to-connect-all-u-s-schools/

71. global citizenship; http://www.unesco.org/new/en/gefi/priorities/global-citizenship/

72. globalized curriculum; https://connectallschools.wordpress.com

73. Agenda 21; https://sustainabledevelopment.un.org/outcomedocuments/ agenda21

74. United Nations Sustainable Development; https://sustainabledevelopment. un.org/content/documents/Agenda21.pdf

75. 2030 Agenda for Sustainable Development; https://sdgs. un.org/2030agenda

76. World Core Curriculum; https://en.unesco.org/themes/education/

77. Westphalian state system; https://www.oxfordreference.com/ view/10.1093/oi/authority.20110803121924198

78. UNESCO; https://thenewamerican.com/un-obama-and-gates-are-

globalizing-education-via-common-core/

79. Pearson Education; https://fortune.com/2015/01/21/everybody-hates-pearson/

80. educational materials; https://plc.pearson.com/purpose/sustainability/

81. *The Impact of Science on Society*; Bertrand Russell, Routledge Classics (2016), pp. 27-28

CHAPTER 16: *Nationalism Is NOT a Dirty Word!*

82. The Four Oxen and the Lion; https://aesopfables.com/cgi/aesop1.cgi?sel&TheFourOxenandtheLion

83. Agenda 21; https://sustainabledevelopment.un.org/content/documents/Agenda21.pdf

84. Agenda 2030's; https://sdgs.un.org/2030agenda

85. Merriam-Webster; https://www.merriam-webster.com/dictionary/nationalism

86. Barack Hussein Obama; http://goudsmit.pundicity.com/20058/barack-hussein-obama-puppet-on-a-string

87. Port Canaveral and the Port of Wilmington; http://goudsmit.pundicity.com/21191/club-k-is-not-for-dancing

CHAPTER 17: *Obama: The Leftist Toothfish of Modern Politics*

88. *Anatomy of a Bolshevik: How Marx & Lenin Explain Obama's Grand Plan*; Alexander Markovsky, Dog Ear Publishing (2012), p.42, p.77, pp. 61-76, pp. 217-219, pp. 235-236

CHAPTER 18: *The Fractal Wrongness of Leftist Ideology*

89. fractal; http://fractalfoundation.org/fractivities/WhatIsaFractal-1pager.pdf

90. Benoit Mandelbrot; https://phys.org/news/2011-10-beautiful-math-fractals.html

91. Menger sponge; https://en.wikipedia.org/wiki/Menger_sponge

92. Fractal wrongness; https://rationalwiki.org/wiki/Fractal_wrongness

CHAPTER 19: *Dialectical Speech: The Language of Leftist Deception*

93. *Politics and the English Language*; George Orwell, Penguin Books (1946), p. 20

CHAPTER 20: *Collectivism: Persuading the Individual to Stop Being an Individual*

94. *The Ayn Rand Lexicon: Objectivism from A to Z*, Penguin (1988) p. 465

95. *The Virtue of Selfishness*, Ayn Rand, Signet (1964), "The Monument Builders," p. 91

96. *The Virtue of Selfishness*, Ayn Rand, Signet (1964), "The Monument Builders," p. 87

97. The Problem of Identity Politics and Its Solution; https://imprimis.hillsdale.edu/the-problem-of-identity-politics-and-its-solution/

98. *The Liberal Mind: The Psychological Causes of Political Madness*, Lyle H. Rossiter, Jr., MD., Free World Books (2006), pp. 320, 321, 329, 330, 374

99. *Abuse of Language–Abuse of Power*, Josef Peiper, Ignatius Press (1992), pp. 34-35

CHAPTER 22: *Leftism's Assault on Parenthood Is an Assault on Adulthood*

100. 411 Pediatrics; https://411pediatrics.com/about-us/baby-411/

101. Memo to K-12 students: Resist; http://www.renewamerica.com/columns/bprice/180909

102. Brave New World; https://en.wikipedia.org/wiki/Brave_New_World

CHAPTER 24: *A Cautionary Tale: And Not a Shot Is Fired*

103. And Not a Shot Is Fired; https://robertwelchuniversity.org/Not%20a%20Shot.pdf

CHAPTER 25: *The Merit of the Meritocracy*

104. The Reimagining Education Summer Institute; https://www.thecollegefix.com/conference-teaches-k-12-educators-combat-whiteness-schools/

105. *White Guilt: How Blacks and Whites Together Destroyed the Promise of the Civil Rights Era*, Shelby Steele, Harper Perennial (2007)

CHAPTER 26: *Who Launched the Cultural Revolution and Hostile Takeover of America?*

106. *Last Will and Testament of Cecil J. Rhodes*; https://info.publicintelligence.net/RhodesLastWill.pdf

107. How the British Invented Globalism; https://www.lewrockwell.com/2021/04/richard-poe/how-the-british-invented-globalism/

108. Locksley Hall; https://www.poetryfoundation.org/poems/45362/locksley-hall

109. The Reisman Institute; https://www.thereismaninstitute.org

110. MKULTRA, KINSEY & ROCKEFELLER: Instruments of the New World Order; http://www.drjudithreisman.com/archives/MKULTRA_Kinsey_Rockefeller.pdf

CHAPTER 27: *The Weapons of the Ruling Class*

111. 'The True Story of the Bilderberg Group' and What They May Be Planning Now; https://www.globalresearch.ca/the-true-story-of-the-bilderberg-group-and-what-they-may-be-planning-now/13808

CHAPTER 28: *The Great Reset for the United States of America*

112. CFR media networks; https://swprs.org/the-american-empire-and-its-media/

113. *The First Global Revolution*; https://wakeup-world.com/wp-content/uploads/2015/12/The-Council-of-The-Club-of-Rome-The-First-Global-Revolution.pdf

114. *The Fourth Industrial Revolution;* Klaus Schwab, Crown Business (2017)

115. January 10, 2016, interview; https://www.youtube.com/watch?v=UmQNA0HL1pw&t=22s

116. The Great Reset; https://www.youtube.com/watch?v=8rAiTDQ-NVY

117. You will OWN NOTHING, and you will be HAPPY; https://www.youtube.com/watch?v=60MzTlrOCXQ

CHAPTER 29: *The Permanent Global Welfare State*

118. *The Managerial Revolution: What is Happening in the World*, James Burnham, John Day Company (1941)

119. Rising Tide Foundation; https://risingtidefoundation.net

120. Strategic Culture Foundation; https://www.strategic-culture.org/contributors/cynthia-chung/

121. The Great Reset: How a 'Managerial Revolution' Was Plotted 80 Years Ago by a Trotsky-turned-CIA Neocon; https://www.strategic-culture.org/news/2021/09/17/the-great-reset-how-managerial-revolution-was-plotted-80-years-ago-by-cia-neocon/

122. How the Great Reset Was First Thought Up by the Original Proselytizer of Totalitarianism and the Father of Neo-Conservatism; https://www.strategic-culture.org/news/2021/09/21/how-great-reset-was-first-thought-up-by-original-proselytizer-totalitarianism-and-father-neo-conservatism/

123. The Managerial Revolution; https://archive.org/details/in.ernet.dli.2015.17923/page/n55/mode/1up?q=ownership+rights

124. The Managerial Revolution; https://archive.org/details/in.ernet.dli.2015.17923/page/n171/mode/1up?q=intellectuals

125. The Ultimate Revolution; https://www.youtube.com/watch?v=5RX-iUfPJ9I

126. How Global Capital's Social Credit Systems Force Corporate America to Lurch Left; https://thefederalist.com/2021/10/22/how-global-capitals-social-credit-systems-force-corporate-america-to-lurch-left/

CHAPTER 30: *Political Medicine Threatens American National Security*

127. Hippocratic Oath; https://absn.northeastern.edu/blog/the-history-of-the-hippocratic-oath/

128. Declaration of Geneva; http://www.cirp.org/library/ethics/geneva/

129. 1964 Hippocratic Oath; https://doctors.practo.com/the-hippocratic-oath-the-original-and-revised-version/

130. New York Medical College; https://www.nymc.edu/school-of-medicine-som/student-life/events–milestones/white-coat/medical-student-oath/

131. What is "Bioethics?"; http://www.lifeissues.net/writers/irv/irv_36whatisbioethics01.html

132. *The Federalist Papers*; https://thefederalistpapers.org/us/the-15-most-shocking-statements-from-obamacare-architect-ezekial-emannuels-die-at-75-article

133. Ezekiel Emanuel Wants to Shut Down the Country Again;

https://www.nationalreview.com/corner/ezekiel-emanuel-wants-to-shut-down-the-country-again/

134. Vaxxed or axed: To protect patients, every health care worker must be vaccinated; https://www.statnews.com/2021/07/14/vaxxed-or-axed-protect-patients-health-care-vaccine-mandate/

135. The Future of Value-Based Payment: A Road Map to 2030; https://ldi.upenn.edu/our-work/research-updates/the-future-of-value-based-payment-a-road-map-to-2030/

136. JAMA 1992; https://www.unlv.edu/sites/default/files/story_attachments/1111/11.08.18%20SOM%20Journal%20Club%20Article.pdf

CHAPTER 31: *Personnel Is Policy*

137. Dr. Anthony Fauci declares Americans should 'give up' individual freedom 'for the greater good of society'; https://washingtonnewsdaily.com/dr-fauci-declares-americans-should-give-up-individual-freedom-for-the-greater-good-of-society/

138. 12-minute video interview; https://www.youtube.com/watch?v=i3HusehOm7c

139. *The Federalist Papers*; https://thefederalistpapers.org/opinion/cdc-recently-changed-definition-vaccine-vaccination-fascinating

140. CDC; https://web.archive.org/web/20210826113846/https://www.cdc.gov/vaccines/vac-gen/imz-basics.htm

141. CDC had switched; https://www.cdc.gov/vaccines/vac-gen/imz-basics.htm

142. Media Research Center; https://www.mrc.org/george-soros-media-mogul

143. reflexivity; https://macro-ops.com/understanding-george-soross-theory-of-reflexivity-in-markets/

144. organizational structure; https://oma.od.nih.gov/DMS/Pages/Organizational-Changes-Org-Chart-Function.aspx

145. *The Book of Humanitarian Hoaxes: Killing America with 'Kindness'*, Linda Goudsmit, Contrapoint Publishing (2020), p. 283

CHAPTER 32: *Psychiatry: Covert Weapon of the Ruling Class*

146. Kurt Lewin's change model; https://www.change-management-coach.com/kurt_lewin.html

147. *Tavistock Institute: Social Engineering the Masses*, Daniel Estulin, Trine Day LLC (2015)

148. farewell address; https://www.ourdocuments.gov/print_friendly.php?flash=false&page=transcript&doc=90&title=Transcript+of+President+Dwight+D.+Eisenhowers+Farewell+Address+%281961%29

149. 1984 interview; https://www.youtube.com/watch?v=bX3EZCVj2XA&t=5s

150. defined; https://www.jerseyconservative.org/blog/2021/1/30/in-1984-yuri-bezmenov-explained-why-this-would-happen-today

151. *The Rape of the Mind*, Dr. Joost Meerloo, Grosset & Dunlap (1956), Martino Publishing (2015)

152. *COVID-19 AND THE GLOBAL PREDATORS: We Are the Prey*, Peter R. Breggin MD and Ginger Ross Breggin, Lake Edge Press (2021)

153. 21-page PowerPoint presentation; https://www.who.int/medicines/ebola-treatment/TheCoalitionEpidemicPreparednessInnovations-an-overview.pdf

154. House Divided Speech; https://www.nps.gov/liho/learn/historyculture/housedivided.htm

CHAPTER 33: *Transhumanism and Technocracy*

155. Internet of Bodies (IoB): Using CRISPR to electrically connect with and control the genome; https://bioengineeringcommunity. nature.com/posts/using-crispr-to-electrically-connect-with-and-control-the-genome

156. A redox-based electrogenetic CRISPR system to connect with and control biological information networks; https://www.nature.com/articles/s41467-020-16249-x?utm_campaign=related_content&utm_source=BIOENG&utm_medium=communities

157. The Fourth Industrial Revolution: What It Means and How to Respond; https://www.weforum.org/agenda/2016/01/the-fourth-industrial-revolution-what-it-means-and-how-to-respond/

158. The Evil Twins of Transhumanism and Technocracy; https://www.technocracy.news/the-evil-twins-of-transhumanism-and-technocracy/

159. *Brave New World*, Aldous Huxley, Chatto & Windus (1932)

CHAPTER 34: *Connecting the Dots ... the Grayson File*

160. From UNESCO Study 11 to UNESCO 2050: Project BEST and the Forty-Year Plan to Reimagine Education for the Fourth Industrial Revolution; https://unlimitedhangout.com/2021/06/investigative-reports/from-unesco-study-11-to-unesco-2050/

161. schoolworldorder.info; https://www.schoolworldorder.info

CHAPTER 35: *Prove That You Love Me*

162. Do or Die; https://www.objectivityistheobjective.com/post/do-or-die

163. an incendiary letter; https://s3.documentcloud.org/

documents/21094557/national-school-boards-association-letter-to-biden.pdf, complete letter; https://web.archive.org/web/20211001143718/https://www.nsba.org/News/2021/federal-assistance-letter

FINAL THOUGHTS: *Freedom Is an Adult Enterprise*

164. *Dear America*; Linda Goudsmit, *Dear America: Who's Driving the Bus?*, Contrapoint Publishing (2011), pp. 13-14

165. Meta: The Final Disconnect from Reality; https://www.technocracy.news/meta-the-final-disconnect-from-reality/

166. *1984*, George Orwell, Signet Classics (1961), pp. 266–267

167. What is the metaverse? And why should we care?; https://www.weforum.org/agenda/2021/10/facebook-meta-what-is-the-metaverse/

168. Carl Sagan; https://www.youtube.com/watch?v=U8HEwO-2L4w

AUTHOR BIO

Linda Goudsmit is the devoted wife of Rob and they are the parents of four children and the grandparents of four. She and Rob owned and operated a girls' clothing store in Michigan for forty years before retiring to the sunny beaches of Florida. A graduate of the University of Michigan in Ann Arbor, Linda has a lifelong commitment to learning and is an avid reader and observer of life. She is the author of the philosophy book *Dear America: Who's Driving the Bus?* and its political sequel, *The Book of Humanitarian Hoaxes: Killing America with 'Kindness'*, along with numerous current affairs articles featured on her websites www.lindagoudsmit.com and www.goudsmit.pundicity.com. *The Collapsing American Family: From Bonding to Bondage* completes Linda's trilogy of insightful books that connect the philosophical, political, and psychological dots of the globalist war on both American and individual sovereignty.

Linda believes the future of our nation requires reviving individualism, restoring meritocracy, and teaching critical-thinking skills to children again. Her illustrated children's book series, *Mimi's Strategy*, offers youngsters new and exciting ways of solving their problems and having their needs met. Mrs. Goudsmit believes that learning to think strategically rather than reacting emotionally is a valuable skill that will empower any child throughout his or her life. Plus, in Linda's words, "I have yet to meet the child who would prefer a reprimand to a kiss."

BOOKS BY LINDA GOUDSMIT

Philosophy/Political science

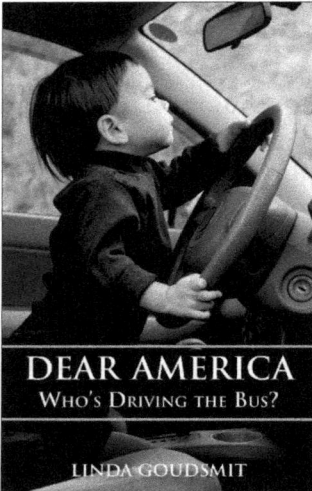

DEAR AMERICA
WHO'S DRIVING THE BUS?
LINDA GOUDSMIT

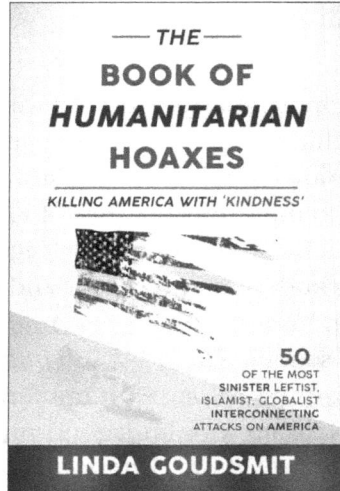

—THE—
BOOK OF
HUMANITARIAN
HOAXES
KILLING AMERICA WITH 'KINDNESS'

50
OF THE MOST
SINISTER LEFTIST,
ISLAMIST, GLOBALIST
INTERCONNECTING
ATTACKS ON AMERICA

LINDA GOUDSMIT

Children's Book Series

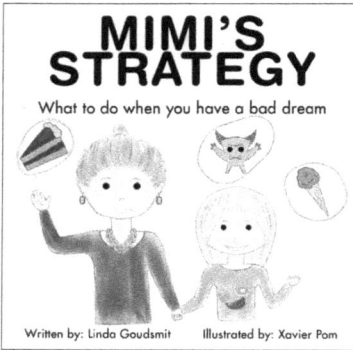

MIMI'S STRATEGY
What to do when you have a bad dream
Written by: Linda Goudsmit   Illustrated by: Xavier Pom

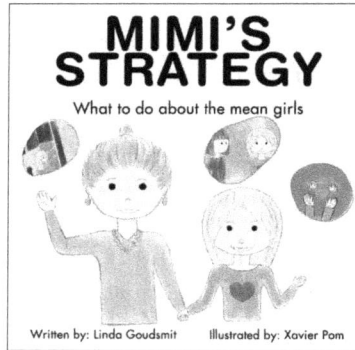

MIMI'S STRATEGY
What to do about the mean girls
Written by: Linda Goudsmit   Illustrated by: Xavier Pom

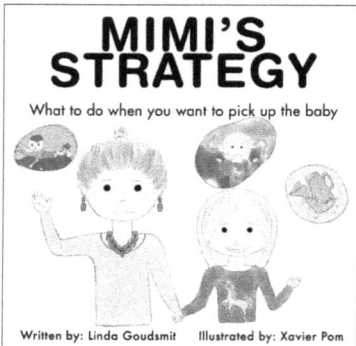

MIMI'S STRATEGY
What to do when you want to pick up the baby
Written by: Linda Goudsmit   Illustrated by: Xavier Pom

MIMI'S STRATEGY
What to do when your sister takes your toys
Written by: Linda Goudsmit   Illustrated by: Xavier Pom

MIMI'S STRATEGY
What to do when the vegetables are green
Written by: Linda Goudsmit   Illustrated by: Xavier Pom

MIMI'S STRATEGY
What to do if Louis says you're stupid
Written by: Linda Goudsmit   Illustrated by: Xavier Pom

MIMI'S STRATEGY
What to do about your imaginary friend
Written by: Linda Goudsmit   Illustrated by: Xavier Pom

MIMI'S STRATEGY
What to do when your birdie dies
Written by: Linda Goudsmit   Illustrated by: Xavier Pom

MIMI'S STRATEGY
What to do about telling tall tales
Written by: Linda Goudsmit   Illustrated by: Xavier Pom

MIMI'S STRATEGY
What to do when you want one more story
Written by: Linda Goudsmit   Illustrated by: Xavier Pom

www.ingramcontent.com/pod-product-compliance
Lightning Source LLC
Chambersburg PA
CBHW062120020426
42335CB00013B/1033